The Best Technology Writing 2010

Julian Dibbell, Editor

The Best Technology Writing 2010

YALE UNIVERSITY PRESS

New Haven and London

Yale University Press books may be purchased in quantity for
educational, business, or promotional use. For information, please
e-mail sales.press@yale.edu (U.S. office) or sales@yaleup.co.uk
(U.K. office).

Set in Granjon type by The Composing Room of Michigan, Inc.,
Grand Rapids, Michigan.
Printed in the United States of America.

Library of Congress Cataloging-in-Publication Data

The best technology writing 2010 / Julian Dibbell, editor.
      p.   cm.
   ISBN 978-0-300-16558-6 (pbk. : alk. paper)   1. Technical
literature.   2. Technological innovations.   3. Digital media.
I. Dibbell, Julian.
   T10.7.B47 2010
   600—dc22   2010017493

A catalogue record for this book is available from the British
Library.

This paper meets the requirements of ANSI/NISO Z39.48-1992
(Permanence of Paper).

10 9 8 7 6 5 4 3 2 1

Contents

The Best Technology Writing 2010

Introduction

Dear reader: You hold in your hands a technology as transformative as any yet invented, and no, I don't mean the Apple iPad or Amazon Kindle on which you may, for all I know, be reading these words. Nor for that matter do I mean the sort of content-delivery system you're more likely looking at just now —the traditional ink-and-paper book, its familiar design essentially unchanged since the time of Augustine. No, what I am talking about is a technology to which the book, electronic or otherwise, has always been and always will be merely a peripheral device. I'm talking about writing itself.

Writing has been with us now for so long that we've lost the habit of thinking of it as an invention. But in the earliest Western civilizations, not yet fully adjusted to the arrival of the written word, its technological origins and implications were keenly felt and hotly discussed. In ancient Egypt, for example, the discovery of writing was ascribed to the god Theuth, "inventor of many arts"—a sort of hacker deity also credited with geometry and board games, among other ancient forms of algorithmic tech. Theuth's arguments with his fellow god Thamus over the merits of this new invention were the stuff of Egyptian myth. Or so, at any rate, reports the philosopher Socrates, in a famous passage of Plato's *Phaedrus*. The passage pits Theuth's claim that writing can only be a boon to the intelligence of mortals ("This . . . will make [them] wiser and give them better memories") against Thamus's retort that, on the contrary, it will only lure its users toward a false and superficial sort of knowledge ("They will be hearers of many things and will have learned nothing; they will appear to be omniscient and will generally know nothing; they will be tiresome company, having the show of wisdom without the reality"). The debate was evidently a live one among Athenians as well as Egyptians. Socrates himself, who saw text as a lifeless replica of speech and much preferred to philosophize in the interactive real-time of his famous dialogues, made no pretense of neutrality: He was Team Thamus all the way.

We moderns, of course, take it for granted that Socrates picked the losing side of an argument now long since settled. But the terms of that same argument will sound almost uncannily familiar to anyone acquainted with the public conversation currently roiling around the arrival of another, equally disruptive new invention: digital technology. And if it's no coincidence that that same conversation happens to be where most of the texts selected for *The Best Technology Writing 2010* live and breathe, then it's also no surprise to find the animating spirits of the enthusiastic Theuth and the doubting Thamus woven through their midst. Steven Johnson's warm, Theuthian appreciation of Twitter's bite-sized contributions to collective human intelligence is a strong response to the latter-day Thamuses who dismiss as "tiresome company" and worse its millions of tweet-happy users. But often as not, in fact, both sides of the argument can be heard to echo in the same, conflicted text—Sam Anderson's giddy but troubled survey of the incursions of tech-driven distraction, for example, or Vanessa Grigoriadis's probing assessment, wistful but wary, of Facebook's growing role in our personal lives—and these echoes resonate all the more fully for it.

New technologies are often controversial, to be sure, yet in the end what links these two technological watersheds—the invention of writing in ancient times and the invention of digital processing in ours—is something more, and much more meaningful, than their sheer novelty. We forget too easily that the digital signal is not reducible to 1s, 0s, and electrons any more than the written word is reducible to ink, paper, and ABCs. Engineers have been known to build functioning digital computers out of clockwork, water pipes, Tinker Toys, just to show they can. Nor is it only in the case of computers or in the two-bit binary code of modern computing that digital technology, in its strictest definitions, can be found. The telegraph, for example, runs on a trinary digital code, the dot, dash, and space of Morse. Our genes use a quaternary digital system, the A, C, T, and G of genetic code, to program our DNA. There's even a hexavigesimal digital code—our own twenty-six-symbol variant of the ancient Latin alphabet, which the Romans derived in turn from the quadrivigesimal version used by the ancient Greeks. Or in other words: yes, the very same form of writing that got Socrates's toga in a twist was already, strictly speaking, a digital technology. And if that's true, then so is the flipside: the digital coding systems that so excite and trouble today's tech watchers do so not only because they transcend traditional writing but because they extend it, radically amplifying what was already exciting and troubling about it. In short, the modern debate about the digital doesn't merely echo the ancient argument about writing: it continues it. And so does *The Best Technology Writing 2010*.

Whatever else this peculiar affinity between writing and computers may account for, however, it begs a question that has gone unanswered since the creation of this series five years ago: Why should a collection that in name, at least, declares itself to be about technology in the broadest sense remain, year after year, so overwhelmingly focused on the digital in particular?

Of course there are selections in this volume, as in every one before it, that bring news from beyond the digital pale. Steve Silberman's investigation of the placebo effect in pharmaceutical testing, for example, deals like many a biotech story with consequences arguably more weighty than anything the microchip has wrought. Jill Lepore, writing on the politics of breastfeeding gadgetry, and Burkhard Bilger, tracking efforts to build a better cook stove for the developing world, both contemplate technologies more viscerally important than the iPod to vast swaths of humanity. Tad Friend's profile of electric-car developer Elon Musk delivers almost the only attempt even indirectly to address what is hands-down the most momentous technological question of our time: How to change our tools and our relationship to them so as to head off environmental catastrophe?

But again, as in every previous year, the nondigital stories are a distinct minority, and if you're thinking it's because the present guest editor, like all four of his predecessors, made his career writing largely about digital subjects, you are only partly right. Believe me, it's not for lack of trying that this year's search committee didn't find more stories about buildings and food and prosthetics and fuel cells. We beat the bushes, we called in chips, and in the end I can only conclude that the reason we found so much more of the digital stuff is, simply, that there's so much more of it to be found. As for why that should be so, I suspect the likeliest explanation is an equally obvious one: The digital story just happens to be the best one technology is telling at the moment. Which, again, is not to say the stakes are any lower in the quest for sustainable energy or the reengineering of the human body. It's just that, for the purpose of grabbing and holding a reader's attention, the story of digital technology has at least one clear advantage: We identify with its protagonist more closely than with any other technology yet contrived. From the moment the first computers were built right up to the latest attempts to design a more brainlike microchip (explored in Douglas Fox's illuminating account of "neural supercomputing"), we've been wondering where and how to draw the line between digital processing and human thought. Meanwhile the proliferation of digital devices (iPods, smart phones, Web sites, game gear) renders the question increasingly moot, infusing our cognitive, imaginative, and social lives with such a mess of auxiliary tech that we might as well admit we're all cyborgs now. More than any other technology, the digital is us.

Yet for that very reason, the digital is also something more. As the technology we most intimately relate to, it has become, additionally, a lightning rod for our feelings about technology in general. Whatever else draws us to the digital story, then, what compels us ultimately is that it focuses the more diffuse intensities of what Kevin Kelly, in his own contribution to this volume, calls our technophilia. By this he doesn't mean the sort of tech-boosting utopianism usually connoted by that phrase—the claims, as old as Theuth, that technology can make us better, smarter, cooler—but something quieter and deeper, beyond ideology or faith or any expectation of a payout. It's a feeling, Kelly suggests, that's as rooted in us as our inborn love of nature and as fundamentally a product of our evolution. "Our transformation from smart hominid into Sapiens was midwifed by our tools," writes Kelly, "and at our human core we harbor an innate affinity for made things. We are embarrassed to admit it, but we love technology. At least sometimes."

Of course what also needs to be said at this point is that technology doesn't love us back. Not really. In fact it's often hardest on those who love it most, sometimes even on those who devote their lives to it, and if you doubt that, consider another awkward reality that year after year haunts this tech-besotted series: technology's ongoing and very probably fatal assault on the same print-based publishing models—the magazine, the newspaper, and the book—that have made possible not only the *Best Technology Writing* series but the professional lives of many if not most of its contributors. Every year, some selection or another in these pages has at least alluded to this trend, and this year never mind allusions: *New York Times*-man David Carr joins us with a full-throated elegy to the dying world of predigital publishing, David Roth reports on an emerging class of digital publishing piecework jobs that makes rag-picking look like a viable alternative, and Clay Shirky's "Thinking the Unthinkable" delivers the most cogent, bracing argument yet written for the inevitability of the commercial newspaper's demise.

But the truly awkward part is this: Most technology writers, perhaps especially the professional ones, take genuine solace and even delight in the thought that commercial publishing's decline makes way for an explosion of passionately amateur online writing, an explosion not just imminent but fully under way. And yet, in each *Best Tech Writing* collection to date, the guest editor has felt obliged to note, with varying degrees of sheepishness, that most of the writing collected in it still comes from well-established print publications and not from the blogs and tumblrs and other deprofessionalized online forms to which we look for glimpses of publishing's future. Now it's my turn. This year, in fact, the awkwardness is starker than ever: Another negligible selection of noncommercial online texts combines with our highest concentration yet of articles from two perennially well-represented publications—*Wired* and *The New Yorker*—that happen both to be owned by the same media corporation. Let a hundred flowers bloom, indeed.

How to explain it? As it happens, my predecessor Clive Thompson already did, having pointed out in his introduction to the third collection that it is difficult to transplant the best online writing into print with its bloom still intact. Though much maligned as exercises in narcissism, blogs, for instance, are in fact defined by dialogue more than monologue; embedded in a conversational universe of links and comments, they are closer in many ways to what Socrates imagined to be the heart of true knowledge. As such, they do not sit well on the printed page. They are antsy and want to play, and for the purposes of an anthology like this, that won't do. When we set out to collect these texts, we knew we were looking for something that knew how to present itself in print, at length and on its own. Print journalism, and especially magazine journalism, tends to succeed in those ways, and it has hit upon certain formulas for that success: a reliance on narrative to engage the reader, an allegiance to the essay as a traditional rhetorical form, an attention to language that is just sufficient to bring the words to life without letting them stand between the reader and the idea. But though we made a point of looking at magazines for sources, we made a point as well of calling for submissions from every type of writing form out there: blogs, forums, comment threads, gadget reviews. We looked everywhere, honest. But you find what you look for, and what we were looking for is still mainly to be found in traditional print media—and perhaps more than ever in the bastions of that tradition upon which the best practitioners of long-form journalism now converge, like polar bears on a shrinking ice floe.

But if it's true that the newest forms of publishing don't, as a rule, translate well into print, it's also true that every rule has its exceptions. And this year, I am pleased to say, the exception comes as close to redeeming the rule as an exception can. This year, we are printing *The Best Technology Writing*'s first Twitter selection, and for my money it's the series' most eloquent encapsulation yet of our contemporary relationship to technology in all its dimensions: This lone tweet sent from the International Space Station by astronaut Mike Massimino leaps from the most intimate of our digital tools (the iPod, Twitter itself) to the most epic of our technological achievements (the domestication of outer space) in the space of 140 characters. And by the time it's done it proves that even a technology as old and familiar as writing can still take us altogether by surprise.

Vanish

For one month, Evan Ratliff shed his identity and tried to disappear. Here's what happened.

I

August 13, 6:40 pm: I'm driving East out of San Francisco on I-80, fleeing my life under the cover of dusk. Having come to the interstate by a circuitous route, full of quick turns and double backs, I'm reasonably sure that no one is following me. I keep checking the rearview mirror anyway. From this point on, there's no such thing as sure. Being too sure will get me caught.

I had intended to flee in broad daylight, but when you are going on the lam, there are a surprising number of last-minute errands to run. This morning, I picked up a set of professionally designed business cards for my fake company under my fake name, James Donald Gatz. I drove to a Best Buy, where I bought two prepaid cell phones with cash and then put a USB cord on my credit card—an arbitrary dollar amount I hoped would confuse investigators, who would scan my bill and wonder what gadgetry I had purchased. An oil change for my car was another head fake. Who would think that a guy about to sell his car would spend $60 at Oil Can Henry's?

I already owned a couple of prepaid phones; I left one of

the new ones with my girlfriend and mailed the other to my parents—giving them an untraceable way to contact me in emergencies. I bought some Just for Men beard-and-mustache dye at a drugstore. My final stop was the bank, to draw a $477 cashier's check. It's payment for rent on an anonymous office in Las Vegas, which is where I need to deliver the check by midday tomorrow.

Crossing the Bay Bridge, I glance back for a last nostalgic glimpse of the skyline. Then I reach over, slide the back cover off my cell phone, and pop out the battery. A cell phone with a battery inside is a cell phone that's trackable.

About 25 minutes later, as the California Department of Transportation database will record, my green 1999 Honda Civic, California plates 4MUN509, passes through the toll-booth on the far side of the Carquinez Bridge, setting off the FasTrak toll device, and continues east toward Lake Tahoe.

What the digital trail will not reflect is that a few miles past the bridge I pull off the road, detach the FasTrak, and stuff it into the duffle bag in my trunk, where its signal can't be detected. Nor will it note that I then double back on rural roads to I-5 and drive south through the night, cutting east at Bakersfield. There will be no digital record that at 4 am I hit Primm, Nevada, a sad little gambling town about 40 minutes from Vegas, where $15 cash gets me a room with a view of a gravel pile.

2

"Author Evan Ratliff Is on the Lam. Locate Him and Win $5,000."
—wired.com/vanish, August 14, 2009 5:38 pm

Officially it will be another 24 hours before the manhunt begins. That's when *Wired*'s announcement of my disappearance will be posted online. It coincides with the arrival on newsstands of the September issue of the magazine, which contains a page of mugshot-like photos of me, eyes slightly vacant. The premise is simple: I will try to vanish for a month and start over under a new identity. *Wired* readers, or whoever else happens upon the chase, will try to find me.

The idea for the contest started with a series of questions, foremost among them: How hard is it to vanish in the digital age? Long fascinated by stories of faked deaths, sudden disappearances, and cat-and-mouse games between investigators and fugitives, I signed on to write a story for *Wired* about people who've tried to end one life and start another. People fret about privacy, but what are the consequences of giving it all up, I wondered. What can investigators glean from all the digital fingerprints we leave behind? You can be anybody you want online, sure, but can you reinvent yourself in real life?

It's one thing to report on the phenomenon of people disappearing. But to really understand it, I figured that I had to try it myself. So I decided to vanish. I would leave behind my loved ones, my home, and my name. I wasn't going off the grid, dropping out to live in a cabin. Rather, I would actually try to drop my life and pick up another.

Wired offered a $5,000 bounty—$3,000 of which would come out of my own pocket—to anyone who could locate me between August 15 and September 15, say the password "fluke," and take my picture. Nicholas Thompson, my editor, would have complete access to information that a private investigator hired to find me might uncover: my real bank accounts, credit cards, phone records, social networking accounts, and email. I'd give Thompson my friends' contact information so he could conduct interviews. He would parcel out my personal details online, available to whichever amateur or professional investigators chose to hunt for me. To add a layer of intrigue, *Wired* hired the puzzle creators at Lone Shark Games to help structure the contest.

I began my planning months in advance. I let my hair and beard grow out, got a motorcycle license, and siphoned off extra cash whenever I visited an ATM, storing it in a hollowed-out book. One day over lunch, a friend from Google suggested software to hide my Internet address—"but all of these things can be broken," he warned—and how best to employ prepaid phones. I learned how to use Visa and American Express gift cards, bought with cash, to make untraceable purchases online. I installed software to mask my Web searches and generated a small notebook's worth of fake email addresses.

I shared my plans with no one, not my girlfriend, not my parents, not my closest friends. Nobody knew the route I was taking out of town, where I was going, or my new name. Not even a hint. If I got caught, it would be by my own mistakes.

Friday afternoon, August 14, I arrive in Vegas wearing a suit and sporting my normal brown hair, a beard, and a pair of rectangular tortoiseshell glasses. Carrying enough electronic equipment to stock a RadioShack, I drive straight to a dreary two-story office complex among the strip malls on South Pecos Road and hand over the cashier's check, securing a tiny windowless office. There I set up two laptops, flip on a webcam to track any activity in the office, and leave.

At CarMax, a used-auto outlet, I then sell my Civic for $3,000. The next day, the first official one of my disappearance, is spent dyeing my hair and goatee jet-black and locking down the security on my laptops—including a third one that I'll carry with me.

At 5 am on Sunday morning, the graveyard shift clerk at the Tropicana hotel hands over my $100 cash deposit, barely looking up. If she had, she might have noticed that the man checking out of room 480—wearing a pair of oversize Harry Potter-style glasses, hazel-colored contact lenses, slicked-back hair, and a belt with $2,000 cash hidden in an underside pocket—bears surprisingly little resemblance to the one who checked in two days before.

wayale *Found #vanish SF apt (http://bit .ly/6yvkR), talked to lady upstairs said he moved to NY. He can't be in NY apt, according to @wired.* 8:27 pm aug 17th

moshi77 *#vanish Evan bought swim trunks for $78, + UPS of $12. 8/10/09 they had a sale on them at gilt.com* 8:10 pm Aug 19th

Xovox *another address: 166 GERMANIA ST SAN FRANCISCO, CA 94117 middle name Donald? ;) #vanish* 8:27 pm Aug 19th

When Sarah Manello heard from a friend about the search for Ratliff, she couldn't resist. A researcher based in Rochester, New York, Manello had long worked with private investigators, digging up information for defense attorneys and tracking down missing people. She quit a few years ago after growing increasingly dissatisfied with the industry's tactics. But her skills remained intact. The initial question she posted on Twitter, under the handle @menacingpickle, was private investigation 101: What was Ratliff's middle name?

The first trickle of discussion among Manello and other hunters appeared by the morning of August 16, 36 hours after news of the hunt was posted on *Wired*.com. The next day it had grown into a deluge. On Twitter, anonymous users dedicated to Ratliff's pursuit sprouted by the hour: @VanishingActo1, @FindEvanRatliff, @EvanOffGrid, @FinderofEvan, @FindThatMan, among others. They organized around the Twitter tag #vanish, which, when placed in a post, allowed the growing horde of investigators to exchange theories, clues, and questions. They created Web sites and blogs and flyers and even a telephone tip line. A programmer in St. Louis, Michael Toecker, started a Facebook group called "The Search for Evan Ratliff." A week later it would have nearly a thousand members. (A countergroup designed to help Ratliff, founded by a banker in Cincinnati named Rich Reder, garnered a few dozen.)

What drew all these people? Some of them were lured by

the $5,000 bounty. Others were intrigued by the technical challenges of online tracking or the thrill of stakeouts. Some felt that a public dare needed to be answered. For many, Ratliff's flight evoked their own fleeting thoughts of starting over. "It was an adventure," says Matty Gilreath, a grant manager at UC San Francisco, referring to the dozens of hours he spent on the pursuit. "I'm grateful for my career. But there are other things I'd like to do, and this brought up a lot of issues about reinventing yourself."

From the *Wired* offices, Thompson began doling out information from Ratliff's accounts onto a blog—starting with the final credit card purchases and the FasTrak data. The would-be hunters dissected it as quickly as Thompson could post it. Using two FedEx tracking numbers from Ratliff's credit card bill, Manello managed, in a few aboveboard telephone calls, to find out where the packages had gone and who had signed for them. Hunters scoured the pictures on Ratliff's Flickr page, writing software code to extract information about the camera used and search for other photos it had taken. They combined the FasTrak data with other clues to build maps of possible routes.

Within days, they knew that Ratliff was a borderline-obsessive US national soccer team fan and a follower of the English team Fulham. That he had celiac disease, a condition under which he ate a diet entirely free of gluten, a protein found in wheat. That he and his girlfriend had bought an apartment in Brooklyn (in fact, the hunters posted a scan of Ratliff's signature from the deed). That he had recently attended a wedding, sporting a beard, in Palo Alto. They knew of his purchases at Best Buy and Oil Can Henry's and bombarded both businesses with calls.

What had started as an exercise in escape quickly became a cross between a massively multiplayer online game and a reality show. A staggeringly large community arose spontaneously, splintered into organized groups, and set to work turning over every rock in Ratliff's life. It topped out at 600 Twitter posts a day. The hunters knew the names of his cat sitter and his mechanic, his favorite authors, his childhood nicknames. They found every article he'd ever written; they found recent videos of him. They discovered and published every address he'd ever had in the US, from Atlanta to Hawaii, together with the full name and age of every member of his family.

They discovered almost every available piece of data about Ratliff, in fact, except his current location.

4

The Search for Evan Ratliff Facebook wall

Michael P. Anderson (Dallas/Fort Worth, TX) wrote at 2:21 pm on August 19th, 2009 *Sooooo. If I am trying to disappear wouldn't it make sense to leave a misdirection? I would arrange in advance to have some packages mailed to someplace where I knew that I would not be. Likewise I would make sure that a tab turned up at a local bar somewhere. What we really need to see is an ATM where he takes cash out.*

Michael Toecker wrote at 7:27 pm on August 19th, 2009 *1999 Honda Civic—4MUN509 CA—Don't ask me how I found out, but it's solid and legal.*

If you are looking to launch a disappearance, I cannot recommend any location more highly than a big-city Greyhound bus station. A mode of transportation Americans have seemingly left to the poor and desperate, it reeks of neglect and disdain. But for anonymity in the post-9/11 world—when the words "I'll just need to see a photo ID" are as common as a handshake—bus travel remains a sanctuary untouched by security. At the station in Las Vegas, I paid cash for a ticket under the name James Gatz, no ID required. Six cramped hours later I was in Los Angeles.

I hopped a city bus to Venice Beach and checked in to 15 Rose, a quaint European-style hostel that I'd found online. The laid-back day manager sympathized with my story of losing my credit cards and driver's license and showed me to a clean, spare room with free Wi-Fi. So began what I thought might be a few pleasant days on the beach: no phone calls to return, no deadlines to hit. Just my new life, stretching leisurely out before me.

When I flipped open my laptop and saw my private information spilling onto the Web, however, I got my first taste of a soon-to-be-permanent state of fitful anxiety. I'd signed up for it, of course. But actually living the new, paranoid reality felt different. Absurd ideas suddenly seemed plausible. They'd contacted my cat sitter; would they kidnap my cat?

Email was choking the inbox of the account *Wired* had made public, eratliff@atavist.net. Most of the messages consisted of efforts to subtly or not-so-subtly trick me into revealing my location by replying or visiting a Web site designed to trap my Internet protocol (IP) address, which maps to a physical location. I also started getting what I came to think of as little plea bargain offers: "Send me a picture and the code word and I'll split the $5K 50/50."

Fortunately, while I was shocked by the intensity of the pursuit, I had anticipated the tactics. To keep my Web surfing from being tracked I often used a piece of free software called Tor, designed to protect the Internet activities of dissidents and whistleblowers around the world. Tor masks a computer's IP address by diverting its requests through designated routers around the world. So when I logged in to Gmail from IP 131.179.50.72 in Los Angeles, the logs showed my request originating from 192.251.226.206 in Germany.

But as my friend from Google had reminded me, no security is unbreakable, so I'd added another layer: Vegas. I used the laptop I carried with me to log in remotely to my computers there, using free software from LogMeIn.com. The Vegas machines, in turn, were running Tor. Anyone clever enough to untangle those foreign routers would get only as far as a laptop sitting in an empty office on South Pecos Road.

Meanwhile, in LA, I meticulously kept up my physical disguise. One afternoon, a few blocks from my hotel, I had a chance to test it. A camera crew, fronted by an Internet news correspondent named Amanda Congdon, was corralling passersby for man-on-the-street interviews about their views on swine flu. I volunteered myself as an interview subject. A few days later, I found my interview on the Sometimesdaily.com site, Venice Beach in the background. It was time to get out of LA.

5

socillion @dimitrirose *the only IP not part of the Tor network is in Los Angeles and is owned by Trit Networks #vanish* 5:33 pm Aug 20th

menacingpickle @alanbly *I personally would not hide out in Vegas as every single movement is captured on camera* 7:15 pm aug 20th

evanoffgrid *Hunch Evan started growing out his hair/grew beard knowing his friends wld give out info, now he's bald or crewcut and blond #vanish* 6:06 pm aug 26th

labfly *on yet another evan stake out :) following a hunch #vanish* 6:27 pm Aug 27th

On August 20, a 16-year-old high school student in Portland, Oregon, named Jonathan Mäkelä saw a link to the story about the *Wired* contest on Hacker News. Mäkelä was a casual participant in the online community 4chan, whose pranks sometimes involved tracking down documents concerning unsuspecting targets. Mäkelä had grown fascinated by how much intel could be legally dug up online. Here was a guy, Ratliff, who invited people to use that same intel to find him. Now that was interesting.

Mäkelä began using a Twitter account under an anonymous handle, @socillion, and started pulling apart Ratliff's IP addresses. He quickly marshaled a collection of online tools with which he could peg IPs to a physical location and Internet service provider, often triangulating between several sites. By now, other hunters had determined that Ratliff's IPs—which Thompson published several times a day after logging in to Ratliff's email—appeared to be useless nodes from the Tor network. But Mäkelä meticulously verified that each was indeed a Tor node. He shared his information with the crowd and then got feedback in return. Eventually, he figured, the target might make a mistake.

Mäkelä quickly became one of the most active investigators, posting ideas to Twitter at least a dozen times a day. But this public collaboration, he soon realized, was itself a problem. The hunters were benefiting from their collective brainpower, but Ratliff could follow their thoughts just as easily. "Groups need to take this private," he posted to Twitter on August 20, "otherwise we are guaranteed never to win." Mäkelä set up a secure chat room and gave the password to only those he could verify weren't Ratliff.

6

To eratliff@atavist.net
From Mike
Date Fri, Aug 21, 2009 1:47 AM
Subject Your Disappearance

I want you to know right now that this is not an attempt to track you down. . . . I want to know firsthand from you, what is it like disappearing? How does it feel? Are you lonely? Do you miss life? Is it liberating to be free from everything? I ask these questions because the idea of leaving and starting a new life entertains me.

My plan involved leaving LA for good by midday Friday, August 21, and heading east. But before I left, I wanted to give my investigators a parting diversion, something to keep them fixated on the West Coast. So at 11:55 pm Thursday night, I inserted my bank card into an ATM in nearby Santa Monica, deposited the $3,000 car check, and took out $300 cash, the maximum single-day withdrawal. Figuring that as long as I was revealing my location to the world, I might as well pad my reserves, I withdrew another $300 at 12:01. Then I treated myself to a credit card purchase: a $13 vodka martini at the nearby Viceroy hotel.

Friday, I woke up at dawn and found the hostel Wi-Fi down. Blind to my pursuers, I decided to risk a last jog; I donned a baseball cap and trotted down along the water's edge. As I turned around to head back, a helicopter came up the beach from the opposite direction, flying low. It stopped and hovered between me and a group of surfers floating idly on their boards.

I'm not sure when the thought entered my head, but when it did, it lodged there: Was it possible that someone had seen my ATM transactions, called up a friend with a helicopter, and sent them out to scan the beach for me?

The correct answer was no. Deep down I knew this. But there the chopper was, hovering. I jogged a little bit farther, and it seemed to ease toward me, staying not-quite-directly overhead. I stopped to see if it would pass over. It didn't. The beach was empty. I jogged up to a lifeguard stand, putting it between me and the helicopter, and waited. A few seconds later, the nose crept around the building and back into my line of sight.

In that moment, reason evaporated. I took off toward the boardwalk, a lone figure sprinting across the sand at dawn. Seen from the air, I must have appeared, at this point, worth following. Whatever the reason, the helicopter kept coming. I reached the pavement and turned down a side street, bolted up one alley and down another, and finally ducked under a tree, lungs burning. I could still hear the thump-thump of the blades. I waited, my thoughts spinning out into ever-wilder fantasies. Were they radioing a ground team to drive by and yell "fluke"? Had they already staked out my hotel? Really? All for $5,000?

A few minutes passed and I heard it drift away. I took off again down the alley and ducked into a convenience store. There was an old pay-by-the-minute Internet terminal, and I slipped in a dollar. The ATM transactions hadn't even posted to my account yet.

7

alanbly *he just hit an ATM in Santa Monica #vanish* 11:51 AM Aug 21st

lookingforevan @*combobulate #vanish. His phone has been off for days. I think he's using a prepaid.* 1:26 PM Aug 21st

labfly *okay now i'm walking up to 30 something guys that look anyting like evan & people r thinking i'm nutz* 4:14 PM Aug 21st

socillion @*RatliffPatrol According to the statements its at 1300 4TH ST SANTA MONICA CA whre thrs a wells fargo. street view blckd by bus tho #vanish* 1:23 AM Aug 22nd

When Thompson posted Ratliff's ATM transactions online, late the morning of August 21, the pursuit kicked into high gear. For the first time, Ratliff had pegged himself to a specific place, and hunters hit the streets to try to nab him. Mäkelä pinpointed the exact location of the ATM in Santa Monica. One man set about frantically calling restaurants in the area, asking whoever picked up the phone to scan the crowd for someone who met Ratliff's description. Manello called the car dealer in Vegas, then she found a bookstore owner who claimed to have seen him.

In the private chat room that Mäkelä ran as Socillion,

however, the consensus seemed to be that Ratliff had moved on. They discussed and discarded strategies ranging from the clever to the outlandish to the completely illegal. Somehow, they had to figure out how to get ahead of him. "Right now, Evan is controlling us," a participant named AtavistTracker wrote. "Evan's had over two months to plan this. We need to alter that plan. I like disinformation."

"Me too," Socillion replied. "Fight with his tools."

8

> EvanOffGrid *remember we can't trust messages from Evan.* 8:46 am Aug 27th
>
> how2stalk *Latest Evan Google Earth file: http://bit.ly/nNh7K* #*vanish* 9:39 am aug 27th
>
> TrackEvan *Update: "Evan's Reading List" now on http://www.trackevan.com/* #*vanish* 7:24 pm Aug 27th
>
> bellyscratcher #*vanish* *Contacting more PIs, will update when done.* 12:13 am Aug 28th

By the end of the first week, the deception had already begun to wear me down. Lying about your identity involves more than just transgressing some abstract prohibition against deceit. It means overcoming a lifetime of built-up habits, from a well-rehearsed life story to the sound of your own name. When I convinced people that I really was James Donald Gatz, I occasionally felt a mischievous thrill. Most of the time, however, I felt awful. The people I encountered weren't credulous; they were just nice.

I left LA with a band called the Hermit Thrushes, trading gas money for a spot onboard a converted retirement-home shuttle van that served as their tour bus. An indie rock group composed of college grads from Philadelphia, they'd responded to an ad I posted on craigslist, under the name Don, needing a ride to Austin or New Orleans. We rattled along

from show to show: LA to Tempe to Las Cruces, up to Lubbock and Tulsa, east to Fayetteville, then north toward Chicago. The band played whiskey bars, coffee shops, and rowdy
house parties. We crashed on living room floors or crammed
into the seats of the bus, and, once, on the grass at a rest stop
in Texas.

The band was serious about its music but unperturbed
about much else, and I settled into a role somewhere between
lazy roadie and moneyed patron, pulling $100 bills from my
belt at gas stations. On board, I staked out the bus's backseat,
where I could use my laptop without anyone looking over my
shoulder. With a $150 wireless broadband card from Virgin
Mobile, the only nationwide service that didn't require a credit
check, I had almost uninterrupted online access.

So I passed the long hours on the road building up an online
life for my new identity. I'd opened a Facebook account under
"GatzJD" and a Twitter account under @jdgatz (which I kept
open to the world for days, cataloging my location for posterity,
before panicking and locking it from public view). For the average person, populating an online social network account is as
easy as finding your friends, connecting to their friends, and
watching the virtual acquaintances pile up. As Gatz, though, I
had no actual friends. Instead, I set about finding people who
would accept my friendship automatically, and soon my profile
was overrun with multilevel marketers and inspirational speakers. Enough, I thought, to convince potential real acquaintances
who didn't look too hard that I wasn't friendless.

I'd been set to depart the tour in Lubbock, Texas, but the
band was cool and I was safe, so I kept going. On the afternoon of August 26, the bus finally pulled into St. Louis, where
the band had a college radio gig scheduled and I had a plan to
get to the train station. A half hour later, listeners to KWUR
heard the Hermit Thrushes dedicate their show to a mysterious single-named traveler, Don, headed for New Orleans.

I looked out my office window (about 6 floors up) about 11AM and spotted Evan walking up 1st avenue from the direction of Qwest Field—he was wearing a backpack and heading into downtown . . . My heart started to race as I ran out of the office and hit the elevator button. Once I got to the street Evan w/ backpack was nowhere to be found . . . Walking to the bus that evening I surveyed the faces of every stranger I walked past—looked at the eyes, the hair, finding at least 3 possible Evans on my 15 minute walk to the bus. I think I was going insane!

—Jeremy Thompson aka @evan_ratliff

On August 24, a former Microsoft group program manager in Seattle named Jeff Reifman read about the hunt in *Wired*. Reifman, self-employed these days, had recently launched a series of grant-funded Facebook applications to study the engagement of young people with the news. From a technical standpoint, the contest seemed intriguing.

On August 27, working on a desktop in his living room, he created Vanish Team, a Facebook app dedicated to information and discussion about Ratliff. He announced it on Twitter, and people began clicking over to check it out. Reifman was late to the party, however; most of the real intel swap stayed on Twitter or in Mäkelä's secure chat room.

Down in Portland, Mäkelä was learning that it wasn't secure enough. One night, as a San Diego–based hunter was making the drive to Las Vegas—where the chat room believed Ratliff was headed—an insider emailed Ratliff to tip him off.

When Thompson posted the anonymous email on the *Wired* blog, it was the hunters' turn to be paranoid. Mäkelä moved to another chat room, and then started another, jettisoning all but a few of his most trustworthy correspondents. One of the people he kicked out, after a set of heated exchanges, was Reifman.

SearchForEvan *Ok, best guesses . . . what is Evan doing RIGHT NOW? #vanish* 9:40 pm aug 28th

From St. Louis I took a bus to Carbondale, Illinois, and caught a train south to New Orleans. To get around Amtrak's mandatory government ID requirements, I booked online, using my real name, and picked up the ticket from a machine at the station. I still might need an ID on the train, so to obscure myself to anyone who might get into the Amtrak database, I booked under my middle name and misspelled my last name ever so slightly, leaving out the *l*.

I'd chosen New Orleans months before, distant enough from the coasts to provide obscurity but familiar to me from trips I'd taken years before. Showing up in a city with no friends, no contacts, no credit cards, and no ID is itself a discomfiting experience, and having a basic grip on the layout eases the alienation. After four days in a vacation condo, rented from an absentee landlord who accepted PayPal, I found a cheap one-bedroom apartment around the corner. The next day I signed my well-practiced J. D. Gatz scrawl on the lease. The landlord, after a friendly chat, was ready to hand over the keys. He would, he said, just need to see my driver's license.

I'd been working for months to establish James Donald Gatz as a separate identity. The name itself—the one that Jay Gatsby sheds to start over in *The Great Gatsby*—was easy for me to remember. More important, due to the prolific amount of Gatsby analysis online, it was basically un-Google-able. The middle name was my own, but Mr. Gatz received an entirely new birthday: July 1, 1976, shaving about a year off my age.

He also got a "research firm," Bespect LLC, registered in the state of New Mexico and complete with a logo—a bespectacled cartoon man with a mustache—and a Web site at Bespect.com. Gatz's PayPal account was funded using gift cards. I'd even ordered up a gift card with his name on it that looked to the casual eye like a real credit card.

My new landlord glanced at the business card and flimsy home-laminated "visiting scholar" credentials that I slid across the table. "Bespect.com, eh?" he said. "Interesting. These will do." He turned around, photocopied them, and dropped the copy in a folder along with my lease.

At this point, my new life seemed, superficially at least, satisfactory. My days were spent jogging along the Mississippi, haunting the coffee shops and jazz bars of my adopted neighborhood, and exploring the city by bike. I located a soccer bar and even got a one-night job selling beer and nachos for tips during a Saints game at the Superdome.

The gnawing flaw in the idyllic life of J. D. Gatz was that I did all of these activities alone. It wasn't just that I had no friends. It was that the interactions I did have were beyond superficial. They were fake. My online social networks were populated with strangers; my girlfriend was thousands of miles away; my family knew about me only from news reports and online speculation.

I'd always prided myself on being comfortable with solitude, but this wasn't normal solitude. It was everyone-is-out-to-get-me isolation. What to the hunters felt like an intricate puzzle felt real enough to me—and there was no one around to laugh and tell me otherwise. Instead there was just me, staring into my laptop all day, wondering if it was safe to go out and get the paper.

For the first time in my life, I couldn't sleep. One night I awoke at 4 am drenched in sweat, having dreamed that a childhood friend turned me in.

> vanishteam *Evan shaved his cat on Aug 19 http://bit.ly/zrO86—* *after shaving his own head? It's the easiest and coolest way to chg appearance #vanish* 11:38 PM Aug 28th
>
> vanishteam *Am pretty certain @theatavist is openly blogging and posting photos of his travels somewhere on the net.* #vanish 2:57 PM Sep 1st
>
> vanishteam *Hope @theatavist returns safely or we're all suspects!* *#vanish* 6:41 PM Sep 2nd

Out in Seattle, Reifman wasn't generating solid leads. Through a convoluted set of clues, some of which later turned out to be inaccurate, he developed a theory that the target had headed to San Diego. Reifman posted it to the Vanish Team site, but nothing came of it.

He decided to try a different tack. Instead of using the Vanish Team application to gather news about Ratliff, he'd use it to track him. He installed 38 lines of new code. It was rudimentary and unlikely to work if Ratliff had set up Tor, his anonymity software, correctly. But it gave Reifman a tool to easily pick out the IP addresses of Facebook visitors to Vanish Team. Ratliff might be among them. He'd be the guy without many friends.

> jdgatz *Just arranged to sublet cool apt yesterday. Upstairs back of shotgun house, called a "camel back" apartment. Sounds dirty, but it's not.* 2:33 PM Aug 30th
>
> jdgatz *I'm not sure I've ever stayed up all night before in order to (partially) re-shave my head before a morning flight. But desperate times...* 12:51 AM Sep 5th
>
> jdgatz *I'm learning to love Amtrak, but anything over 5 hrs w/out sleeping car = yearning for the development of air travel. Wait, they have that?* 12:51 AM Sep 5th

In constructing a proper disguise, there is no place for vanity or pride. Altering your appearance, after all, is not about convincing people. It's about misdirection, diverting their attention from the physical features you are unable to change and toward the ones you can. Success often involves making yourself look older, fatter, nerdier, sleazier, or otherwise more unpleasant than you were before. The goal is to be overlooked, ignored, or, sometimes, noticed and then dismissed with a chuckle.

It was the last to which I aspired as I walked through security at the Memphis airport, on Saturday morning, September 5, barely resembling the face on the real ID I showed at the security line. My hair was shaved clean on top with a razor but left short-cropped on the sides and back, in the manner of advanced male pattern baldness. The bald spot had been enhanced with tanning cream, compensation for the sudden paleness of my newly shorn dome. I wore a borderline-creepy mustache, above which a new set of prescriptionless glasses were backed by brown prescription contacts. I twirled a fake wedding band on my finger. A hands-free cell phone headset dangled from my ear.

Unable to completely abandon the hobbies of my previous life, I was headed to Salt Lake City for the US World Cup qualifying soccer match against El Salvador. The logistics had been complicated: a train to Memphis, followed by a flight to San Francisco (which needed to be under $250, the maximum gift card available) that stopped in Salt Lake.

The greater problem would be avoiding the hunters. They had long speculated that I might attend the game, and I'd seen stakeout rumors on Twitter. So I bought two fully refundable tickets to Salt Lake on my credit card for September 4, originating in LA and Portland—misdirections I knew they'd discover and that I hoped would lead them to the airport on the wrong day. I'd anonymously emailed a prominent hunter a link to the Venice Beach "swine flu video" to fix my previous appearance in their minds. Finally, I'd unmasked my computers' address in Las Vegas several times, turning off Tor while visiting Web sites that I knew were trapping IPs.

But it was my disguise that gave me confidence as I breezed off the plane in Salt Lake City, dressed in a suit and tie, jabbering loudly to imaginary business contacts on my hands-free. I met an accomplice, an old friend also dressed as a low-rent sales rep; we dodged a suspicious lurker at the baggage claim. Then we checked in to a downtown hotel and changed into our game-day disguises. For him: a red, white, and blue afro wig. For me: waving stars and stripes painted atop my head, augmented with a bulky pair of American flag sunglasses and a red clown nose.

Walking to the stadium, we passed several people who seemed to be doing nothing other than scanning the crowd. "I've already seen a few people that I thought could be him," one man murmured as we passed a few feet away.

1 3

> socillion @*nxthompson* #*vanish* a *Wired reader/tw telecoms hostmaster tells me that the LV IPs are from a biz @ 4760 S. Pecos Road, Las Vegas 89121* 3:48 pm sEp 3rd

> viequense @*EvanOffGrid We were pretty sure we saw Evan last nt but we were also pretty drunk. Got pick & password.* #*vanish* 8:06 am sep 5th

> viequense @*EvanOffGrid It was last night, maybe about 11pm at a bar in SLC where we were having a USMNT party for the game tomorrow.* 8:16 am sep 5th

For the hunters, it was again time to put boots on the ground. But where? Mäkelä, jumping on the real IP address, called a technician at an ISP in Las Vegas who happily revealed the address on South Pecos Road. The hunters puzzled over the businesses listed there, wondering if Ratliff somehow had a friend among them.

For now, though, the action was headed for Salt Lake City. One woman bought a refundable ticket to get through security and stake out departure gates at the Portland airport. A man did the same for arrivals in Salt Lake City, waiting for seven hours over two days. Mäkelä generated a map of all the known gluten-free eateries in the area, and hunters hit pre-game parties. All that turned up were look-alikes.

That Friday afternoon in Seattle, Reifman was sorting through more Facebook profiles. Recalling Thompson's statement that Ratliff would not just be hiding but trying to make new friends, Reifman had decided to expand his search to include Vanish Team visitors with up to 50 Facebook friends. He pulled up the profile for a James Donald Gatz, who seemed to be visiting Vanish Team regularly. The name didn't ring a bell, but the photo looked familiar. Then he realized where he'd seen that look before: the swine flu video. He flipped back and forth between the two, and soon he was positive. Gatz was Ratliff.

At first, he was giddy. All he needed to do was friend one of Gatz's friends or convince one to reveal their new pal's location. Looking through the profile, though, he realized that Ratliff had populated his account with what amounted to Facebook automatons. Reifman tried sending messages to a few, telling them about the hunt. No luck.

He decided to try Twitter. Eventually, he typed in "jdgatz" and found the account, locked from public view. Friends of @jdgatz could see his posts, but the general public, including Reifman, couldn't. With a simple Google search for "jdgatz," Reifman located an archived, unprotected version of jdgatz's posts from the previous week. Gatz, at least at that point, had been revealing his location as he moved around. Maybe he'd do it again.

Currently, though, gaining access to Gatz's daily feed would require his permission. Not wanting to spook the target, Reifman tried to enlist the help of one of Gatz's current connections, who would already have access. Again, most were multilevel marketers or auto-reply bots. But he managed to find three real people among them: a Hawaii real estate agent, a Segway aficionado in New Zealand, and a blogger in Atlanta. Reifman convinced all three to keep him apprised of whatever Gatz wrote.

At 4 am on Sunday morning, Reifman's girlfriend came downstairs and found him staring into the screen. "What are you doing?"

"I think I've found Evan."

14

The Search for Evan Ratliff Facebook wall

Landon Anderson (Salt Lake City, UT) wrote at 8:26pm on September 6, 2009 *EVERYBODY!!!!! I do not know how to use Twitter, so I am posting this information here so that someone can post it on Twitter. Evan is in ATLANTA. He landed there at about 8:10 pm Atlanta time today. He showed up to SLC airport this morning, canceled the itinerary from SLC to SFO, purchased a new ticket to Atlanta via Denver. I am sure my knowledge will soon be confirmed by Nicholas. I did nothing illegal . . . just have connections.*

The morning after the soccer game, I caught a flight to Atlanta via Denver. After landing at Hartsfield Airport, I rushed off the jetway, a businessman in a hurry. Safely a few gates away, I opened my laptop for a routine check of the *Wired* blog. Headline: "Evan Ratliff will arrive in Atlanta in 5 minutes." I slammed the laptop shut and took off.

All of the Hartsfield terminals funnel out to a single exit.

But as a former Atlanta resident, I knew one other way out, a solitary revolving door from the T Gates leading to a remote part of baggage claim. It was eerily empty when I got there. I slipped out, hustled to the public transit station at the far end, and caught a train into town. Only later would I learn that a hunter in Atlanta arrived minutes after I'd left, sprinted to the trains, and frantically canvassed the passengers.

I crashed for a few hours at the house of a friend—one of only a few I was willing to reach out to, knowing that Thompson was posting interview transcripts of his talks with them. The next morning I caught the first Amtrak train out, sinking down in my seat for the 12-hour ride back to New Orleans. A few times en route I opened my laptop to check on reports of the hunters scurrying furiously around Atlanta. On Twitter, the guy running the Vanish Team Facebook application kept announcing new scoops, exhorting people to check out his site. Each time, I'd click over to Facebook, using James Gatz's account. What scoops? Vanish Team seemed like all bluster.

At this point, I'd stopped logging in to my Vegas computers for anything but the riskiest Web surfing. This was partly out of a growing laziness; the whole process took longer than dialup circa 1993. I also figured that I could freely visit Facebook pages like Vanish Team. Anyone who built an application to use on a corporate site, I assumed, would need cooperation from the company to track their users.

Once back safely in New Orleans, I decided to redouble my efforts to socialize, both online and in real life. For starters, I opened up my @jdgatz Twitter feed to the public—maybe I could connect with some local friends. I searched for New Orleans businesses I might follow. One was a local gluten-free pizza place I'd wanted to go to called NakedPizza.

From Jeff Reifman
Date Mon, Sep 7, 2009 9:48 PM
Subject Re: ALERT Evan in Jacksons Gap, Alabama—Got a
clear lead just now

By Monday, Jeff Reifman had mentioned the @jdgatz account
to a few active hunters, including Sarah Manello and Mäkelä,
with whom he'd patched things up. When Ratliff opened his
Twitter feed to the public, Reifman created two fake accounts
of his own—crafted to look like automated Twitter bots, so as
not to raise Ratliff's suspicion—and started following the account.

Then Monday night, Reifman noticed James Gatz logging in from a new IP address: 74.180.70.233. According to
the database Reifman was using, the address pointed to Jacksons' Gap, Alabama. After he emailed his select group of
trusted hunters, Mäkelä ran the address through his own little triangulated system and discovered where it actually originated from. Two minutes later he sent a one-line response to
Reifman: "That IP is in New Orleans."

Reifman flipped over to the @jdgatz Twitter feed and
noticed that the number of accounts Gatz was following had
gone up by three—all New Orleans businesses. He looked
up NakedPizza's Web site and fired off an email explaining
the hunt. "I have accurate information that Evan has arrived
in New Orleans and plans to go to NakedPizza Tuesday or
Wednesday," he wrote. A few minutes later, he followed
up. "I forgot to mention," he said, "that we know Evan has
shaved his head either partially (male pattern bald) or fully."
Reifman informed his fellow hunters, and Manello spent the
evening dialing 50 hotels near the restaurant, asking for a
James Gatz.

The next morning when Jeff Leach, cofounder of Naked-

Pizza and a tech-savvy entrepreneur, got the email, he thought at first it was a scam. But he passed it along to his business partner, and after delving into the hunt information online, they concluded it was real. Leach decided to help.

1 6

> *To* Jeff Reifman
> *From* Jeff Leach
> *Date* Tue, Sep 8, 2009 8:17 AM
> *We will catch him.*

Tuesday, September 8, 7 am: Just seven days to go. I awake in my apartment in New Orleans, relieved to find no online indication of anyone wise to my location. Aside from a few random new followers to my Twitter feed, all of whom seem like automated bots, nobody seems to be paying attention to my fake accounts either.

I use a gift card to book a flight to New York City on September 15, the final day of my disappearance, and hatch plans to surprise Thompson in his office using a fake security badge. I've been communicating sporadically with my editor through a public blog—I'd post something, he'd read it, delete it, and then post his response. Before Salt Lake City, I'd boasted that I could survive the month, "just by keeping my head down and being careful with my phones and IPs."

Now *Wired* has decided to up the stakes, offering me $400 for each of a series of challenges I complete. And I could use it. As much as any other factor—personal gall, or endurance, or discipline—staying on the run requires an abundance of cash. I've already nearly spent the three grand I brought with me. Besides, I made it through the Salt Lake City gauntlet and survived a near miss in Atlanta. I can do this.

The first two challenges—clues to which are embedded,

with the help of Will Shortz and Lone Shark Games, for the hunters to find in the *New York Times* crossword puzzle—are to go to the 50th story of a building and to attend a book reading. Checking online, I identify only two buildings in downtown New Orleans of 50 stories or taller, and I choose One Shell Square. At the security desk, back in my businessman disguise, I step up and announce that I'm here to visit the law firm occupying the upper floors. "Just sign in here. And we'll need to see your ID."

"Well, I've lost mine. Will a business card and a credit card do?"

In two minutes, I'm on the 50th floor, video camera rolling. Later, as I wander home through the French Quarter, a street vendor sidles up beside me with some friendly unsolicited advice. "Hey buddy," he says, gesturing to my haircut. "You gotta shave the rest of that off, man."

That same morning, Leach, of NakedPizza, calls Reifman, and the two begin comparing notes. Leach searches through his Web site's logs, finding that IP address 74.180.70.233— aka James Gatz—visited NakedPizza.biz late the previous evening.

By 11 am, Leach has briefed all of his employees on the hunt. If they see the target, he explains, they need to say "fluke" and take a photo. He creates a folder on the company network with pictures for them to study. One is a Photoshopped mock-up of Ratliff, bald.

Brock Fillinger, also a cofounder, whose own pate is clean-shaven, heads over to stake out the tours at Old New Orleans Rum, another business Ratliff was following on Twitter and that Reifman had contacted. "Hey," the woman behind the desk says as Fillinger lingers nearby, "are you that *Wired* writer?"

Snide street comments aside, I've already decided to shave the rest of my head and mustache. My acquisition of actual friends will require looking less creepy. I change into casual clothes, grab a fedora, and ride my bicycle to the barber.

At 5:20 I'm completely bald, and I'll have to hustle to make it across town for the book reading I plan to attend.

At 5:48, Leach and Fillinger are watching both entrances to the Garden District BookShop. They're expecting someone "wigged up," someone who looks like he doesn't quite belong. But the reading started promptly at 5:30, and there is no sign of Ratliff.

Leach sends a text message to Fillinger. This looks like a bust. They meet up out front, ready to move on.

It's surreal, in those moments when I stop to think about it. Scores of people have studied my picture, stared into those empty eyes in the hopes of relieving me of thousands of dollars. They have stood for hours, trying to pick out my face in a crowd. They've come to know me like we've been friends for years. It's weirdly thrilling, in a narcissistic kind of way, but also occasionally terrifying.

I almost ride past the bookshop before I see the sign, tucked into a tiny shopping center. I stop at the corner and pull out my bike lock. Two men stand on the stairs outside, facing the street. They glance over at me.

My first impulse is to ride away. But at what point do I separate caution from self-delusion? Not every out-of-place person is looking for me.

Tired from the bike ride, tired of the corrosive suspicion, I decide to walk past them on the sidewalk, making no move toward the bookstore. Just a local, heading down the street to visit a friend.

"Hey," Leach calls out from the stairs, taking a hesitant step toward me. I freeze and stare back helplessly. "You wouldn't happen to know a guy named Fluke, would you?"

17

To Nicholas Thompson
From Laurie Ambrose
Date Wed, Sep 9, 2009 12:54 PM
Subject My #Vanish Story

> *Why would a middle-aged woman with virtually no technical knowledge be interested in following the Evan's Vanished story on Twitter? You see, my father walked out one morning in Sumter, South Carolina, kissed the wife and two young children good-bye as if he was going to work as always, and disappeared for 12 years. He was around Evan's age. He sent the family a telegraph a few days later asking them not to look for him. To this day, no one knows anything about his personal life during those years. I guess I'm hoping to have some clues to some of my questions.*

At first I was angry: at myself for getting caught and losing the money, at *Wired* for tempting me with the challenges. But that was soon replaced by the thrill of being redeposited in my own identity, with a family, a partner, friends, and a past I didn't have to hide. I packed up my apartment, rented a car, and visited my parents in Florida. Then I bought a plane ticket home.

Leach and Reifman had agreed to split the prize money, but they both ended up giving it all to Unity of Greater New Orleans, a charity helping the city recover from Hurricane Katrina. Socillion started his junior year of high school. The online chatter dissolved as quickly as it had formed.

And what of our original questions? Had I shown that a person, given enough resources and discipline, could vanish from one life and reinvent himself in another? I thought I had, though only up to a point. Obviously the smarts and dedication of the hunters had overwhelmed my planning and endurance. Along the way they'd also proven my privacy to be a modern fiction. It turns out that people—ordinary people—really can gather an incredible dossier of facts about you. But a month later, life was back to normal and no one was taking any interest.

More than all that, I'd discovered how quickly the vision of total reinvention can dissolve into its lonely, mundane reality. Whatever reason you might have for discarding your old self and the people who went with it, you'll need more than a made-up backstory and a belt full of cash to replace them.

For weeks after the hunt ended, I still paused when introducing myself and felt a twinge of panic when I handed over my credit card. The paranoid outlook of James Donald Gatz was hard to shake. Even now, my stomach lurches when I think back to the night I got caught. "You wouldn't happen to know a guy named Fluke, would you?"

Right after it happened, I rode my bike back to my apartment and sat in the air-conditioning, unsure what to do. Finally I got online and logged in to the hunters' private chat room for the first time. Rich Reder, founder of the Facebook countergroup designed to help me stay hidden, had infiltrated the room and sent me the password. Just a little too late.

I found Mäkelä there, still logged in. I asked him why he was hanging around a chat room dedicated to catching a guy who'd already been caught. "Just lurking," he wrote. "Working out the moles."

After a while I signed off, closed my laptop, and walked down the street to J. D. Gatz's local dive bar. I ordered a whiskey and tried to tell the bartender how I abandoned my life and then got it back. For the first time in weeks, someone didn't seem to believe my story.

Steven Johnson

Why We Tweet

What Twitter can teach us about the future of innovation.

The one thing you can say for certain about Twitter is that it makes a terrible first impression. You hear about this new service that lets you send 140-character updates to your "followers," and you think, Why does the world need this, exactly? It's not as if we were all sitting around four years ago scratching our heads and saying, "If only there were a technology that would allow me to send a message to my 50 friends, alerting them in real time about my choice of breakfast cereal."

I, too, was skeptical at first. I had met Evan Williams, Twitter's co-creator, a couple of times in the dotcom '90s when he was launching Blogger.com. Back then, what people worried about was the threat that blogging posed to our attention span, with telegraphic, two-paragraph blog posts replacing long-format articles and books. With Twitter, Williams was launching a communications platform that limited you to a couple of sentences at most. What was next? Software that let you send a single punctuation mark to describe your mood?

And yet as millions of devotees have discovered, Twitter turns out to have unsuspected depth. In part this is because hearing about what your friends had for breakfast is actually more interesting than it sounds. The technology writer Clive Thompson calls this "ambient awareness": by following these quick, abbreviated status reports from members of your extended social network, you get a strangely satisfying glimpse of their daily routines. We don't think it at all moronic to start a phone call with a friend by asking how her day is going. Twitter gives you the same information without your even having to ask.

The social warmth of all those stray details shouldn't be taken lightly. But I think there is something even more profound in what has happened to Twitter over the past two years, something that says more about the culture that has embraced and expanded Twitter at such extraordinary speed. Yes, the breakfast-status updates turned out to be more interesting than we thought. But the key development with Twitter is how we've jury-rigged the system to do things that its creators never dreamed of.

In short, the most fascinating thing about Twitter is not what it's doing to us. It's what we're doing to it.

THE OPEN CONVERSATION

Earlier this year I attended a daylong conference in Manhattan devoted to education reform. Called Hacking Education, it was a small, private affair: 40-odd educators, entrepreneurs, scholars, philanthropists and venture capitalists, all engaged in a sprawling six-hour conversation about the future of schools. Twenty years ago, the ideas exchanged in that conversation would have been confined to the minds of the participants. Ten years ago, a transcript might have been published weeks or months later on the Web. Five years ago, a handful of participants might have blogged about their experiences after the fact.

But this event was happening in 2009, so trailing behind

the real-time, real-world conversation was an equally real-time conversation on Twitter. At the outset of the conference, our hosts announced that anyone who wanted to post live commentary about the event via Twitter should include the word #*hackedu* in his 140 characters. In the room, a large display screen showed a running feed of tweets. Then we all started talking, and as we did, a shadow conversation unfolded on the screen: summaries of someone's argument, the occasional joke, suggested links for further reading. At one point, a brief argument flared up between two participants in the room—a tense back-and-forth that transpired silently on the screen as the rest of us conversed in friendly tones.

At first, all these tweets came from inside the room and were created exclusively by conference participants tapping away on their laptops or BlackBerrys. But within half an hour or so, word began to seep out into the Twittersphere that an interesting conversation about the future of schools was happening at #hackedu. A few tweets appeared on the screen from strangers announcing that they were following the #hackedu thread. Then others joined the conversation, adding their observations or proposing topics for further exploration. A few experts grumbled publicly about how they hadn't been invited to the conference. Back in the room, we pulled interesting ideas and questions from the screen and integrated them into our face-to-face conversation.

When the conference wrapped up at the end of the day, there was a public record of hundreds of tweets documenting the conversation. And the conversation continued—if you search Twitter for #*hackedu,* you'll find dozens of new comments posted over the past few weeks, even though the conference happened in early March.

Injecting Twitter into that conversation fundamentally changed the rules of engagement. It added a second layer of discussion and brought a wider audience into what would have been a private exchange. And it gave the event an afterlife on the Web. Yes, it was built entirely out of 140-character messages, but the sum total of those tweets added up to something truly substantive, like a suspension bridge made of pebbles.

THE SUPER-FRESH WEB

The basic mechanics of Twitter are remarkably simple. Users publish tweets—those 140-character messages—from a computer or mobile device. (The character limit allows tweets to be created and circulated via the SMS platform used by most mobile phones.) As a social network, Twitter revolves around the principle of followers. When you choose to follow another Twitter user, that user's tweets appear in reverse chronological order on your main Twitter page. If you follow 20 people, you'll see a mix of tweets scrolling down the page: breakfast-cereal updates, interesting new links, music recommendations, even musings on the future of education. Some celebrity Twitterers—most famously Ashton Kutcher—have crossed the million-follower mark, effectively giving them a broadcast-size audience. The average Twitter profile seems to be somewhere in the dozens: a collage of friends, colleagues and a handful of celebrities. The mix creates a media experience quite unlike anything that has come before it, strangely intimate and at the same time celebrity-obsessed. You glance at your Twitter feed over that first cup of coffee, and in a few seconds you find out that your nephew got into med school and Shaquille O'Neal just finished a cardio workout in Phoenix.

In the past month, Twitter has added a search box that gives you a real-time view onto the chatter of just about any topic imaginable. You can see conversations people are having about a presidential debate or the *American Idol* finale or Tiger Woods—or a conference in New York City on education reform. For as long as we've had the Internet in our homes, critics have bemoaned the demise of shared national experiences, like moon landings and "Who Shot J.R." cliff hangers—the folkloric American living room, all of us signing off in unison with Walter Cronkite, shattered into a million isolation booths. But watch a live mass-media event with Twitter open on your laptop and you'll see that the futurists had it wrong. We still have national events, but now when we have them, we're actually having a genuine, public conversation with a group that extends far beyond our nuclear family and our next-door neighbors. Some of that conversation is juvenile, of course, just as it was in our living room when we heckled Richard Nixon's Checkers speech. But some of it is moving, witty, observant, subversive.

Skeptics might wonder just how much subversion and wit is conveyable via 140-character updates. But in recent months Twitter users have begun to find a route around that limitation by employing Twitter as a pointing device instead of a communications channel: sharing links to longer articles, discussions, posts, videos—anything that lives behind a URL. Websites that once saw their traffic dominated by Google search queries are seeing a growing number of new visitors coming from "passed links" at social networks like Twitter and Facebook. This is what the naysayers fail to understand: it's just as easy to use Twitter to spread the word about a brilliant 10,000-word *New Yorker* article as it is to spread the word about your Lucky Charms habit.

Put those three elements together—social networks, live searching and link-sharing—and you have a cocktail that poses what may amount to the most interesting alternative to Google's near monopoly in searching. At its heart, Google's system is built around the slow, anonymous accumulation of authority: pages rise to the top of Google's search results according to, in part, how many links point to them, which tends to favor older pages that have had time to build an audience. That's a fantastic solution for finding high-quality needles in the immense, spam-plagued haystack that is the contemporary Web. But it's not a particularly useful solution for finding out what people are saying *right now,* the in-the-moment conversation that industry pioneer John Battelle calls the "super fresh" Web. Even in its toddlerhood, Twitter is a more efficient supplier of the super-fresh Web than Google. If you're looking for interesting articles or sites devoted to Kobe Bryant, you search Google. If you're looking for interesting comments from your extended social network about the three-pointer Kobe just made 30 seconds ago, you go to Twitter.

FROM TOASTERS TO MICROWAVES

Because Twitter's co-founders—Evan Williams, Biz Stone and Jack Dorsey—are such a central-casting vision of start-up savvy (they're quotable and charming and have the extra glamour of using a loft in San Francisco's SoMa district as a headquarters instead of a bland office park in Silicon Valley) much of the media interest in Twitter has focused on the company. Will Ev and Biz sell to Google early or play long ball? (They have already turned down a reported $500 million from Facebook.) It's an interesting question but not exactly a new plotline. Focusing on it makes you lose sight of the much more significant point about the Twitter platform: the fact that many of its core features and applications have been developed by people who are not on the Twitter payroll.

This is not just a matter of people finding a new use for a tool designed to do something else. In Twitter's case, the users have been redesigning the tool itself. The convention of grouping a topic or event by the "hashtag"—#hackedu or #inauguration—was spontaneously invented by the Twitter user base (as was the convention of replying to another user with the @

symbol). The ability to search a live stream of tweets was developed by another start-up altogether, Summize, which Twitter purchased last year. (Full disclosure: I am an adviser to one of the minority investors in Summize.) Thanks to these innovations, following a live feed of tweets about an event—political debates or *Lost* episodes—has become a central part of the Twitter experience. But just 12 months ago, that mode of interaction would have been technically impossible using Twitter. It's like inventing a toaster oven and then looking around a year later and seeing that your customers have of their own accord figured out a way to turn it into a microwave.

One of the most telling facts about the Twitter platform is that the vast majority of its users interact with the service via software created by third parties. There are dozens of iPhone and BlackBerry applications—all created by enterprising amateur coders or small start-ups—that let you manage Twitter feeds. There are services that help you upload photos and link to them from your tweets, and programs that map other Twitizens who are near you geographically. Ironically, the tools you're offered if you visit Twitter.com have changed very little in the past two years. But there's an entire Home Depot of Twitter tools available everywhere else.

As the tools have multiplied, we're discovering extraordinary new things to do with them. Last month an anticommunist uprising in Moldova was organized via Twitter. Twitter has become so widely used among political activists in China that the government recently blocked access to it, in an attempt to censor discussion of the 20th anniversary of the Tiananmen Square massacre. A service called SickCity scans the Twitter feeds from multiple urban areas, tracking references to flu and fever. Celebrity Twitterers like Kutcher have directed their vast followings toward charitable causes (in Kutcher's case, the Malaria No More organization).

Social networks are notoriously vulnerable to the fickle tastes of teens and 20-somethings (remember Friendster?), so it's entirely possible that three or four years from now, we'll have moved on to some Twitter successor. But the key elements of the Twitter platform—the follower structure, link-sharing, real-time searching—will persevere regardless of Twitter's fortunes, just as Web conventions like links, posts and feeds have endured over the past decade. In fact, every major channel of information will be Twitterfied in one way or another in the coming years:

News and opinion. Increasingly, the stories that come across our radar—news about a plane crash, a feisty Op-Ed, a gossip item—will arrive via the passed links of the people we follow. Instead of being built by some kind of artificially intelligent software algorithm, a customized newspaper will be compiled from all the articles being read that morning by your social network. This will lead to more news diversity and polarization at the same time: your networked front page will be more eclectic than any traditional-newspaper front page, but political partisans looking to enhance their own private echo chamber will be able to tune out opposing viewpoints more easily.

Searching. As the archive of links shared by Twitter users grows, the value of searching for information via your extended social network will start to rival Google's approach to the search. If you're looking for information on Benjamin Franklin, an essay shared by one of your favorite historians might well be more valuable than the top result on Google; if you're looking for advice on sibling rivalry, an article recommended by a friend of a friend might well be the best place to start.

Advertising. Today the language of advertising is dominated by the notion of impressions: how many times an advertiser can get its brand in front of a potential customer's eyeballs, whether on a billboard, a Web page or a NASCAR hood. But impressions are fleeting things, especially compared with the enduring relationships of followers. Successful businesses will have millions of Twitter followers (and will pay good money to attract them), and a whole new language of tweet-based customer interaction will evolve to keep those followers engaged: early access to new products or deals, live customer service, customer involvement in brainstorming for new products.

Not all these developments will be entirely positive. Most of us have learned firsthand how addictive the micro-events of our personal e-mail inbox can be. But with the ambient awareness of status updates from Twitter and Facebook, an entire new empire of distraction has opened up. It used to be that you compulsively checked your BlackBerry to see if anything new had happened in your personal life or career: e-mail from the boss, a reply from last night's date. Now you're compulsively checking your BlackBerry for news from other people's lives. And because, on Twitter at least, some of those people happen to be celebrities, the Twitter platform is likely to expand that strangely delusional relationship that we have to fame. When Oprah tweets a question about getting ticks off her dog, as she did recently, anyone can send an @ reply to her, and in that exchange, there is the semblance of a normal, everyday conversation between equals. But of course, Oprah has more than a million followers, and that isolated query probably elicited thousands of responses. Who knows what small fraction of her @ replies she has time to read? But from the fan's perspective, it feels refreshingly intimate: "As I was explaining to Oprah last night, when she asked about dog ticks . . . ."

END-USER INNOVATION

The rapid-fire innovation we're seeing around Twitter is not new, of course. Facebook, whose audience is still several times as large as Twitter's, went from being a way to scope out the most attractive college freshmen to the Social Operating System of the Internet, supporting a vast ecosystem of new applications created by major media companies, individual hackers, game creators, political groups and charities. The Apple iPhone's long-term competitive advantage may well prove to be the more than 15,000 new applications that have been developed for the device, expanding its functionality in countless ingenious ways.

The history of the Web followed a similar pattern. A platform originally designed to help scholars share academic documents, it now lets you watch television shows, play poker with strangers around the world, publish your own newspaper, rediscover your high school girlfriend—and, yes, tell the world what you had for breakfast. Twitter serves as the best poster child for this new model of social creativity in part because these innovations have flowered at such breathtaking speed and in part because the platform is so simple. It's as if Twitter's creators dared us to do something interesting by giving us a platform with such draconian restrictions. And sure enough, we accepted the dare with relish. Just 140 characters? I wonder if I could use that to start a political uprising.

The speed with which users have extended Twitter's platform points to a larger truth about modern innovation. When we talk about innovation and global competitiveness, we tend to fall back on the easy metric of patents and Ph.D.s. It turns out the U.S. share of both has been in steady decline since peaking in the early '70s. (In 1970, more than 50% of the world's graduate degrees in science and engineering were issued by U.S. universities.) Since the mid-'80s, a long progression of doomsayers have warned that our declining market share in the patents-and-Ph.D.s business augurs dark times for American innovation. The specific threats have changed. It was the Japanese who would destroy us in the '80s; now it's China and India.

But what actually happened to American innovation during that period? We came up with America Online, Netscape, Amazon, Google, Blogger, Wikipedia, Craigslist, TiVo, Netflix, eBay, the iPod and iPhone, Xbox, Facebook and Twitter itself. Sure, we didn't build the Prius or the Wii, but if you measure global innovation in terms of actual lifestyle-changing hit products and not just grad students, the U.S. has been lapping the field for the past 20 years.

How could the forecasts have been so wrong? The answer is that we've been tracking only part of the innovation story. If I go to grad school and invent a better mousetrap, I've created value, which I can protect with a patent and capitalize on by selling my invention to consumers. But if someone else figures out a way to use my mousetrap to replace his much more expensive washing machine, he's created value as well. We tend to put the emphasis on the first kind of value creation because there are a small number of inventors who earn giant paydays from their mousetraps and thus become celebrities. But there are hundreds of millions of consumers and small businesses that find value in these innovations by figuring out new ways to put them to use.

There are several varieties of this kind of innovation, and they go by different technical names. MIT professor Eric von Hippel calls one "end-user innovation," in which consumers actively modify a product to adapt it to their needs. In its short life, Twitter has been a hothouse of end-user innovation: the hashtag; searching; its 11,000 third-party applications; all those creative new uses of Twitter—some of them banal, some of them spam and some of them sublime. Think about the community invention of the @ reply. It took a service that was essentially a series of isolated microbroadcasts, each individual tweet an island, and turned Twitter into a truly conversational medium. All of these adoptions create new kinds of value in the wider economy, and none of them actually originated at

Twitter HQ. You don't need patents or Ph.D.s to build on this kind of platform.

This is what I ultimately find most inspiring about the Twitter phenomenon. We are living through the worst economic crisis in generations, with apocalyptic headlines threatening the end of capitalism as we know it, and yet in the middle of this chaos, the engineers at Twitter headquarters are scrambling to keep the servers up, application developers are releasing their latest builds, and ordinary users are figuring out all the ingenious ways to put these tools to use. There's a kind of resilience here that is worth savoring. The weather reports keep announcing that the sky is falling, but here we are —millions of us—sitting around trying to invent new ways to talk to one another.

Jill Lepore

Baby Food

*If breast is best, why are women bottling their
milk?*

There are some new rules governing what used to be called
"mother's milk," or "breast milk," including one about what
to call it when it's no longer in a mother's breast. A term, then,
nomenclatural: "expressed human milk" is milk that has been
pressed, squeezed, or sucked out of a woman's breast by hand
or by machine and stored in a bottle or, for freezing, in a plastic bag secured with a twist tie. Matters, regulatory: Can a
woman carry containers of her own milk on an airplane? Before the summer of 2007, not more than three ounces, because
the Transportation Security Administration classed human
milk with shampoo, toothpaste, and Gatorade, until a Min-
neapolis woman heading home after a business trip was reduced to tears when a security guard at LaGuardia poured a
two-day supply of her milk into a garbage bin. Dr. Ruth
Lawrence, of the breast-feeding committee of the American
Academy of Pediatrics, promptly told the press, "She needs
every drop of that precious golden fluid for her baby"; lac-
tivists, who often stage "nurse-ins," sent petitions; and the
T.S.A. eventually reclassified human milk as "liquid medication." Can a woman sell her milk on eBay? It has been done,

and, so far, with no more consequence than the opprobrium of the blogosphere, at least until the F.D.A. decides to tackle this one. The Centers for Disease Control and Prevention, however, does provide a fact sheet on "What to Do If an Infant or Child Is Mistakenly Fed Another Woman's Expressed Breast Milk," which can happen at day-care centers where fridges are full of bags of milk, labelled in smudgeable ink. (The C.D.C. advises that a switch "should be treated just as if an accidental exposure to other bodily fluids had occurred.") During a nine-hour exam, can a woman take a break to express the milk uncomfortably filling her breasts? No, because the Americans with Disabilities Act does not consider lactation to be a disability. Can a human-milk bank pay a woman for her milk? (Milk banks provide hospitals with pasteurized human milk.) No, because doing so would violate the ethical standards of the Human Milk Banking Association of North America. If a nursing woman drinks to excess—some alcohol flows from the bloodstream into the mammary glands—can she be charged with child abuse? Hasn't happened yet, but there's been talk. Meanwhile, women who are worried can test a few drops with a product called milkscreen; if the alcohol level is too high, you're supposed to wait and test again, but the temptation is: pump and dump.

An observation, historical: all this is so new that people are making up the rules as they go along. Before the nineteen-nineties, electric breast pumps, sophisticated pieces of medical equipment, were generally available only in hospitals, where they are used to express milk from women with inverted nipples and from mothers of infants too weak and tiny to suck. Today, breast pumps are such a ubiquitous personal accessory that they're more like cell phones than like catheters. Last July, Stephen Colbert hooked up to a breast pump on *The Colbert Report*. In August, the Republican Vice-Presidential nominee, Sarah Palin, told *People* that she has often found herself having to "put down the BlackBerries and pick up the breast pump." Pumps, in short, abound.

A treatise, mercantile: Medela, a Swiss company that has long been a breast-pump industry leader, introduced its first non-hospital, electric-powered, vacuum-operated breast pump in the United States in 1991; five years later it launched the swank Pump In Style. Since then, its sales have quadrupled. The traffic in pumps is brisk, although accurate sales figures are hard to come by, not least because many people buy the top-of-the-line models secondhand. (Manufacturers argue that if you wouldn't buy a used toothbrush you shouldn't buy a used breast pump, but a toothbrush doesn't cost three hundred dollars.) Then, there's the swag. "Baby-friendly" maternity wards that used to send new mothers home with free samples of infant formula now give out manual pumps: plastic, one-breast-at-a-time gizmos that work like a cross between a straw and a bicycle pump. Wal-Mart sells an Evenflo electric pump for less than forty dollars. Philips makes one "featuring new iQ Technology"; the pitch is: the pump's memory chip makes it smart, but the name also plays on dubious claims that human milk raises I.Q. scores. State-of-the-art pumps whose motors, tubes, and freeze packs are wedged into bags disguised to look like black leather Fendi briefcases and Gucci backpacks are a must-have at baby showers; the Medela Pump In Style Advanced Metro model—"the C.E.O. of breast pumps"—costs $329.99 at Target. Medela also sells Pump & Save storage bags and breast shields. (The shield is the plastic part of the contraption that fits over the breast; it looks like a horn of plenty.) Medela's no-hands model can be powered by your car's cigarette lighter. Strenuous motherhood is de rigueur. Duck into the ladies' room at a conference of, say, professors and chances are you'll find a flock of women with matching "briefcases," waiting, none too patiently and, trust me, more than a little sheepishly, for a turn with the electric outlet. Pumps come with plastic sleeves, like the sleeves in a man's wallet, into which a mother is supposed to slip a photograph of her baby, because, Pavlov-like, looking at the picture aids "let-down," the release of milk normally triggered by the presence of the baby, its touch, its cry. Staring at that picture when your baby is miles away, well, it can make you cry, too. Pumping is no fun—whether it's more boring or more lonesome I find hard to say—but it has recently become so common that even some women who are home with their babies all day long express their milk and feed it in a bottle. Behind closed doors, the nation begins to look like a giant human dairy farm.

This makes it all the more worrying that the evolving rules governing human milk, including the proposed Breast-feeding Promotion Act of 2007, look a muddle. They indulge in a nomenclatural sleight of hand, conflating "breastfeeding" and "feeding human milk." They are purblind, unwilling to eye whether it's his mother or her milk that matters more to a baby. They suffer from a category error. Is human milk an elixir, a commodity, a right? The question is, at heart, taxonomical. And it has been asked before.

In 1735, when the Swedish naturalist Carl Linnaeus first sorted out the animal kingdom, he classed humans in a category called *Quadrupedia:* four-footed beasts. Even those of Linnaeus's contemporaries who conceded the animality of man averred that people have two feet, not four. Ah, but hands are just feet that can grip, Linnaeus countered. This proved unpersuasive. By 1758, in a process that the Stanford historian of science Londa Schiebinger has reconstructed, Linnaeus had abandoned *Quadrupedia* in favor of a word that he made up, *Mammalia:* animals with milk-producing nipples. (The Latin root, *mamma,* meaning breast, teat, or udder, is closely related to the onomatopoeic *mama*—"mother"—

thought to derive from the sound that a baby makes while suckling.) As categories go, "mammal" is an improvement over "quadruped," especially if you're thinking about what we have in common with whales. But, for a while, at least, it was deemed scandalously erotic. (Linnaeus's classification of plants based on their reproductive organs, stamens and pistils, fell prey to a similar attack. "Loathsome harlotry," one botanist called it.) More important, the name falls something short of capacious: only female mammals lactate; males, strictly speaking, are not mammals. Plenty of other features distinguish mammals from Linnaeus's five other animal classes —birds, amphibians, fish, insects, and worms. (*Tetracoilia*, animals with a four-chambered heart, proposed by a contemporary of Linnaeus's, the Scottish surgeon John Hunter, was at least as good an idea.) Linnaeus had his reasons. Naysayers might doubt that humans are essentially four-footed (whether on scriptural or arithmetic grounds), but no man born of woman, he figured, would dare deny that he was nourished by mother's milk.

Then, too, while Linnaeus was revising his *Systema Naturae* from the twelve-page pamphlet that he published in 1735 to the two-thousand-page opus of 1758—and abandoning *Quadrupedia* in favor of *Mammalia*—his wife was, not irrelevantly, lactating. Between 1741 and 1757, she bore and nursed seven children. Her husband, meanwhile, lectured and campaigned against the widespread custom of wet-nursing. The practice is ancient; contracts for wet nurses have been found on scrolls in Babylonia. A very small number of women can't breast-feed, and wet nurses also save the lives of infants whose mothers die in childbirth. But, in Linnaeus's time, extraordinary numbers of European mothers—as many as ninety per cent of Parisian women—refused to breast-feed their babies and hired servants to do the work. In 1752, Linnaeus wrote a treatise entitled "Step Nurse," declaring wet-nursing a crime against nature. Even the fiercest beasts nurse their young, with the utmost tenderness; surely women who resisted their mammalian destiny were to be ranked as lowlier than the lowliest brute.

Enlightenment doctors, philosophers, and legislators agreed: women should nurse their children. In *Émile* (1762), Rousseau prophesied, "When mothers deign to nurse their own children, then morals will reform themselves." (Voltaire had a quibble or two about Rousseau's own morals: the author of *Émile* had abandoned his five illegitimate children at birth, depositing them at a foundling hospital.) "There is no nurse like a mother," Benjamin Franklin wrote in 1785, after discovering an infant-mortality rate of eighty-five per cent at the foundling hospital in Paris that relied on wet nurses (the hospital where Rousseau's children all but certainly died), a discovery that explains why Franklin, in his autobiography, went to the trouble of remarking of his own mother, "She suckled all her 10 Children." But wet nurses were not nearly as common in Colonial America as they were in eighteenth-century Europe. "*Suckle* your Infant your Self if you can," Cotton Mather commanded from the pulpit. Puritans found milk divine: even the Good Book gave suck. "Spiritual Milk for Boston Babes, Drawn Out of the Breasts of Both Testaments" was the title of a popular catechism. By the end of the eighteenth century, breast-feeding had come to seem an act of citizenship. Mary Wollstonecraft, in her *Vindication of the Rights of Woman* (1792), scoffed that a mother who "neither suckles nor educates her children, scarcely deserves the name of a wife, and has no right to that of a citizen." The following year, the French National Convention ruled that women who employed wet nurses could not apply for state aid; not long afterward, Prussia made breast-feeding a legal requirement.

There was also a soppy side to the Age of Reason. In 1794, Erasmus Darwin offered in *Zoonomia; or The Laws of Organic*

Life a good summary of the eighteenth century's passionate attitude toward the milky breast:

> When the babe, soon after it is born into this cold world, is applied to its mother's bosom; its sense of perceiving warmth is first agreeably affected; next its sense of smell is delighted with the odour of her milk; then its taste is gratified by the flavour of it; afterwards the appetites of hunger and of thirst afford pleasure by the possession of their objects, and by the subsequent digestion of the aliment; and, lastly, the sense of touch is delighted by the softness and smoothness of the milky fountain, the source of such variety and happiness.

A half century later, across the Atlantic, this kind of thing had turned into a cult of motherhood, abundantly illustrated in daguerreotypes from the eighteen-fifties that showed babies suckling beneath the unbuttoned bodices of prim, sober American matrons, looking half Emily Dickinson, half Leonardo's *Madonna and Child.*

Then, bizarrely, American women ran out of milk. "Every physician is becoming convinced that the number of mothers able to nurse their own children is decreasing," one doctor wrote in 1887. Another reported that there was "something wrong with the mammary glands of the mothers in this country." It is no mere coincidence that this happened just when the first artificial infant foods were becoming commercially available. Cows were proclaimed the new "wet nurse for the human race," as the historian Adrienne Berney has pointed out in a study of the "maternal breast." Tragically, many babies fed on modified cow's milk died. But blaming those deaths on a nefarious alliance of doctors and infant-food manufacturers, as has become commonplace, seems both unfair and unduly influenced by later twentieth-century scandals (most infamously, Nestlé's deadly peddling of infant formula in Africa and elsewhere, which led, in 1981, to the landmark International Code for Marketing Breastmilk Substitutes). In the United States, nineteenth- and early-twentieth-century physicians, far from pressing formula on their patients, told women that they ought to breast-feed. Many women, however, refused. They insisted that they lacked for milk, mammals no more.

In 1871, Erasmus Darwin's grandson Charles published *Descent of Man,* in which he speculated that the anomalous occurrence in humans of extra nipples represented a reversion to an earlier stage of evolution. If our ancestors once suckled litters of four or six, and if—as was supposed—men had nipples because male mammals once produced milk, maybe women, too, were evolving out of the whole business. In 1904, one Chicago pediatrician argued that "the nursing function is destined gradually to disappear." Gilded Age American women were so refined, so civilized, so delicate. How could they suckle like a barnyard animal? (By the turn of the century, the cow's udder, or, more often, its head, had replaced the female human breast as the icon of milk.) Behind this question lay another: how could a white woman nurse a baby the way a black woman did? (Generations of black women, slave and free alike, not only nursed their own infants but also served as wet nurses to white babies.) Racial theorists ran microscopic tests of human milk: the whiter the mother, chemists claimed, the less nutritious her milk. On downy white breasts, rosy-red nipples had become all but vestigial. It was hardly surprising, then, that well-heeled women told their doctors that they had insufficient milk. By the nineteen-tens, a study of a thousand Boston women reported that ninety per cent of the poor mothers breast-fed, while only seventeen per cent of the wealthy mothers did. (Just about the opposite of the situation today.)

Doctors, pointing out that evolution doesn't happen so fast, tried to persuade these Brahmins to breast-feed, but by then it was too late.

The American epidemic of lactation failure depended, too, on the evolving design of baby bottles: so sleek, so clean, so scientific, so modern. The first U.S. patent for a baby bottle was issued in 1841; the device, shaped like a breast, could be held close to a mother's chest, almost like a prosthetic. Year by year, bottles became less like breasts. The familial cylindrical bottle, called the Stork Nurser, dates from 1910 and is tied to the rise of the stork myth: milk comes from the milkman; babies come from storks. Perversely, Freud's insistence that infants experience suckling as sexual pleasure proved a boon to stork-style repression, too: mothers, eager to keep infantile incestuous desire at arm's length, propped their babies up in high chairs and handed them bottles.

Meanwhile, more and more women were giving birth in hospitals, which meant that, for the first time in human history, infants born prematurely, or very small, had a chance of survival—if only there were enough milk and a way to get it into the belly of a baby that was too tiny to suck at the breast.

In 1910, a Boston doctor, Fritz Talbot, spent three days searching for a wet nurse. He failed. Exasperated, Talbot established a placement service, the Boston Wet Nurse Directory. Across town, Francis Parkman Denny, caring for a sick baby, asked a neighbor to hand-express her milk for him. When the infant improved after drinking just three ounces, Denny, a bacteriologist, became convinced of the "bactericidal power" of human milk. The year after Talbot started his Wet Nurse Directory, Denny opened the first human-milk bank in the United States, collecting milk from donors using a breast pump whose design was inspired by bovine milking machines. (Milking machines are still cited in breast-pump patents; mechanically, Medela's Pump In Style has much in common with DairyMaster's Swiftflo.) Denny's plan worked better: families who needed and could afford human milk did not generally like having poor women live with them; they preferred to have the milk delivered in bottles. Talbot stopped placing wet nurses and instead began distributing their milk; he renamed his agency the Directory of Mother's Milk.

Once milk banks replaced wet nurses, human milk came to be treated, more and more, as a medicine, something to be prescribed and researched, tested and measured in flasks and beakers. Denny's bottled, epidemiological model prevailed. Laboratory-made formulas improved, and aggressive marketing of processed infant food—not just bottles of formula but jars of mush and all manner of needless pap—grew to something between badgering and downright coercion. By the middle of the twentieth century, the majority of American women were feeding their babies formula. But, all the while, Erasmus Darwin's rhapsodic view of the milky breast endured. "With his small head pillowed against your breast and your milk warming his insides, your baby knows a special closeness to you," advised *The Womanly Art of Breastfeeding,* originally published by La Leche League in 1958, just two years after the league's first meeting. "He is gaining a firm foundation in an important area of life—he is learning about love." In the nineteen-sixties, nursing as a mammalian love-in began making a comeback, at least among wealthier women. (A brief history of food: when the rich eat white bread and buy formula, the poor eat brown bread and breast-feed; then they trade places.) In the decades since, the womanly art of breast-feeding has yielded, slowly but surely, to the medical science of human milk.

In 1997, the American Academy of Pediatrics issued a policy statement on "Breastfeeding and the Use of Human Milk," declaring human milk to be "species-specific" and recommending it as the exclusive food for the first six months of a baby's life, to be followed by a mixed diet of solid foods and human milk until at least the end of the first year. In that statement, and in a subsequent revision, the A.A.P. cited research linking breast-feeding to the reduced incidence and severity of, among other things, bacterial meningitis, diarrhea, respiratory-tract infection, ear infection, urinary-tract infection, sudden-infant-death syndrome, diabetes mellitus, lymphoma, leukemia, Hodgkin's disease, obesity, and asthma. The benefits of breast-feeding are unrivalled; breast-feeding rates in the United States are low; the combination makes for a public-health dilemma. In 2000, the Department of Health and Human Services announced its goal of increasing the proportion of mothers who breast-feed their babies "at initiation" (i.e., before they leave the hospital) from a 1998 baseline of sixty-four per cent to a 2010 target of seventy-five per cent; until the age of six months, from twenty-nine per cent to fifty per cent; at one year, from sixteen per cent to twenty-five per cent. (The same targets were announced in 1990; they were not reached.) Attempts to improve initiation rates have met with much, if spotty, success. The Rush University Medical Center, in Chicago, which runs a peer-counselling program called the Mother's Milk Club, has achieved an astonishing initiation rate of ninety-five per cent; nationally, the rate is not quite seventy-five per cent. More difficult has been raising the rates at six and twelve months. The C.D.C., which issues an annual Breastfeeding Report Card, has announced that for babies born in 2005 the rate of exclusive breast-feeding at six months was only twelve per cent (although the rate of *some* breast-feeding at six months had risen to forty-three per cent).

One big reason so many women stop breast-feeding is that more than half of mothers of infants under six months old go to work. The 1993 Family and Medical Leave Act guarantees only twelve weeks of (unpaid) maternity leave and, in marked contrast to established practice in other industrial nations, neither the government nor the typical employer offers much more. To follow a doctor's orders, a woman who returns to work twelve weeks after childbirth has to find a way to feed her baby her own milk for another nine months. The nation suffers, in short, from a Human Milk Gap.

There are three ways to bridge that gap: longer maternity leaves, on-site infant child care, and pumps. Much effort has been spent implementing option No. 3, the cheap way out. Medela distributes pumps in more than ninety countries, but its biggest market, by far, is the United States, where maternity leaves are so stinting that many women—blue-, pink-, and white-collar alike—return to work just weeks after giving birth. (Breasts supply milk in response to demand; if a woman is unable to put her baby to her breast regularly, she will stop producing milk regularly. Expressing not only provides milk to be stored for times when she is away; it also makes it possible for a working woman to keep nursing her baby at night and on weekends.) In 1998, Congress authorized states to use food-stamp funds granted to the U.S.D.A.'s Special Supplemental Nutrition Program for Women, Infants, and Children (WIC) to buy or rent breast pumps for eligible mothers. Breast-feeding rates rise with maternal age, education, and income. Medela offers a Corporate Lactation Program, free advice for employers seeking to reduce absenteeism and health-insurance costs by establishing "Mother's Rooms," equipped, ideally, with super-duper electric pumps, because "breastpumps with double-pumping options save time and can even help increase a mother's milk supply." The loss of productivity, Medela promises, is slight: "If each employee uses safe, effective, auto-cycling breastpumps, each visit to the Mother's Room should last no longer than 10 to 15 minutes."

Even more intensive has been the energy directed toward legislative reform. Many states have recently passed laws about breast-feeding, having to do with option No. 3. Must companies supply employees with refrigerators to store milk expressed during the workday? Twenty-one states, along with Puerto Rico and the District of Columbia, require employers to make a "reasonable effort" to accommodate nursing mothers and their bottled milk, although these laws are, generally, toothless. As a rule, the posher the employer, the plusher the pump station. Traders at Goldman Sachs can use an online booking service to reserve time in dedicated lactation rooms, equipped with pumps and chairs; baristas at Starbucks are left to line up to use the customers' loo. In 2007, Oregon became the first state to pass a law requiring companies with more than twenty-five employees to provide "non-bathroom" lactation rooms. (A national media campaign asks, reasonably enough, if you wouldn't make your kid a sandwich in a public rest room, why would you expect a woman to bottle her baby's milk in one?) Virginia and Maryland recently joined twenty-three other states and the Virgin Islands in exempting women who expose their breasts while suckling infants from indecency laws. Whether pumping in public is obscene has not yet been tested—honestly, who would want to? —but, what with all these lactation rooms, maybe that won't come up.

More rules are under consideration. Can a woman or her employer get a tax break for producing or storing milk? Maryland exempts breast pumps from its sales tax, but a congressional sub-committee is still mulling over the Breastfeeding Promotion Act. The goals of the bill are to add the word "lactation"—defined as "the feeding of a child directly from the breast or the expressing of milk from the breast"—to the Civil Rights Act of 1964, and to allow a tax credit of up to ten thousand dollars per year to companies that provide their employees with pumps or pump rooms. A better title for the proposed legislation might be the Breast Pump Promotion Act.

The cynical politics of pump promotion would seem, at first, to be obvious. Breast pumps can be useful, even indispensable and, in some cases, lifesaving. But a thing doesn't have to be underhanded to feel cold-blooded. Non-bathroom lactation rooms are such a paltry substitute for maternity leave, you might think that the craze for pumps—especially pressing them on poor women while giving tax breaks to big businesses—would be met with skepticism in some quarters. Not so. The National Organization for Women wants more pumps at work: NOW's president, Kim Gandy, complains that "only one-third of mega-corporations provide a safe and private location for women to pump breast milk for their babies." (When did "women's rights" turn into "the right to work"?) The stark difference between employer-sponsored lactation programs and flesh-and-blood family life is difficult to overstate. Pumps put milk into bottles, even though many of breast-feeding's benefits to the baby, and all of its social and emotional benefits, come not from the liquid itself but from the smiling and cuddling (stuff that people who aren't breast-feeding can give babies, too). Breast-feeding involves cradling your baby; pumping involves cupping plastic shields on your breasts and watching your nipples squirt milk down a tube. But this truth isn't just rarely overstated; it's rarely stated at all. In 2004, when Playtex débuted a breast pump called the Embrace, no one bothered to point out that something you plug into a wall socket is a far cry from a whisper and a kiss. Rhode Island's Physicians' Committee for Breastfeeding gives an annual award for the most "Breastfeeding-Friendly Workplace," a merit measured, in the main, by the comforts provided in pumping rooms, like the gold-medal winner's "soothing room," equipped with "a sink, a lock on the door, and literature." It appears no longer within the realm of the imaginable that, instead of running water and a stack of magazines, "breastfeeding-friendly" could mean making it possible for women and their babies to be together. Some lactation rooms even make a point of banning infants and toddlers, lest mothers smuggle them in for a quick nip. At the University of Minnesota, staff with keys can pump their milk at the Expression Connection, but the sign on the door warns: "This room is not intended for mothers who need a space to nurse their babies."

Lately, some WIC officers have begun to worry that pump promotion might be backfiring, having "the unintended effect of discouraging breastfeeding." But such cautions have hardly stopped the anti-formula fire and brimstone. Between 2004 and 2006, a National Breastfeeding Awareness Campaign included TV ads that likened a mother feeding her baby formula to a pregnant woman riding a mechanical bull: "You'd never take risks before your baby is born. Why start after?" No one seems especially worried about women whose risk assessment looks like this: "Should I take three twenty-minute pumping 'breaks' during my workday, or use formula and get home to my baby an hour earlier?"

Pumps can be handy; they're also a handy way to avoid privately agonizing and publicly unpalatable questions: is it the mother, or her milk, that matters more to the baby? Gadgets are one of the few ways to "promote breast-feeding" while avoiding harder—and divisive and more stubborn—social and economic issues. Is milk medicine? Is suckling love? Taxonomical questions are tricky. Meanwhile, *mamma ex machina*. Medela's newest models offer breakthrough "2-Phase Expression" technology: phase one "simulates the baby's initial rapid suckling to initiate faster milk flow"; phase two "simulates the baby's slower, deeper suckling for maximum milk flow in less time." These newest machines, the company promises, "work less like a pump and more like a baby." More like a baby? Holy cow. We are become our own wet nurses.

Thinking Machine

*The future of computing may depend on embracing
the chaos that defines human thinking.*

Kwabena Boahen's love affair with digital computers began
and ended in 1981, when he was 16.

Boahen lived outside the city of Accra in the West African
nation of Ghana. His family's sprawling block house stood in
a quiet field of mango and banana trees. One afternoon Boahen's father rolled down the driveway with a surprise in the
trunk of his Peugeot: a RadioShack TRS-80—the family's
first computer—purchased in England.

Young Boahen parked the machine at a desk on the
porch, where he usually dismantled radios and built air guns
out of PVC pipe. He plugged the computer into a TV set to
provide a screen and a cassette recorder so he could store programs on tapes, and soon he was programming it to play Ping-
Pong. But as he read about the electronics that made it and all
other digital computers work, he soured on the toy.

Moving the Ping-Pong ball just one pixel across the screen
required thousands of 1s and 0s, generated by transistors in
the computer's processor that were switching open and shut
2.5 million times per second. Boahen had expected to find elegance at the heart of his new computer. Instead he found a

Lilliputian bureaucracy of binary code. "I was totally disgusted," he recalls. "It was so brute force." That disillusionment inspired a dream of a better solution, a vision that would eventually guide his career.

Boahen has since crossed the Atlantic Ocean and become a prominent scientist at Stanford University in California. There he is working to create a computer that will fulfill his boyhood vision—a new kind of computer, based not on the regimented order of traditional silicon chips but on the organized chaos of the human brain. Designing this machine will mean rejecting everything that we have learned over the past 50 years about building computers. But it might be exactly what we need to keep the information revolution going for another 50.

The human brain runs on only about 20 watts of power, equal to the dim light behind the pickle jar in your refrigerator. By contrast, the computer on your desk consumes a million times as much energy per calculation. If you wanted to build a robot with a processor as smart as the human brain, it would require 10 to 20 megawatts of electricity. "Ten megawatts is a small hydroelectric plant," Boahen says dismissively. "We should work on miniaturizing hydroelectric plants so we can put them on the backs of robots." You would encounter similar problems if you tried to build a medical implant to replace just 1 percent of the neurons in the brain, for use in stroke patients. That implant would consume as much electricity as 200 households and dissipate as much heat as the engine in a Porsche Boxster.

"Energy efficiency isn't just a matter of elegance. It fundamentally limits what we can do with computers," Boahen says. Despite the amazing progress in electronics technology —today's transistors are 1/100,000 the size that they were a half century ago, and computer chips are 10 million times faster—we still have not made meaningful progress on the energy front. And if we do not, we can forget about truly intelligent humanlike machines and all the other dreams of radically more powerful computers.

Getting there, Boahen realized years ago, will require rethinking the fundamental balance between energy, information, and noise. We encounter the trade-offs this involves every time we strain to hear someone speaking through a crackly cell phone connection. We react instinctively by barking more loudly into the phone, trying to overwhelm the static by projecting a stronger signal. Digital computers operate with almost zero noise, but operating at this level of precision consumes a huge amount of power—and therein lies the downfall of modern computing.

In the palm of his hand, Boahen flashes a tiny, iridescent square, a token of his progress in solving that problem. This silicon wafer provides the basis for a new neural supercomputer, called Neurogrid, that he has nearly finished building. The wafer is etched with millions of transistors like the ones in your PC. But beneath that veneer of familiarity hides a radical rethinking of the way engineers do business.

Traditional digital computers depend on millions of transistors opening and closing with near perfection, making an error less than once per 1 trillion times. It is impressive that our computers are so accurate—but that accuracy is a house of cards. A single transistor accidentally flipping can crash a computer or shift a decimal point in your bank account. Engineers ensure that the millions of transistors on a chip behave reliably by slamming them with high voltages—essentially, pumping up the difference between a 1 and a 0 so that random variations in voltage are less likely to make one look like the other. That is a big reason why computers are such power hogs.

Radically improving that efficiency, Boahen says, will involve trade-offs that would horrify a chip designer. Forget about infinitesimal error rates like one in a trillion; the transistors in Neurogrid will crackle with noise, misfiring at rates as high as 1 in 10. "Nobody knows how we're going to compute with that," Boahen admits. "The only thing that computes with this kind of crap is the brain."

It sounds cockamamy, but it is true. Scientists have found that the brain's 100 billion neurons are surprisingly unreliable. Their synapses fail to fire 30 percent to 90 percent of the time. Yet somehow the brain works. Some scientists even see neural noise as the key to human creativity. Boahen and a small group of scientists around the world hope to copy the brain's noisy calculations and spawn a new era of energy-efficient, intelligent computing. Neurogrid is the test to see if this approach can succeed.

Most modern supercomputers are the size of a refrigerator and devour $100,000 to $1 million of electricity per year. Boahen's Neurogrid will fit in a briefcase, run on the equivalent of a few D batteries, and yet, if all goes well, come close to keeping up with these Goliaths.

The problem of computing with noise first occurred to a young neuroscientist named Simon Laughlin three decades ago. Laughlin, then at the Australian National University in Canberra, spent much of 1975 sitting in a black-walled, windowless laboratory with the lights off. The darkness allowed him to study the retinas of blowflies captured from Dumpsters around campus. In hundreds of experiments he glued a living fly to a special plastic platform under a microscope, sunk a wisp-thin electrode into its honeycombed eye, and recorded how its retina responded to beams of light. Laughlin would begin recording at noon and finish after midnight. As he sat in the gloomy lab, watching neural signals dance in green light across an oscilloscope, he noticed something strange.

Each fly neuron's response to constant light jittered up and down from one millisecond to the next. Those fluctuations showed up at every step in the neurons' functioning, from the unreliable absorption of light by pigment molecules to the sporadic opening of electricity-conducting proteins called ion channels on the neurons' surfaces. "I began to realize that noise placed a fundamental limit on the ability of neurons to code information," Laughlin says.

Boosting a crackly signal so that it stands above background noise requires energy. Whether you are a neuron or the operator of a ham radio, doubling your signal-to-noise ratio demands quadrupling your energy consumption—a law of rapidly diminishing returns. "The relationship between information and energy is rather deep, and grounded in thermodynamics," says Laughlin, who now works at the University of Cambridge in England. He has spent the last 12 years studying how brains perform the three-way balancing act among information, energy, and noise.

That balance is critical to survival. Neurons are far more efficient than computers, but despite that, the brain still consumes a tremendous amount of energy. While accounting for just 2 percent of our body weight, the human brain devours 20 percent of the calories that we eat.

Functionally, most neurons have a lot of properties similar to those of transistors. Both act as switches that can either transmit or not transmit electrical pulses, depending on signals they receive. The trade-offs that have evolved in humans could not be more different from those that engineers made in designing conventional computers, however. Engineers chose accuracy. Brains, shaped by natural selection, minimize energy consumption at all costs. Skinny neurons require less energy, so evolution shrank them, and brains adapted to operate barely above the noise threshold.

With great efficiency, though, came a lot of mistakes. Ideally, for example, neurons should fire off electric spikes only when they receive signals from other cells telling them to do so. But the brain's skinniest neurons sometimes send out random spikes triggered by ion channel proteins' popping open accidentally. The smaller the neuron, the more sensitive it is to these random channel openings, and the more often these hiccups occur. The brain's smallest neurons operate "at the limit of biophysics," Laughlin says. In 2005 he found that shrinking those neurons a tiny bit more meant they would burp out more than 100 random spikes per second.

This flaky behavior places a fundamental limit on how we function. Compensating for random neural noise has shaped the human brain—and human intelligence—from the bottom up: the size and shape of neurons, the wiring pattern of neural circuits, and even the language of spikes that encodes information. In the most basic sense, the brain manages noise by using large numbers of neurons whenever it can. It makes important decisions (such as "Is that a lion or a tabby cat?") by having sizable groups of neurons compete with each other—a shouting match between the lion neurons and the tabby cat neurons in which the accidental silence (or spontaneous outburst) of a few nerve cells is overwhelmed by thousands of others. The winners silence the losers so that ambiguous, and possibly misleading, information is not sent to other brain areas.

The brain also filters out errors using a neural code based on coincidences in timing. Consider the "Bill Clinton cells" that neuroscientists have found in the brain's medial temporal lobe. These neurons fire whenever you see a picture of Bill Clinton, hear his voice, or read his name. (You have similar neurons for each of the hundreds of other people you are familiar with.) A Clinton neuron might give off a spike whenever it receives, say, 100 or more simultaneous spikes from other neurons. Even if the false-positive rate for each incoming spike is as high as 1 in 2, the collective false-positive rate for 100 spikes arriving at the same time is considerably less.

Laughlin and David Attwell at University College London estimate that neural signaling accounts for 80 percent of the brain's energy use, whereas keeping those neurons charged and ready to fire takes only 15 percent. This finding has major implications. It means that the brain can save energy by containing large numbers of neurons that it rarely uses.

With many extra neurons lying around, each spike can travel along any one of many different routes through the brain. Each of these power-consuming spikes can transmit information along multiple paths, so your brain can project the same amount of information by firing fewer of them overall. (Think about it: If you are writing in a language that has only two letters, each word has to be pretty long in order to have a unique spelling; if you have 26 letters to choose from, your words can be shorter, and a given sentence, or paragraph, or novel will also contain fewer keystrokes overall.) The brain achieves optimal energy efficiency by firing no more than 1 to 15 percent—and often just 1 percent—of its neurons at a time. "People hadn't considered that most neurons in the brain have to be inactive most of the time," Laughlin says.

The Neurogrid chip mimics the brain by using the same analog process that neurons use to compute. This analog process occurs until a certain threshold is reached, at which point a digital process takes over, generating an electric spike (the spike is like a 1, and lack of a spike is like a 0).

Instead of using transistors as switches the way digital computers do, Boahen builds a capacitor that gets the same voltage a neuron makes. "By using one transistor and a capacitor, you can solve problems that would take thousands of transistors in a modern digital computer," Boahen says.

Following the discovery in the 1980s of the brain's amazingly efficient method of noisy computing, an engineer and physicist named Carver Mead tried to do the same thing using transistors. Mead, now professor emeritus at Caltech and one of the fathers of modern silicon chips, wanted to find more-efficient ways to compute. When he applied low voltages to a regular transistor, he could coax it to produce currents that had the same dependence on voltage as neuronal membrane currents had. The field now known as neuromorphic engineering was born.

Boahen arrived at Mead's laboratory in 1990 to pursue his doctorate. Mead's lab has produced many leaders in the field of neuromorphic electronics, including Boahen, Rahul Sarpeshkar (now at MIT), Paul Hasler (now at Georgia Tech), and Shih-Chii Liu (now at the Institute of Neuroinformatics in Zurich). Mead's grad students wore sandals and cowboy boots, worked until 1 a.m., and often spent seven or eight years, rather than the usual four or five, earning their Ph.D.s. "It was a fantastically creative environment," says Sarpeshkar, who graduated a year after Boahen. "We were all having a good time. We weren't necessarily in a great hurry to graduate."

Mead's students read biological journals religiously and then attempted to construct silicon versions of the neural circuits that brain scientists were mapping out. One of Sarpeshkar's first chips was an early analog of the cochlea, which processes sound in the inner ear. Boahen was working on retina chips, which produced fuzzy signals and grainy, salt-and-pepper images. These silicon-chip mimics faced the same problems of noise that real neurons face. In silicon the noise arises from manufacturing imperfections, random variations, and thermal fluctuations in the devices. This problem is exacerbated by large variations in electronic currents. "The currents of two transistors are supposed to be identical," Boahen says, "but at low power they can differ by a factor of two, and that makes everything quite random."

Recently Sarpeshkar adapted one of his audio chips into a biologically inspired radio frequency cochlea chip, which enables applications for cognitive and ultrahigh-band radios in the future. The chip, unveiled in June, will allow radios to simultaneously listen to a wide range of frequencies—spanning all radio and television broadcasts, along with all cell phone traffic—the way that ears listen to and analyze many sound frequencies at once. Boahen and his students have developed increasingly realistic silicon chips for the retina, which provides primary input to the visual cortex (which identifies objects that we see) and several other brain areas. These chips might one day provide a foundation for medical implants that restore vision in people with eye or brain injuries. For now, they serve as research tools for learning, by trial and error, how the brain encodes information and manages noise.

These chips use anywhere from 1/10,000 to 1/500 of the power that would be used by equivalent digital circuitry. Still, they represent mere baby steps on the road to building a brain-inspired computer. Until this year, the largest neural machines contained no more than 45,000 silicon neurons. Boahen's Neurogrid supercomputer, in contrast, contains a million neurons. That tremendous increase in computing power will allow him to test ideas about the brain, and about how to manage noise, on an entirely new scale.

On a sunny Friday afternoon, Boahen walks, in jeans and Ghanaian sandals, into the computer lab at Stanford where his team is putting the final touches on Neurogrid. One of the computer stations is ringed by a shrine of empty Peet's coffee cups, evidence of the serious amount of caffeine consumed here. "We're on a chip deadline," Boahen says, "so we're pulling 15-hour days."

John Arthur, an engineer and former Ph.D. student of Boahen's, sits at the Peet's shrine. Arthur's computer monitor displays a schematic of triangles and squares: part of the Neurogrid chip design. The on-screen blueprint of transistors and capacitors represents a single neuron. "It's 340 transistors per neuron," he says.

These circuits are simple compared with living neurons, but they are advanced enough to illustrate the vast gulf in efficiency between digital and neural computing. The mathematical equations that Arthur and others are using to simulate the chip's behavior and test its blueprint for flaws would quickly bog down a regular digital computer. At full speed, even the high-end Dell Quad-core computers in Boahen's lab cannot simulate more than one of Neurogrid's silicon neurons at a time—and the complete chip contains 65,536 neurons.

A few months ago Boahen's team received the first batch of newly fabricated Neurogrid chips. On that pivotal day everything changed. The group finally said good-bye to the pesky equations they had been compelled to run, for months and months, using unwieldy software on energy-hogging conventional computers. At last they could take the leap from simulating neurons using software to embodying those neurons in a low-power silicon chip.

When the first of the Neurogrid chips was plugged in, its silicon neurons came to life, chattering back and forth with trains of millisecond electric spikes, which were then relayed onto a computer monitor through a USB cable. Just as spikes ripple down the branching tendrils of a neuron, pulses of electricity cascaded like flash floods through the chip's transistors and nanowires. This activity had no more to do with equations or programming than does water tumbling down Yosemite's Bridal Veil Falls. It happened automatically, as a result of the basic physics of electricity and conductors.

In its first experiment, Boahen's team coaxed the neurons on a single chip to organize themselves into the familiar "gamma rhythm" that scientists pick up with EEG electrodes on a person's scalp. Like members of a 65,536-member chorus, each silicon neuron adjusted its spiking rate to match the 20- to 80-wave-per-second gamma tempo. The researchers recently mounted 16 Neurogrid chips on a single board to emulate 1 million neurons, connected by a tangle of 6 billion synapses. By 2011 they hope to create a second-generation

Neurogrid containing 64 million silicon neurons, about equal to the total brain of a mouse.

Just a few miles down the road, at the IBM Almaden Research Center in San Jose, a computer scientist named Dharmendra Modha recently used 16 digital Blue Gene supercomputer racks to mathematically simulate 55 million neurons connected by 442 billion synapses. The insights gained from that impressive feat will help in the design of future neural chips. But Modha's computers consumed 320,000 watts of electricity, enough to power 260 American households. By comparison, Neurogrid's 1 million neurons are expected to sip less than a watt.

Neurogrid's noisy processors will not have anything like a digital computer's rigorous precision. They may, however, allow us to accomplish everyday miracles that digital computers struggle with, like prancing across a crowded room on two legs or recognizing a face.

The lessons of Neurogrid may soon start to pay off in the world of conventional computing too. For decades the electronics industry has hummed along according to what is known as Moore's law: As technology progresses and circuitry shrinks, the number of transistors that can be squeezed onto a silicon chip doubles every two years or so.

So far so good, but this meteoric growth curve may be headed for a crash.

For starters, there is, again, the matter of power consumption. Heat, too, is causing headaches: As engineers pack transistors closer and closer together, the heat they generate threatens to warp the silicon wafer. And as transistors shrink to the width of just a few dozen silicon atoms, the problem of noise is increasing. The random presence or absence of a single electricity-conducting dopant atom on the silicon surface can radically change the behavior of a transistor and lead to errors, even in digital mode. Engineers are working to solve these problems, but the development of newer generations of chips is taking longer. "Transistor speeds are not increasing as quickly as they used to with Moore's law, and everyone in the field knows that," Sarpeshkar says. "The standard digital computing paradigm needs to change—and is changing."

As transistors shrink, the reliability of digital calculation will at some point fall off a cliff, a result of the "fundamental laws of physics," says Sarpeshkar. Many people place that statistical precipice at a transistor size of 9 nanometers, about 80 silicon atoms wide. Some engineers say that today's digital computers are already running into reliability problems. In July a man in New Hampshire bought a pack of cigarettes at a gas station, according to news reports, only to discover his bank account had been debited $23,148,855,308,184,500. (The error was corrected, and the man's $15 overdraft fee was refunded the next day.) This is exactly the kind of error that silicon-chip designers fear could arise from a single transistor accidentally flipping from a 1 to a 0 in a large computer system.

"Digital systems are prone to catastrophic errors," Sarpeshkar says. "The propensity for error is actually much greater now than it ever was before. People are very worried."

Neurally inspired electronics represent one possible solution to this problem, since they largely circumvent the heat and energy problems and incorporate their own error-correcting algorithms. Corporate titans like Intel are working on plenty of other next-generation technologies, however. One of these, called spintronics, takes advantage of the fact that electrons spin like planets, allowing a 1 or 0 to be coded as a clockwise versus counterclockwise electron rotation.

The most important achievement of Boahen's Neurogrid, therefore, may be in re-creating not the brain's efficiency but its versatility. Terrence Sejnowski, a computational neuroscientist at the Salk Institute in La Jolla, California, believes that neural noise can contribute to human creativity.

Digital computers are deterministic: Throw the same equation at them a thousand times and they will always spit out the same answer. Throw a question at the brain and it can produce a thousand different answers, canvassed from a chorus of quirky neurons. "The evidence is overwhelming that the brain computes with probability," Sejnowski says. Wishy-washy responses may make life easier in an uncertain world where we do not know which way an errant football will bounce, or whether a growling dog will lunge. Unpredictable neurons might cause us to take a wrong turn while walking home and discover a shortcut, or to spill acid on a pewter plate and during the cleanup to discover the process of etching.

Re-creating that potential in an electronic brain will require that engineers overcome a basic impulse that is pounded into their heads from an early age. "Engineers are trained to make everything really precise," Boahen says. "But the answer doesn't have to be right. It just has to be approximate."

Lawrence Weschler

David Hockney's iPhone Passion

An elder master still at the cutting edge.

After two decades of regularly finding himself caught up in all sorts of seemingly extraneous side-passions (photocollages, operatic stage design, fax extravaganzas, homemade photo-copier print runs, a controversial revisionist art-historical in-vestigation, and a watercolor idyll), David Hockney, now age seventy-two, has finally taken to painting once again, doing so, over the past three or four years, with a vividness and a sheer productivity perhaps never before seen in his career. This recent body of work consists almost entirely of seasonal landscapes of the rolling hills, hedgerows, tree stands, valley wolds, and farm fields surrounding the somewhat déclassé onetime summer seaside resort of Bridlington, England, on the North Sea coast, where he now lives. Some are intimately scaled but many are among the largest, most ambitious can-vases of his entire career.

The paintings have been widely exhibited—in London (at the Tate and the Royal Academy), in Los Angeles, a broad overview in a small museum in Germany this past summer— though not yet in New York, a situation that will be rectified in late October by a major show, his first there in ten years, slated to take up both the uptown and downtown spaces at

PaceWildenstein ("David Hockney: Recent Paintings," October 23–December 24, 2009). The buildup toward these shows has found Hockney busier than ever (he is still in the process of completing a dozen fresh canvases as I write), but not so busy that he hasn't managed to become fascinated by yet another new (and virtually diametrically opposite) technology, one that he is pursuing with almost as much verve and fascination: drawing on his iPhone.

Hockney first became interested in iPhones about a year ago (he grabbed the one I happened to be using right out of my hands). He acquired one of his own and began using it as a high-powered reference tool, searching out paintings on the Web and cropping appropriate details as part of the occasional polemics or appreciations with which he is wont to shower his friends.

But soon he discovered one of those newfangled iPhone applications, entitled Brushes, which allows the user digitally to smear, or draw, or fingerpaint (it's not yet entirely clear what the proper verb should be for this novel activity), to create highly sophisticated full-color images directly on the device's screen, and then to archive or send them out by e-mail. Essentially, the Brushes application gives the user a full colorwheel spectrum, from which he can choose a specific color. He can then modify that color's hue along a range of darker to lighter, and go on to fill in the entire backdrop of the screen in that color, or else fashion subsequent brushstrokes, variously narrower or thicker, and more or less transparent, according to need, by dragging his finger across the screen, progressively layering the emerging image with as many such daubings as he desires. (Recently Brushes issued an upgrade, Brushes 2.0, much to Hockney's dismay. As with many such applications, he prefers the original.)

Over the past six months, Hockney has fashioned literally

hundreds, probably over a thousand, such images, often sending out four or five a day to a group of about a dozen friends, and not really caring what happens to them after that. (He assumes the friends pass them along through the digital ether.) These are, mind you, not second-generation digital copies of images that exist in some other medium: their digital expression constitutes the sole (albeit multiple) original of the image.

The flood of images has more or less resolved itself into three streams. To begin with, portraits, and mainly self-portraits at that—perhaps playing on the way that an iPhone's blackened screen, when off, already functions as a sort of Claude Lorrain–style darkened glass, reflecting back a ghostly image of the user's face. (Intriguingly, the reflected face in the blackened screen is approximately twice the size of the same face if one turns the iPhone around to snap a photographic self-portrait. "But that's how it always is with photography," Hockney points out. "It inevitably pushes the world away. That's just one of its many problems." Hockney's drawings, as it were, bring the face back to full scale.)

Early on, however, Hockney became much more interested in bunches of cut flowers and plants ranged in brick pots, ceramic vases, and glass jars. These became the occasion for his extensive investigations into the types of effects possible in this new medium. "Although the actual drawing, when I do it, goes quite quickly," he explains, "some days it might be preceded by hours and hours of thinking through just how one might achieve a certain play of light, texture, or color." Indeed, the range of results is dazzlingly various, colorful, and instantaneously evocative.

Increasingly, over the past several months, it is the summer dawn, rising over the seabay outside his bedroom window, that has been capturing Hockney's attention. "I've always wanted to be able to paint the dawn," Hockney explains.

After all, what clearer, more luminous light are we ever afforded? Especially here where the light comes rising over the sea, just the opposite of my old California haunts. But in the old days one never could, because, of course, ordinarily it would be too dark to see the paints; or else, if you turned on a light so as to be able to see them, you'd lose the subtle gathering tones of the coming sun. But with an iPhone, I don't even have to get out of bed, I just reach for the device, turn it on, start mixing and matching the colors, laying in the evolving scene.

He has now accomplished dozens of such sequential studies, sending them out in real time, so that his friends in America wake to their own account of the Bridlington dawn—two, five, sometimes as many as eight successive versions, sent out minutes apart, one after the next.

I've noticed that most users of the Brushes application tend to trace out their brushstrokes with their pointer finger. (The screen measures changes in electrical charge, and can be operated only with a conductive object—like a finger—rather than a pen-like stylus.) As I discovered on a recent visit, Hockney limits his contact with the screen exclusively to the pad of his thumb. "The thing is," Hockney explains, "if you are using your pointer or other fingers, you actually have to be working from your elbow. Only the thumb has the opposable joint which allows you to move over the screen with maximum speed and agility, and the screen is exactly the right size, you can easily reach every corner with your thumb." He goes on to note how people used to worry that computers would one day render us "all thumbs," but it's incredible the dexterity, the expressive range, lodged in "these not-so-simple thumbs of ours."

Hockney, who has carried small notebooks in his pockets

since his student days, along with pencils, crayons, pastel sticks, ink pens, and watercolor bottles—and smudged clean-up rags—is used to working small, but he delights in the simplicity of this new medium:

> It's always there in my pocket, there's no thrashing about, scrambling for the right color. One can set to work immediately, there's this wonderful impromptu quality, this freshness, to the activity; and when it's over, best of all, there's no mess, no clean-up. You just turn off the machine. Or, even better, you hit Send, and your little cohort of friends around the world gets to experience a similar immediacy. There's something, finally, very intimate about the whole process.

I asked Hockney whether he'd mind my sharing some of these images with a wider audience across a printed medium, and he said, not really, he more or less assumed that the pictures would one by one find their way into the world. "Though it is worth noting," he adds, lighting one of his perennial cigarettes, "that the images always look better on the screen than on the page. After all, this is a medium of pure light, not ink or pigment, if anything more akin to a stained glass window than an illustration on paper." He continues:

> It's all part of the urge toward figuration. You look out at the world and you're called to make gestures in response. And that's a primordial calling: goes all the way back to the cave painters. May even have preceded language. People are always asking me about my ancestors, and I say, Well there must have been a cave painter back there somewhere. Him scratching away on his cave wall, me dragging my thumb over this iPhone's screen. All part of the same passion.

He laughs, stubs out his cigarette, snaps off the iPhone, and heads back over to a vast set of painted canvases arrayed against the far wall of his hangarlike studio: a view of a forest road lined with felled trees, a gridded combine of fifteen canvases, three high and five long. He daubs a long paintbrush with fresh creamy glops of paint, and begins working *from his shoulder*. "People from the village," he says, craning back over that shoulder, "come up to me and tease me, 'We hear you've started drawing on your telephone.' And I tell them, 'Well, no, actually, it's just that occasionally I speak on my sketch pad.'"

Javier Marías
Translated by Margaret Jull Costa

Airships

A writer overcomes his fear of flying.

A few years ago, I wrote an article in which I confessed, in rather jocular fashion, to a fear of flying, even though—with no little show of courage—I board a plane about twenty times a year. I'm pleased to say that I now feel much more confident during flights, perhaps because I've grown used to it or perhaps, as the trail of years behind us grows, we become more scornful about our possible future life and more satisfied with the life we've already accumulated. However, over a period of at least twenty years, plane journeys—of fifty minutes, two, seven or even twelve hours—could be relied upon to transform me into a highly superstitious little boy, who reached his various destinations feeling utterly drained after the hours of tension and the indescribable effort of having to "carry" the plane.

What I've always found so odd about my fear—although it might also be the explanation—is that I first flew in a plane when I was only one month old, in the days when, for most people, flying was still a rare experience. I was born in Madrid on September 20, 1951 and on that very date—it had been planned beforehand, so it wasn't that he took one look at me

and fled—my father set off on the first of his Atlantic cross-
ings and travelled to America with a contract to teach at
Wellesley College, Massachusetts—a college for young ladies
—for the academic year of 1951–2. My mother followed a
month later, taking with her my two older brothers, Miguel
and Fernando, as well as me, the newborn baby. I don't know
what the travelling conditions were like (apart from the fact
that I was dressed all in pink, because they had been expecting a girl), or whether I cried a little or a lot as we crossed the
ocean, or whether the crew members of Iberia or TWA made
a fuss of me or loathed me. And I recall nothing, either, of the
return journey—New York–Madrid—nine or ten months
later. I do, however, have a vague recollection of my third trip
by plane. I was just four years old, had acquired another
brother, Álvaro, and my father had decided to take us all to
New Haven, Connecticut, at the behest of Yale University.
It's not a very pleasant memory: I can see myself—not crying,
but very, very angry—lying in the aisle, refusing to get up and
doubtless obstructing crew and passengers alike. I don't know
how long the tantrum lasted—possibly a couple of minutes,
possibly much longer—but I'm sure that if, as an adult, I had
seen the child that was me, I would have hated him for blocking the aisle; more than that, I would have thought it a bad
omen, which is always rather worrying in mid-flight.

It's probably a well-known fact—although I can't be sure because people don't talk about it much—that those of us who
suffer in planes tend to invest a great deal of feverish, ex-
hausting mental activity in our role as, how can I put it, "imaginary co-pilots." As I said, my fear of flying is now abating,
but throughout my life I've spent many hours on board in a
state of permanent alertness, attentive not only to any possible
changes of mood in the engines, or to the plane's recognizable
or unexpected noises, or to its scheduled or unscheduled ups

and downs, but also to everything else around me, in particular the air hostesses and the stewards and even the captain's variable tones of voice over the intercom—whether he sounds calm or nervous.

I have tended to see "signs" or "premonitions" in the tiniest details and, given that all superstitions are arbitrary, it always used to make me feel uneasy if a passenger stood talking in the aisle for too long, especially if he or she was Japanese, don't ask me why. Nor was I soothed, particularly on long-haul flights, by the sight of other excessively relaxed and uninhibited passengers who, far from keeping a close eye on our flight path, as is the duty of all caring and committed travellers, laughed and drank, moved around the cabin, played cards or performed other equally grave and reckless acts, or so it seemed to me. In short, I spend, or have spent, the entire journey "controlling" and "helping" and "protecting" the whole hazardous crossing with my tireless thoughts. A four-year-old child blocking the aisle would definitely have strained my nerves. I'm not sure I would have been able to refrain from giving him a good slap.

No, I would doubtless have contained my irritation because since I reached the age of shaving, I've always behaved myself on board planes, unlike the callow creature I was then. I have limited myself to keeping a firm grip on an open newspaper (of the broadsheet variety, so that there's no chance of my sneaking a glance out of the windows), either pretending to read it or actually reading it—although without taking in a single word—meanwhile fending off any attempts at conversation (one doesn't want to become distracted and neglect one's duty as lookout), demolishing at high speed whatever food is placed in front of me, and all the while clutching some wooden object I've brought with me for the purpose, since there doesn't tend to be any wood—a major oversight—on those flying submarines.

It was a similar remark, made in that earlier article, and my subsequent confession that I'd worn out the wooden toothpicks and matches I grasped between my fingers, that provoked a charming Iberia air hostess into sending me a letter and a little wooden key ring in the form of a plane, so that, in future, I wouldn't have to make a fool of myself abroad, holding those grubby matches and toothpicks. And that same air hostess, as well as recounting a few anecdotes from her long experience in the air, made me think of planes, for the first time, as relatively "humanizable" objects, which one could, in a way, and depending on the circumstances, mentally direct. Not that there's anything very remarkable about that. Indeed, it's perfectly normal. She told me in her letter that whenever the plane she was on lurched or bumped about a bit or jolted, she would issue a silent order: "Down, boy!" Yes, an order, an exorcism, a persuasive word.

In *The Mirror of the Sea*—a magnificent book I translated into Spanish several years ago now—the great Polish-English novelist Joseph Conrad speaks of ships having their own character and spirit, their own norms of behaviour, their caprices, rebellions and gratitudes. Of how, in large measure, their performance and reliability depend on the treatment they receive from captain and crew.

If treated with respect, affection, consideration, care and tact, a ship, says Conrad, is grateful and responds by trying hard and giving of its best (or, rather, her best, since curiously and significantly almost the only objects that merit a gender in the English language are ships, which are always referred to as "she" and not, as would be more natural, as "it"). If, on the contrary, the relationship between them is one of superiority, disdain or is simply too demanding, authoritarian or neglectful, abusive, inconsiderate or even despotic, ships react badly, and feel no "loyalty" and fail to "protect" their crews at moments of risk or danger.

Ships, writes Conrad, are "not exactly what men make them. They have their own nature; they can of themselves minister to our self-esteem by the demand their qualities make upon our skill and their shortcomings upon our hardiness and endurance." Further on, he adds:

The love that is given to ships is profoundly different from the love men feel for every other work of their hands—the love they bear to their houses, for instance —because it is untainted by the pride of possession. The pride of skill, the pride of responsibility, the pride of endurance there may be, but otherwise it is a disinterested sentiment. No seaman ever cherished a ship, even if she belonged to him, merely because of the profit she put in his pocket. No one, I think, ever did; for a ship-owner, even of the best, has always been outside the pale of that sentiment embracing in a feeling of intimate, equal fellowship the ship and the man, backing each other against the implacable, if sometimes dissembled, hostility of their world of waters.

Later still, Conrad describes the touching words, tantamount to a funeral oration, uttered by the captain of a brig that had sunk:

"No ship could have done so well . . . She was small, but she was good. I had no anxiety. She was strong. Last voyage I had my wife and two children in her. No other ship could have stood so long the weather she had to live through for days and days before we got dismasted a fortnight ago. She was fairly worn out, and that's all. You may believe me. She lasted under us for days and days, but she could not last for ever. It was long enough.

I am glad it is over. No better ship was ever left to sink at sea on such a day as this."

Conrad sums up by saying: "She had lived, he had loved her; she had suffered, and he was glad she was at rest."

We air passengers are not accustomed to perceiving, or even imagining, planes in this way, as almost animate beings, with a capacity for suffering and endurance, requiring consideration and esteem, and being sensitive, almost, to gratitude and rancour. We board them and can barely distinguish between them; we know nothing of their age or their past history; we don't even notice their names, which, in Spain at least, are chosen in such a bureaucratic, pious spirit, so lacking in poetry, adventure and imagination, that they're hard to retain and recognize if ever we entrust ourselves to them again. I would like to ask Iberia, in this the twenty-first century, to abandon their anodyne patriotic gestures and adulatory nods to the Catholic Church—all those planes called *Our Lady of the Pillar* and *Our Lady of Good Remedy, The City of Burgos* and *The City of Tarragona*—and instead choose names that are more cheerful and more literary. I, for one, would feel safer and more reassured, more protected, if I knew I was flying in *The Red Eagle* or *The Fire Arrow* or even *Achilles* or *Emma Bovary* or *Falstaff* or *Liberty Valance* or *Nostromo*.

Perhaps reading that air hostess's epistolary revelations had something to do with the diminution of my fear. Until that comment of hers it had never occurred to me that captains might have a similar relationship with their planes as old seadogs do with their ships, and that air crews are like sailors. Perhaps the things that surprised and disturbed me during my long watches as a fearful traveller—a murmur, a squeak, a bump, a lurch—were perfectly recognizable to them, familiar, customary, the reactions of each individualized and distinguishable plane, just as we recognize the people close to us by their gestures and intonations, their silences and vacillations, so much so that, often, we don't even need them to speak to know what's wrong, what's going through their minds, what they're suffering or worrying about or plotting or waiting for.

This possibility soothes me. We live in an age that tends to depersonalize even people and is, in principle, averse to anthropomorphism. Indeed, such a tendency is often criticized, erroneously and foolishly in my view, since that "rapprochement" between the human and the non-human is quite natural and spontaneous, and far from being an attempt to deprive animals, plants and objects of their respective selves, it places them in the category of the "humanizable," which is, for us, the highest and most respectable of categories.

I know people who talk to, question, spoil, threaten or even quarrel with their computers, saying things like: "Right now, you behave yourself," or thanking them for their help. There's nothing wrong with that, it's perfectly understandable. In fact, given how often we travel in planes, the odd thing about our relationship with them—those complex machines endowed with movement to which we surrender ourselves and that transport us through the air—is that it isn't more "personal," or more "animal," or more "sailor-like," if you prefer. Perhaps those who crew them haven't known how to communicate this to us. I've never seen them pat a plane, as you might pat a horse to calm or reward it; I've never seen planes being groomed and cleaned and tidied, except very hurriedly and impatiently; I've never seen them loved as Conrad's captain loved his sunken brig; I've never seen air hostesses— who spend a lot of time on-board—treat them with the respect and care, at once fatherly and comradely, enjoyed by ships.

That's what I would like to see, less cool efficiency and more affection, and I'm sure that I, along with many other tense, vigilant passengers, would become infected by their confidence and be able to relax, because then planes, like ships in the old days, would have their "reputation," and we would know something of their voyages, their history, their deeds, their past and their future. The pilots, instead of frightening us with their usual litany of cold, hair-raising facts ("We will be flying at an absurdly high altitude, the temperature outside is unbelievably cold, etc."), could say: "This plane, the Pierre Ménard, has had an amazing life so far. It was born ten years ago, has made five hundred flights and crossed the Atlantic on sixty-three previous occasions. It has always responded well to us, even in the most unfavourable of circumstances. It's a docile plane by nature, but very sensitive as well. Why, I remember once . . ."

Well, I leave the rest up to the airlines. Perhaps it isn't too much to ask for a little more literature or—which comes to the same thing—a little uniqueness; a little history and background; a little life.

Ben Greenman

Naked Truth

Mr. Skin refines his business with Blu-ray.

Even the greatest art works can be revitalized by new technologies. As a result of carbon dating and infrared analysis, a painting once credited to an obscure nineteenth-century artist is believed to be a long-lost work of Leonardo da Vinci. This year's Beatles remasters applied modern recording technology to the group's iconic albums. And then there's the epiphanic experience of watching *Road House,* the 1989 bouncer/philosopher drama starring the late Patrick Swayze, on Blu-ray. Just ask Mr. Skin.

Mr. Skin, also known as Jim McBride, has spent the past decade overseeing his popular Web site of the same name, which meticulously catalogues nude scenes in films. Give McBride an actress's name, and he'll tell you when she lifted her shirt or dropped her trousers. For instance, Maureen Mc-Cormick, better known as Marcia Brady, of *The Brady Bunch:* "There's a movie called *Texas Lightning,* which came out in 1981," McBride said over the phone recently from Chicago, where his company is based. "At about the hour-and-four-minute mark, in a scene in a motel, a group of thugs pull down McCormick's top and you see both of her breasts." Or take Anne Hathaway. McBride said, "Three movies: *Brokeback*

Mountain, Havoc, and *Rachel Getting Married.*" Times are good for Mr. Skin. His Web site made a cameo in Judd Apatow's *Knocked Up,* in 2007—Seth Rogen and his friends dreamed of launching a similar project, only to discover that McBride was already on the scene—and a new edition of the site's companion book, the *Skincyclopedia,* comes out this month.

When McBride launched his site, in 1999, it was exclusively a VHS operation. "It had to be," he said, "because I didn't have a DVD player." As the business grew, VHS was supplanted by DVD, which offered better picture quality. In the past year, as the video industry has begun to shift to Blu-ray, the new high-definition format, Mr. Skin has had to rethink his entire modus operandi.

"Blu-ray quality is six times better than DVD," he said. "If you watch a movie on Blu-ray, something you thought was just a shadow will suddenly be revealed as a breast or a butt." He sighed. "*Road House,*" he said. "There's a scene at the hour-and-four-minute mark"—Mr. Skin has noticed that nudity tends to crop up more commonly at certain points in films, perhaps when audiences' attention is lagging—"where Patrick Swayze is sitting outside smoking a cigarette, and Kelly Lynch gets out of bed and starts to walk toward him. All the other times we saw this movie, on video or even DVD, you could only see her butt as she was walking toward him. When we were reviewing it on Blu-ray, we decided to get a closeup of her butt, and when we blew up the scene we could clearly see more. We had previously rated the movie as Breast and Buns, but we had to change it to Breast, Buns, and Bush." He went on, "Or take *Fatal Attraction.* There's a scene where Glenn Close is rolling around on the bed with Michael Douglas. There's always been breast nudity visible, but on Blu-ray you can really make out even more."

McBride's content department—eight guys who spend

their workweek capturing screen shots of any flash of flesh—is working hard to keep up with the new technology. "Studios are releasing about five or six Blu-ray titles a week," McBride said, "so we're able to be pretty comprehensive, at least so far. In *Thunderball,* for example, there's a scene with the French actress Claudine Auger on a raft with Sean Connery, and the bottom of her bathing suit is askew. It's not visible to the naked eye, but it's obvious in the Blu-ray, so that film got immediately upgraded from No Nudity to Brief Nudity."

How much extra dishabille will Blu-ray eventually reveal? "Some nudity, as it turns out, is like a tree falling in the forest with no one around," McBride said. "If you've never seen it before, does it really exist? We're going to keep looking at all these movies as technology makes them better and better, and who knows? We may even discover something in *The Sound of Music.* That would be the Holy Grail for me, to find a nude scene in a G-rated movie."

Clay Shirky

Newspapers and Thinking the Unthinkable

If the old model is broken, what will work in its place? Nothing. Nothing will work.

Back in 1993, the Knight-Ridder newspaper chain began investigating piracy of Dave Barry's popular column, which was published by the *Miami Herald* and syndicated widely. In the course of tracking down the sources of unlicensed distribution, they found many things, including the copying of his column to alt.fan.dave_barry on usenet; a 2000-person strong mailing list also reading pirated versions; and a teenager in the Midwest who was doing some of the copying himself, because he loved Barry's work so much he wanted everybody to be able to read it.

One of the people I was hanging around with online back then was Gordy Thompson, who managed internet services at the *New York Times.* I remember Thompson saying something to the effect of "When a 14 year old kid can blow up your business in his spare time, not because he hates you but because he loves you, then you got a problem." I think about that conversation a lot these days.

The problem newspapers face isn't that they didn't see the internet coming. They not only saw it miles off, they figured out early on that they needed a plan to deal with it, and during the early 90s they came up with not just one plan but several. One was to partner with companies like America Online, a fast-growing subscription service that was less chaotic than the open internet. Another plan was to educate the public about the behaviors required of them by copyright law. New payment models such as micropayments were proposed. Alternatively, they could pursue the profit margins enjoyed by radio and TV, if they became purely ad-supported. Still another plan was to convince tech firms to make their hardware and software less capable of sharing, or to partner with the businesses running data networks to achieve the same goal. Then there was the nuclear option: sue copyright infringers directly, making an example of them.

As these ideas were articulated, there was intense debate about the merits of various scenarios. Would DRM or walled gardens work better? Shouldn't we try a carrot-and-stick approach, with education *and* prosecution? And so on. In all this conversation, there was one scenario that was widely regarded as unthinkable, a scenario that didn't get much discussion in the nation's newsrooms, for the obvious reason.

The unthinkable scenario unfolded something like this: The ability to share content wouldn't shrink, it would grow. Walled gardens would prove unpopular. Digital advertising would reduce inefficiencies, and therefore profits. Dislike of micropayments would prevent widespread use. People would resist being educated to act against their own desires. Old habits of advertisers and readers would not transfer online. Even ferocious litigation would be inadequate to constrain massive, sustained law-breaking. (Prohibition redux.) Hardware and software vendors would not regard copyright holders as allies, nor would they regard customers as enemies. DRM's requirement that the attacker be allowed to decode the content would be an insuperable flaw. And, per Thompson, suing people who love something so much they want to share it would piss them off.

Revolutions create a curious inversion of perception. In ordinary times, people who do no more than describe the world around them are seen as pragmatists, while those who imagine fabulous alternative futures are viewed as radicals. The last couple of decades haven't been ordinary, however. Inside the papers, the pragmatists were the ones simply looking out the window and noticing that the real world increasingly resembled the unthinkable scenario. These people were treated as if they were barking mad. Meanwhile the people spinning visions of popular walled gardens and enthusiastic micropayment adoption, visions unsupported by reality, were regarded not as charlatans but saviors.

When reality is labeled unthinkable, it creates a kind of sickness in an industry. Leadership becomes faith-based, while employees who have the temerity to suggest that what seems to be happening is in fact happening are herded into Innovation Departments, where they can be ignored *en masse.* This shunting aside of the realists in favor of the fabulists has different effects on different industries at different times. One of the effects on the newspapers is that many of their most passionate defenders are unable, even now, to plan for a world in which the industry they knew is visibly going away.

The curious thing about the various plans hatched in the '90s is that they were, at base, all the same plan: "Here's how we're going to preserve the old forms of organization in a world of cheap perfect copies!" The details differed, but the core assumption behind all imagined outcomes (save the unthinkable one) was that the organizational form of the newspaper, as a general-purpose vehicle for publishing a variety of news and opinion, was basically sound, and only needed a digital facelift. As a result, the conversation has degenerated into the enthusiastic grasping at straws, pursued by skeptical responses.

"The *Wall Street Journal* has a paywall, so we can too!" (Financial information is one of the few kinds of information whose recipients don't want to share.) "Micropayments work for iTunes, so they will work for us!" (Micropayments work only where the provider can avoid competitive business models.) "The *New York Times* should charge for content!" (They've tried, with QPass and later TimesSelect.) "*Cook's Illustrated* and *Consumer Reports* are doing fine on subscriptions!" (Those publications forgo ad revenues; users are paying not just for content but for unimpeachability.) "We'll form a cartel!" (. . . and hand a competitive advantage to every ad-supported media firm in the world.)

Round and round this goes, with the people committed to saving newspapers demanding to know "If the old model is broken, what will work in its place?" To which the answer is: Nothing. Nothing will work. There is no general model for newspapers to replace the one the internet just broke.

With the old economics destroyed, organizational forms perfected for industrial production have to be replaced with structures optimized for digital data. It makes increasingly less sense even to talk about a publishing industry, because the core problem publishing solves—the incredible difficulty, complexity, and expense of making something available to the public—has stopped being a problem.

Elizabeth Eisenstein's magisterial treatment of Gutenberg's invention, *The Printing Press as an Agent of Change,* opens with a recounting of her research into the early history of the printing press. She was able to find many descriptions of life in the early 1400s, the era before movable type. Literacy was limited, the Catholic Church was the pan-European political force, Mass was in Latin, and the average book was the Bible. She was also able to find endless descriptions of life in the late 1500s, after Gutenberg's invention had started to spread. Literacy was on the rise, as were books written in contemporary languages, Copernicus had published his epochal work on astronomy, and Martin Luther's use of the press to reform the Church was upending both religious and political stability.

What Eisenstein focused on, though, was how many historians ignored the transition from one era to the other. To describe the world before or after the spread of print was child's play; those dates were safely distanced from upheaval. But what was happening in 1500? The hard question Eisenstein's book asks is "How did we get from the world before the printing press to the world after it? What was the revolution *itself* like?"

Chaotic, as it turns out. The Bible was translated into local languages; was this an educational boon or the work of the devil? Erotic novels appeared, prompting the same set of questions. Copies of Aristotle and Galen circulated widely, but direct encounter with the relevant texts revealed that the two sources clashed, tarnishing faith in the Ancients. As novelty spread, old institutions seemed exhausted while new ones seemed untrustworthy; as a result, people almost literally didn't know what to think. If you can't trust Aristotle, who can you trust?

During the wrenching transition to print, experiments were only revealed in retrospect to be turning points. Aldus Manutius, the Venetian printer and publisher, invented the smaller *octavo* volume along with italic type. What seemed like a minor change—take a book and shrink it—was in retrospect a key innovation in the democratization of the printed word. As books became cheaper, more portable, and therefore more desirable, they expanded the market for all publishers, heightening the value of literacy still further.

That is what real revolutions are like. The old stuff gets

broken faster than the new stuff is put in its place. The importance of any given experiment isn't apparent at the moment it appears; big changes stall, small changes spread. Even the revolutionaries can't predict what will happen. Agreements on all sides that core institutions must be protected are rendered meaningless by the very people doing the agreeing. (Luther and the Church both insisted, for years, that whatever else happened, no one was talking about a schism.) Ancient social bargains, once disrupted, can neither be mended nor quickly replaced, since any such bargain takes decades to solidify.

And so it is today. When someone demands to know how we are going to replace newspapers, they are really demanding to be told that we are not living through a revolution. They are demanding to be told that old systems won't break before new systems are in place. They are demanding to be told that ancient social bargains aren't in peril, that core institutions will be spared, that new methods of spreading information will improve previous practice rather than upending it. They are demanding to be lied to.

There are fewer and fewer people who can convincingly tell such a lie.

If you want to know why newspapers are in such trouble, the most salient fact is this: Printing presses are terrifically expensive to set up and to run. This bit of economics, normal since Gutenberg, limits competition while creating positive returns to scale for the press owner, a happy pair of economic effects that feed on each other. In a notional town with two perfectly balanced newspapers, one paper would eventually generate some small advantage—a breaking story, a key interview—at which point both advertisers and readers would come to prefer it, however slightly. That paper would in turn find it easier to capture the next dollar of advertising, at lower expense, than the competition. This would increase its dominance, which would further deepen those preferences, repeat chorus. The end result is either geographic or demographic segmentation among papers, or one paper holding a monopoly on the local mainstream audience.

For a long time, longer than anyone in the newspaper business has been alive in fact, print journalism has been intertwined with these economics. The expense of printing created an environment where Wal-Mart was willing to subsidize the Baghdad bureau. This wasn't because of any deep link between advertising and reporting, nor was it about any real desire on the part of Wal-Mart to have their marketing budget go to international correspondents. It was just an accident. Advertisers had little choice other than to have their money used that way, since they didn't really have any other vehicle for display ads.

The old difficulties and costs of printing forced everyone doing it into a similar set of organizational models; it was this similarity that made us regard *Daily Racing Form* and *L'Osservatore Romano* as being in the same business. That the relationship between advertisers, publishers, and journalists has been ratified by a century of cultural practice doesn't make it any less accidental.

The competition-deflecting effects of printing cost got destroyed by the internet, where everyone pays for the infrastructure, and then everyone gets to use it. And when Wal-Mart, and the local Maytag dealer, and the law firm hiring a secretary, and that kid down the block selling his bike, were all able to use that infrastructure to get out of their old relationship with the publisher, they did. They'd never really signed up to fund the Baghdad bureau anyway.

Print media does much of society's heavy journalistic lifting, from flooding the zone—covering every angle of a huge story

—to the daily grind of attending the City Council meeting, just in case. This coverage creates benefits even for people who aren't newspaper readers, because the work of print journalists is used by everyone from politicians to district attorneys to talk radio hosts to bloggers. The newspaper people often note that newspapers benefit society as a whole. This is true, but irrelevant to the problem at hand; "You're gonna miss us when we're gone!" has never been much of a business model. So who covers all that news if some significant fraction of the currently employed newspaper people lose their jobs?

I don't know. Nobody knows. We're collectively living through 1500, when it's easier to see what's broken than what will replace it. The internet turns 40 this fall. Access by the general public is less than half that age. Web use, as a normal part of life for a majority of the developed world, is less than half *that* age. We just got here. Even the revolutionaries can't predict what will happen.

Imagine, in 1996, asking some net-savvy soul to expound on the potential of craigslist, then a year old and not yet incorporated. The answer you'd almost certainly have gotten would be extrapolation: "Mailing lists can be powerful tools," "Social effects are intertwining with digital networks," blah blah blah. What no one would have told you, could have told you, was what actually happened: craiglist became a critical piece of infrastructure. Not the idea of craigslist, or the business model, or even the software driving it. Craigslist itself spread to cover hundreds of cities and has become a part of public consciousness about what is now possible. Experiments are only revealed in retrospect to be turning points.

In craigslist's gradual shift from "interesting if minor" to "essential and transformative," there is one possible answer to the question "If the old model is broken, what will work in its place?" The answer is: Nothing will work, but everything might. Now is the time for experiments, lots and lots of experiments, each of which will seem as minor at launch as craigslist did, as Wikipedia did, as *octavo* volumes did.

Journalism has always been subsidized. Sometimes it's been Wal-Mart and the kid with the bike. Sometimes it's been Richard Mellon Scaife. Increasingly, it's you and me, donating our time. The list of models that are obviously working today, like *Consumer Reports* and NPR, like ProPublica and Wiki-Leaks, can't be expanded to cover any general case, but then nothing is going to cover the general case.

Society doesn't need newspapers. What we need is journalism. For a century, the imperatives to strengthen journalism and to strengthen newspapers have been so tightly wound as to be indistinguishable. That's been a fine accident to have, but when that accident stops, as it is stopping before our eyes, we're going to need lots of other ways to strengthen journalism instead.

When we shift our attention from "save newspapers" to "save society," the imperative changes from "preserve the current institutions" to "do whatever works." And what works today isn't the same as what used to work.

We don't know who the Aldus Manutius of the current age is. It could be Craig Newmark, or Caterina Fake. It could be Martin Nisenholtz, or Emily Bell. It could be some 19 year old kid few of us have heard of, working on something we won't recognize as vital until a decade hence. Any experiment, though, designed to provide new models for journalism is going to be an improvement over hiding from the real, especially in a year when, for many papers, the unthinkable future is already in the past.

For the next few decades, journalism will be made up of overlapping special cases. Many of these models will rely on amateurs as researchers and writers. Many of these models will rely on sponsorship or grants or endowments instead of revenues. Many of these models will rely on excitable 14 year olds distributing the results. Many of these models will fail. No one experiment is going to replace what we are now losing with the demise of news on paper, but over time, the collection of new experiments that do work might give us the journalism we need.

Vanessa Grigoriadis

Do You Own Facebook?
Or Does Facebook Own You?

Trust is a fragile commodity.

Let's begin with a typical parable of life in the era of web 2.0.
On Presidents' Day, Julius Harper turned on his computer at
9 a.m. This was later than usual, but he had the day off from
his job as a video-game producer in Los Angeles. He began
his daily "blog check"—Digg, Reddit, "anything interesting,
disasters, plane crashes"—before turning to a post on the Con-
sumerist, a consumer-advocacy blog, about the finer points of
user privacy on Facebook.com. "Facebook's New Terms of
Service: 'We Can Do Anything We Want With Your Content. Forever,'" it read. "Facebook's terms of service used to
say that when you closed an account on their network, any
rights they claimed to the original content you uploaded
would expire. Not anymore. Now, anything you upload to
Facebook can be used by Facebook in any way they deem fit,
forever, no matter what you do later."

Harper, a 25-year-old graduate of the University of Southern California, didn't like this too much. "I thought, *This is
bull-crap,*" he says. With a few clicks of his mouse, he created
a protest group on Facebook, which came to be called People
Against the New Terms of Service. "That's the first group like

that I started," he says. "The other ones I've made are just for my friends, like Hey Guys, Let's Go See *Watchmen* This Weekend." Around 10 a.m., he drove to Wal-Mart, where he bought several Healthy Choice lunches for the upcoming workweek. By the time he arrived home, at noon, over 800 people had joined his group. Soon the membership rolls reached 20,000. The next day, *NBC Nightly News* came to his home in Valencia, California. He checked their I.D.'s at the door. "I thought they might be from *The Daily Show* or playing a joke on me," he says. "I mean, I've seen *Borat.*"

Overnight, Harper had become a consumer-rights activist, and his protest was turning into a PR disaster for Facebook, a social-networking site of about 200 million members that is both based on an expansive idea of community and invested in controlling it for commercial purposes. Soon, the company's 24-year-old paterfamilias, Mark Zuckerberg, who also owns over 20 percent of the company's shares, joined the discussion. We're family, he seemed to be saying. On his blog, he protested that there was nothing to worry about because "in reality, we wouldn't share your information in a way you wouldn't want"—a version of the "Trust us" comment that Google's Eric Schmidt made to Charlie Rose last year—but, if anything, his remarks only threw fuel on the fire: Why change the terms if it didn't matter who owned what? And anyway, the issue was more a matter of a kind of pre-rational emotion than any legalistic parsing of rights. What people put up on Facebook was themselves: their personhood, their social worlds, what makes them distinctive and singular. It was a pursuit-of-happiness type of thing. No one else should be permitted to own it.

But Facebook is as sensitive as any politician to feedback from its constituents, especially on the issue of privacy. No other social-networking site provides users the kind of granular privacy settings for their profiles and applications that

Facebook does. After Harper received a call from privacy experts who wanted his support in a $5 million FTC complaint —"I was like, 'Whoa, we don't care about money,'" he says, "'we're just trying to get the TOS changed'"—he heard from a Facebook spokesperson, who asked him for a memo summarizing his group's complaints. Harper put these together carefully. He thought that Facebook should allow users to decide whether their information could be used for commercial purposes, inform them of which third parties have access to their content, and delete a user's information the moment he closes his account. Furthermore, changes to the TOS should be made visibly and put to a vote before implementation. Also, it was important that Facebook write its legal documents in a straightforward way. "No Latin!" he wrote. "I'm not sure what *forum non conveniens* means, and I shouldn't have to."

But Zuckerberg made a bold move, aligned with Facebook's corporate image: He turned the site into a democracy. He decided to reinstate the former TOS, then released a new version a week later that took broad latitude to use our content while we were on the site but fell short of claiming ownership, and that Facebook revoked its rights to our content when we delete our accounts. This version was open for user comments until March 29. Facebook will release its response to the comments by April 10 and put the entire document to a vote by all users during the week of April 20.

With the vote, though, Zuckerberg set a high bar—perhaps an impossibly high bar—for user voices to be heard: It will be binding only if 30 percent of members cast a ballot. That's about 60 million people. "You can't get 60 million people to agree on anything, so the fact that Facebook is requiring it makes this all seem a little fake," says Harper, over lunch at a Hawaiian fast-food restaurant near his office in Burbank, California. Harper is stiff and proper, with a pressed shirt and a silver cross around his neck, yet now he shifts his eyes downward uneasily. Facebook listened to him, and he is uncomfortable judging it. "I have to think that they are showing good faith here," he says, then nods his head. "I'm going to give them the benefit of the doubt."

If there were one word to describe what Facebook has added to my life, I would use it. It's a multidimensional pleasure: It's given me a tool for exceptionally mindless, voyeuristic, puerile procrastination; crowd-sourced pesky problems like finding a new accountant; stoked my narcissism; warmed my heart with nostalgia; and created a euphoric, irrational, irresistible belief in the good in men's hearts among the most skeptical people I know—people who should know better. As the dominant social network on the web (the Internet began, essentially, as a social network, with Usenet in the late seventies) Facebook has created a space similar to a college quad, where members can check each other out, talk about culture, gossip, and pass mash notes. Users really like Facebook; they believe in it so strongly that they want to protect it from itself. That much is clear from the anger over the redesign, released a couple of weeks ago, meant to outmaneuver Twitter in the realm of speedy exchange of information—a redesign that, ironically, created a much louder protest, at two-and-a-half-million users and counting, than Harper's protest about the security of one's personal information. As of now, Harper's group has around 148,000 users. Organizing has basically come to a standstill. "We're waiting to see what Facebook does next," he says.

This is a crucial moment for Facebook, and a delicate one, because We, the users, are what Facebook is selling. "Facebook is walking a fine line of keeping the trust of its members, and wanting to exploit them for profit," says Nicholas Carr, author of *The Big Switch*. "It's having a tough time balancing the two." In 2007, the company was valued at $15 billion, after Microsoft bought a 1.6 percent stake for $240 million, but profit has been elusive. If they can solve this problem, come up with a viable business model—one might note that if they charged $1 a month for the service and even half its users stuck around, it would take in $100 million each month—it could go public and even become the first big IPO to reinvigorate the market; if Facebook doesn't, Zuckerberg & Co. will struggle to resist a takeover by a very rich tech company (well, Microsoft) for a fire-sale price of a billion or two. After CFO Gideon Yu announced his exit last week, the company claimed that it was looking for a replacement with public-company experience, but the way forward is far from clear. The history of social networks is an absurd one of missed opportunities, from Tripod to Geocities to AOL, though Facebook thus far has avoided their pitfalls. It's been unaffected by Friendster's technical glitches and its taint of uncoolness; Facebook's antiseptic design clears away the lascivious, spam-ified, knife-wielding clutter of MySpace, a site that was double Facebook's size in the U.S. eight months ago but whose technological innovation has been stymied by News Corp until recently.

Facebook is exceptional at public relations. Harper may think that it's impossible to get millions of people to join hands, but Facebook's particular genius has been convincing 200 million people to color within the lines, to behave a certain way without being told to. When it moved the lines a bit with the redesign, the company issued a statement that it only meant well—"Whenever we build something new or tweak something old, our motivation is the same: to help you share with the people you care about," it said—which wasn't strictly true; advertisers seemed to be more prominent on the home page, for one thing, and group pages were redesigned to look like "friends." For users, it can feel like information is rushing toward us as through a beer funnel, too much information about too many people, much as on Twitter, though that's part of why Twitter is still largely used by tech-heads, nerds, and those who work in marketing or want to market themselves (though all bets are off regarding Twitter when the war over social networks on mobile heats up).

Still, Facebook was clearly spooked by Twitter—and spooked, also, by the fact that we were spooked. Because this is how social networks collapse. Do things feel uncomfortable? Am I oversharing? Are others oversharing? Or is the company stealing my soul by mining my personal information? Wispy perceptions. A slight paranoia. And then, for no rational reason, a queasiness sets in, the comfort level drops, and people start to drift away. One day the numbers are growing exponentially, and the next they're stagnant, none of the users are actually showing up, and there's another network that's getting all the buzz. Friendster had numbers. AOL had numbers. It's like the Yogi Berra line: Nobody goes there anymore, it's too crowded. It's easy to join on the web and just as easy to leave.

I'm part of one of the fastest-growing segments on Facebook, users over 30, and I'm a late-adopter. About three years ago, a trendy 22-year-old colleague who wore T-shirts with slogans like THIS IS WHAT A FEMINIST LOOKS LIKE over her ample chest invited me to join, but I did not accept, as we were friends of no sort. Soon, my e-mail box began to fill with weekly requests from slightly more mature friends—or, at least, people I know vaguely—to "Check out my Facebook profile!" Just like the boomers who missed out on the Summer of Love finally threw on some tie-dye and flocked to EST in the seventies, Gen-Xers have eagerly embraced Facebook as a chance to join millennial culture—the Paris Hilton–posey, authority-loving, hive mind of kids today—through Facebook. Says a friend in her forties, "Facebook makes us feel very young, which feels really great. Connecting with old crushes, even younger." I'm not a joiner by nature—I have never been to a high-school or college reunion—but by last year, acquaintances at parties were no longer asking me "What's your e-mail?" the way they have for the past few years, since they stopped asking "What's your phone number?" (No one can be bothered to use phones anymore, even cell phones.) Now they were saying "I'll find you on Facebook." And if you weren't on Facebook—where were you?

Because on Facebook, people are doing things. Their "status updates" say they are at the Cardio Barre, or haggling over prices at the Range Rover dealership, or making soup from scratch at home; in fact, it seems to me that someone is always making soup. This information scrolled rapidly down my screen when I was staring at my computer at work, and maybe it wasn't quite as fast as Twitter, but the people providing the information were twice as important to me. It formed a constant reminder that there was still a real world out there with real people walking around in it, even if they had chosen to leave that world for a moment to join me in the pretend, Facebook world. On Facebook, I didn't have to talk to anyone, really, but I didn't feel alone, and I mean "alone" in the existential use of the word; everyone on Facebook wished me well, which I know not to be the case in the real world; and, most important, there was nothing messy or untoward or unpleasant—the technology controlled human interaction, keeping everyone at a perfect distance, not too close and not too far away, in a zone where I rarely felt weird or lame or like I had said the wrong thing, the way one often feels in the real world. This is the promise of Facebook, the utopian hope for it: the triumph of fellowship; the rise of a unified consciousness; peace through superconnectivity, as rapid bits of information elevate us to the Buddha mind, or at least distract us from whatever problems are at hand. In a time of deep economic, political, and intergenerational despair, social cohesion is the only chance to save the day, and online social networks like Facebook are the best method available for reflecting—or perhaps inspiring—an aesthetic of unity.

In any case, these status updates formed a pleasant collage, a kind of poetry, like first-draft scribbles in Gertrude Stein's notebook—the poetry of the mundane. *Emily is in the heavenly land of Williamsburg; Brian is tired and sweaty from a day of playing the Safety Ape and a clam and garlic pizza; Elizabeth is reading, happily, with sunshine through a windowpane*—and then got sucked into the vortex that is Facebook. This microknowledge of others has been termed "ambient awareness" by sociologists, a new kind of social proprioception or ethereal limb, and I learned to flex it with ease. But I thought that I would take a different angle for my first status update, something suitably ironic and a little bit outré: *Vanessa is doing cocaine and piercing her nipples.* A Facebook faux pas, I quickly realized. My fellow users pretended not to hear.

This safe and happy community is very much a product of design. The old web, the frontier world of autonomy, anarchy, fantasies, and self-made porn, is being tamed. The flaming, snarky, commenter-board culture that dips in periodically to bang heads against the floor and foster self-hate among humanity's ranks has been deemed not good for business. Facebook's relentless emphasis on literal representation—the site maintains a "blacklist" of celebrity names to discourage impersonation and reserves the right to delete anyone who claims to be someone he is not, or who creates multiple accounts—turns out to be the weapon to quell the web's chaos. Now online life is a series of Victorian drawing rooms, a well-tended garden where you bring your calling card and make polite conversation with those of your kind, a sanitized city on a hill where amity reigns, irony falls flat, and sarcasm is remarkably rare. We prepare our faces, then come and go, sharing little bits of data, like photos, haikus, snippets of conversations—the intellectual property that composes our lives.

Sharing is actually not my word. It's the most important Newspeak word in the Facebook lexicon, an infantilizing phrase whose far less cozy synonym is "uploading data." Facebook's entire business plan, insofar as it is understood by anyone, rests upon this continued practice of friends sharing with friends, and as such it is part of the company's bedrock belief, as expressed in the first line of its principles: "People should have the freedom to share whatever information they want." "A lot of times users—well, I don't want to say they undervalue sharing, but a lot of times they don't want to share initially," said Chris Cox, Facebook's 26-year-old director of products. "And then eventually, they say, 'Okay, I'll put a profile picture up here. I'll do it.' Immediately, their friends comment on it, and there are no tacky, weird strangers around, and suddenly they start to realize, 'Hey, wait, this is different. I am on the Internet, but I am in a safe place.'"

Cox, a dropout from Stanford's graduate program in symbolic systems, is known professionally as Zuckerberg's better half and twice as handsome. We were talking at the Facebook offices in Palo Alto earlier this year, when I spent three hours in a windowless conference room meeting with executives in one of the company's ten small buildings near the campus of Stanford University (the company is moving to an office park next month). Colorful graffiti of Facebook-cap-wearing kids waving Facebook flags line the corridors, and semi-ironic signs like THANKS, SILICON VALLEY, FOR INVENTING THE INTERNET! hang on office doors. It's all very Facebook-y: intimate, twee, and above all friendly, like the research offices of a well-funded postdoctoral project.

I took a trip to visit Facebook because I was interested in the way it is remaking social groups of old friends, so I mostly wanted to talk about that, but all these executives wanted to talk about was sharing. And privacy. And control. (Although I did learn the biggest user complaint on the site: the inability to remove unflattering photos of themselves posted by friends.) They said this kind of stuff: "People have been traditionally too scared to share on the web," that from another executive, Chris Kelly, the company's chief privacy officer at the moment, though he is widely rumored to be leaving soon to run for attorney general of California. "They lost all control because they were too open with sharing information," he continued. "We give them back that control, so they will share again, and we think people will soon be much more comfortable about sharing more with more people." He cleared his throat. "Ultimately, human beings are very social," said Kelly. "They want to share. They just want to share with people that they know and trust."

For all the talk of sharing, it was a slightly tense environment, a little like being in a capsule, hurtling into the great unknown, which is the future of the web. It was all a little vertiginous. In our conversation, we marveled at Facebook's runaway growth of about a million new members a day, which Kelly called an "explosion." It's an astonishing number, but things are moving and changing incredibly fast on the web right now. They know that Facebook's massive cultural footprint could be washed away tomorrow by forces not yet understood, not least by the micro-choices and preconscious perceptions of its users.

Then again, these are smart guys who have thought deeply about the ways their little planet can perish. They're not wicked corporate invaders; they're behaviorists and lawyers, psychology majors and big thinkers. There's a moral undercurrent to their pronouncements—this is what they're selling, of course—and they talk the talk so well, it's hard to imagine they're not walking the walk, too. "I don't think of our users as customers," says Cox. "That reminds me of someone coming into a store and buying a sandwich. We're all Facebook users here, and our parents, friends, colleagues, and loved ones are Facebook users. This is a much more intimate relationship, frankly. We take it very personally."

When we first use Facebook, we're back in college, and just like the first day there, we really want to make friends. We love sharing: We'll talk to the loser girl down the hall who only listens to the Eagles, the kid who sits next to us in physics, the R.A. who doesn't seem as cool as an R.A. should be. Within a week on the service, I had 50 friend requests, many from people I did not recall from any particular time in my life, and there was a certain loss of innocence as I realized this wasn't a sign of brain freeze: I really didn't know these people. They were just nice people using the site as they thought it should be used, for social networking, though this isn't the way cool people use the site, so I quickly de-friended them. (Although one could argue that deciding who to be and not to be friends with on Facebook is the most uncool thing in the world.)

This is part of the magic of Facebook, where many actions that take on weight in the real world simply don't pack the same punch: You can reconnect with long-lost friends without a gooey, uncomfortable e-mail about why you grew apart; you can forget to return Facebook e-mail and nobody minds; you can click obsessively on someone's profile and there's no way for him to know it. "Stalking on Facebook doesn't feel like stalking," says Rachel Zabar, my friend from high school. "It feels innocent, like when you were a kid and had a crush on someone and you'd call him and hang up." At lunch with girlfriends, we talked endlessly about negotiating the boundaries of this new social world: which estranged friends had most recently come out of the woodwork; whose profile was cool and whose was too "Facebook-y"; who was a

"Facebook abuser": "He tried to get all of the people on his friend list to send his mom a birthday note!" The dark art of stalking ex-boyfriends on Google began to shift over to Facebook, as many more personal details were suddenly available there. "I saw Facebook pictures of my ex with his new wife and their new baby on a private jet!" wails a friend. "That was too much for me." She sighs. "I can't believe I'm stalking people's babies on Facebook."

The deeply voyeuristic pleasure of Facebook, wherein one feels as though one were sucking the very life out of the person whose profile one is viewing, was only part of the story, and many of the conversations that I had with friends about Facebook quickly catapulted past Jane Austen and into the territory of Eckhart Tolle, as we confessed the details of deep exchanges that we'd had on the site, the healing that was going on. A friend got back together with her ex-husband, who had resettled in Norway; another reconnected with a friend who had supported her when she was experiencing sexual abuse as an adolescent. Facebook wants you to form these bonds; it wants to create "folksonomies," an academic term for what we're doing when we tag people's photos and write Facebook haikus to lovers and in general pass the network more and more information, because, by the law of network effects, the more that you parse out your relationships to other people, the stronger their networks become.

Here is another parable about web 2.0 culture: In nursery school at Bank Street on 112th and Broadway, a kid used to bite me—a lot. It was a progressive preschool in the seventies, and crazy stuff happened there—one day, my friend's mother jumped in front of the subway after she dropped her off at school, and Bank Street chose to share this information with us in class. Gabe would bite my arm while we playing during recess; he would bite my leg when I was coloring in my book; he would bite me when we lined up by size in the hallway, where I, the runt, was always first. (He also put another kid in an empty refrigerator in the teacher's lounge, briefly.) It took six months for the school to figure out that he was biting me, because the penalty for biting was getting sent home for the rest of the day, at which point the torture abated.

Gabe ended up at Fieldston, and I'd seen him a few times on the Manhattan prep-school social circuit, but I never knew much about him. One day he friended me on Facebook. We agreed to meet for a drink, and he looked sheepish as he told me things that I never knew. He had a learning disability as a kid and suffered from severe ear infections. When we knew each other, he couldn't speak in full sentences and every day after school he had to meet with a speech therapist. "I was confused and angry as a kid," he said. "I was so traumatized by my health problems that I didn't mind fighting. I wasn't scared of anything, because it couldn't possibly hurt worse than my ear infections already did."

This is part of who I am now—somebody who knows that her nursery-school tormentor wasn't a bully without a heart. It will get logged into my profile, and that profile will become part of the "social graph," which is a map of every known human relationship in the universe. Filling it in is Facebook's big vision, a typically modest one for Silicon Valley. It's too complex for a computer scientist to build. Just as our free calls to GOOG-411 helped Google build its voice-recognition technology, we are creating the graph for Facebook, and I'm not sure that we can take ourselves out once we've put ourselves on there. We have changed the nature of the graph by our very presence, which facilitates connections between our disparate groups of friends, who now know each other. "If you leave Facebook, you can remove data objects, like photographs, but it's a complete impossibility that you can control all of your data," says Fred Stutzman, a teaching fellow studying social networks at the University of North Carolina at Chapel Hill. "Facebook can't promise it, and no one can promise it. You can't remove yourself from the site because the site has, essentially, been shaped by you."

This graph, this most intimate of databases, is so immensely valuable, and powerful—if in ways as yet impossible to comprehend—that it is hard to imagine it being held in the hands of a 24-year-old eager to make his stamp on the world. Facebook may thicken social bonds, but it was founded on the ruins of a relationship. Zuckerberg, a confident, privileged programmer and fencer from Dobbs Ferry who graduated from Exeter, started the site in 2004, as a Harvard sophomore studying computer science and psychology. After he created a stir on campus with a mean-spirited comparison of Harvard students' relative attractiveness (quickly shut down by university administrators), a trio of entrepreneurial classmates, including Olympian rowing twins, approached him to write code for an online Harvard Facebook that they planned to call Harvard Connection. According to the Connection guys, Zuckerberg agreed to the project, then blew them off for a couple months. Then he launched TheFacebook.com. (The three students settled with him for $65 million in June 2008; they are now suing one of their law firms for making them a questionable deal, as the sum was awarded partially in Facebook stock.)

A slight five foot eight with a cocky attitude but a halting way of speaking, and a near-daily uniform of a fleece paired with a tie, Zuckerberg enjoys his position of power immensely, though a friend says that he doesn't care about money at all —except he really wants a jet. He used to have a business card that read I'M CEO . . . BITCH. Sweeping proclamations fall from his lips, as when he declared he had started a "movement" when he opened Facebook's API to developers, or that "once every hundred years, media changes," upon the release of

Beacon, an ad program that he had to cancel because of user discontent (it was reintroduced as an opt-in program a few months later, and continues with a small number of participating sites today). At his core, he is a programmer—he loves the nerd widgets on the site, like (fluff)Friends—and like most programmers, he believes that more information makes a better world, and a more tolerant one. And he could be right. Your digital self could be even more sensitive, and powerful, than your real self: It could possess more information, and more information is power; it could push progressive cultural norms, like the Saudi women who organized for driving privileges with the help of Facebook; more friends on Facebook already mean more job opportunities, and will likely produce free iPods for those who are identified as influencers by marketers.

But web cognoscenti tend to think that people who worry too much about privacy are sentimentalists who should grow up, and while maintaining a sense of privacy is Facebook's core strength, it's hard to believe that Zuckerberg and the Facebook staff are all that different. Facebook does not give advertisers access to personal information, but third-party widget developers are allowed to scrape some of it with user consent (they are prevented from accessing information like e-mails and IM addresses). The U.S. government, plus criminal attorneys and divorce lawyers, don't technically have access to it either, but it's not hard to get a subpoena in this country these days. And the developers are sometimes located in foreign countries, which means that they could pass our information to foreign governments. I asked Kelly about this, too, and perhaps he found me too credulous. "So the Indian government knows that you like Bon Jovi, and that's a threat to national security?" he asked, laughing.

I get his point, but I still don't like it. Kubrick dreamed of villains like this: nerds in fleece, controlling the information, calling their cult a family. It was an image, a kind of inchoate anxiety about the future, rather than anything you could put your finger on. In many conversations with privacy experts, it was hard to see what, specifically, was upsetting them so much; part of their strategy is clearly to pressure the big dog to set good policies now, so that others follow them later. Twenty years down the road, as algorithms and filtering mechanisms are significantly stronger and we've moved from PCs to home monitors with information stored in remote locations—"the cloud"—we will entrust ever more of ourselves to large data centers, many of which are already built around the Columbia River. Facebook already has tens of thousands of servers in a few data centers throughout the country, but this pales in comparison to Microsoft's facility in Quincy, Washington: Their data center is the area of ten football fields, 1.5 metric tons of batteries for backup power, and 48 megawatts of electricity, enough to power 40,000 homes. An uncanny simulacrum of your life has been created on the web. It may not be too hyperbolic to talk about a digital self, as a fourth addition to mind, body, and spirit. It's not the kind of thing that one wants to give away.

To get to this endgame, though, Facebook has to get through the current phase, which involves keeping people interested. I enjoyed myself on Facebook until a couple of months ago, when I went to a dentist with a little dog in her office, which she put in my lap during my exam. I found this odd enough to justify writing a status update. Several of my friends commented appropriately—"Not so hygienic, I'm thinking, LOL" —but my friend Judd took offense. "And then what happened, Vanessa?" he sneered. "I mean in a moment like that, there's you, the dentist, the dog. It puts dog-lovers and dental fanatics and probably some perverts on the edge of their chairs. So go on, WHAT HAPPENED NEXT?"

"This is why you have 100 friends on Facebook and two in real life," I replied, somewhat lamely. "Oops—now you have one!"

He quickly chastised me. "Suggestion," he shot back. "Start a group called Everybody Please Hate Judd. I'll join it! Or rehabilitate me, via Facebook: Encourage me to share, with the kind of warm, dull, 12-steppish type comments that real Facebookers offer each other every day. The truth is, everyone here has gone back to high school, but now they've read some books, got some cool corporate skills, and this time, they're going to win this game. You go girl!"

This was the beginning of the end. Suddenly, Facebook began to irk me—the way friends always posted about procrastinating, being stuck in traffic, needing a nap or a vacation, or seemed to formulate their updates in declarative yet vague form, like "Michelle is upset" or "Roya is pouting," thus coming off like a needy jerk and making us take time out of our day to plead with them to answer the burning question: "Why are you pouting?" There was the day someone posted about bowel movements. There were too many days when friends, in pathetic attempts to rattle their cages, posted joke updates like "I'm gay!" or "I just got arrested!" There was the day that a friend of mine posted the passport of their newborn, because it was supercute, but I thought of the jpeg finding its way into one of Facebook's servers and it was just . . . creepy.

Friends of mine began to freak out, like a guy with intimacy issues who dropped his girlfriend after reading a list that she had posted on Facebook about her favorite memories; another woman became so addicted to the site that she appeared blank-faced and wobbly in the real world, suddenly uncomfortable with unmediated experience. Other friends started to react poorly as well. "One day, I finally sent a Facebook message to the guy who is the love of my life, even though technically I broke his heart," says a friend, 38. "I said, 'I know you work at IAC, and I've just moved down the street from where you work—do you want to get coffee?' He wrote me back, 'I think it would hurt too much. Plus you and I were never the coffee kind of people anyway.'" Because he had responded to her message, Facebook allowed her to see the guy's profile—and, for the first time, she found out that he was married. "I had no idea, and I was so devastated," she says. "I cried for days."

Why has the number of MySpace visitors remained essentially flat in the past year? Why do social networks fail? Maybe it's claustrophobic to know this much about other people. Maybe we like the way we've been able to live over the past 50 years, the freedom to move where we want, date who we like, and insert ourselves into any number of social cliques, before we cast aside those who bore us and never look back. Independence is a gift, even if it's lonely sometimes, and solving childhood mysteries may make people happier, but it doesn't necessarily turn them into the people they dream of being. So we keep perpetuating the cycle of birthing and abandoning new online communities, drawing close and then pulling away, on a perpetual search for the perfect balance of unity and autonomy on the web.

I don't want to leave Facebook—reloading personal photos and making new friends on another site feels very junior high; it would be a drag. But it's easy to imagine a circumstance—the wrong ads, too much information about too many people, some invisible level where being commodified starts to drive me nuts—when I might stop showing up, living my life in the real world, checking the site every couple of months. Monetize that . . . bitch.

Facebook may well turn out to be some sort of democracy, or at least, as Cox says, a "democracy in spirit." "I think there's a little-*d* democratic analogy here, to the U.S. government for instance," says Chris Kelly. "You don't get to vote on every budget item: You get to vote for your representatives, and you can rise up in constitutional convention, if you want to organize one of them, but on a foundational level, there's a consent to be governed." This might be as much as we can expect on the web. If it is, then our fates are already tied together, because we can either rise up in large numbers, or remain silent —rule-followers, faceless Facebook members.

It's possible that even Harper will go back being nobody, to doing as he's told. After all, it's a big victory, getting an important company to change its Terms of Service, even if it didn't take all of his suggestions. He's a busy guy, and apolitical; he didn't vote in the presidential election, but says that if he had, he would have chosen Barack Obama or Alan Keyes. Last week, Facebook called him again to ask him if he would look over a summary of user feedback before they publish the new Terms of Service on April 10, and told him that it was consulting an independent auditor for the upcoming vote. "I think they wanted some kind of comment like, 'This totally restores my faith in Facebook,'" he says. "I was like, 'Okay, I'm happy you're doing this, but I'm not going to be your mouthpiece.'" Harper may not fully understand what he's fighting, but he still wants to fight. He's not ready to blend in the crowd. Now, he's even thinking about applying to law school. "I like that my claim to fame is something that helps people, that I'm not Omarosa from *The Apprentice*," he says, his brown eyes lighting up. "I'd like to be a person who makes decisions. That would be cool."

Daniel Roth

The Answer Factory

*Demand media and the fast, disposable, and
profitable-as-hell media model.*

Christian Muñoz-Donoso is going to make this job pay, he's
got to move quickly. He has a list of 10 videos to shoot on this
warm June morning, for which he'll earn just $200. To get
anything close to his usual rate, he'll have to do it all in two
hours. As he sets up his three video cameras on the rocky shore
of a man-made lake in Huntington, Massachusetts, he thinks
about the way things used to be. He once spent two weeks in
a bird blind in his native Chile to capture striking footage of
a rarely seen Andean condor. But those jobs are almost as en-
dangered as that bird. Now he trades finesse for speed.

Today's topic is kayaking. Muñoz-Donoso has enlisted a
local instructor to meet him and to bring along four of his
boats. Every five minutes, Muñoz-Donoso's assistant shouts a
new subject—"Kayak basics!" "Paddling tips!"—and the expert, sitting in one of his rigs in the bourbon-colored water,
riffs off the top of his head. Muñoz-Donoso gets most of his
shots in one take. But conditions are working against him.
Shifting winds and changing light require him to adjust his
setup. The instructor keeps switching kayaks and gear. Finally, the entire shoot has to be put on hold as three bearded

fishermen loudly and slowly drag their boats into the lake, directly into the frame. Muñoz-Donoso hoped to finish his shoot by 11, but it's already 12:45 when he crams his equipment into the back of his SUV and speeds back to his office, 20 miles away.

He climbs a flight of stairs to his studio above a strip mall, unloads his gear, and keeps up his breakneck pace. As he opens his files in Final Cut Pro, he winces. "Normally I'd eliminate the wind or the kid screaming in the background," he says. "But in this case we don't do any of that." He points out that the focus is off: The rippling water is sharp while the kayaking instructor is slightly blurred. But the company he's working for won't care, he says, so why should he—especially for $20 a clip? Within a few hours, he has uploaded his work to Demand Media, his employer for the day. It isn't Scorsese, but it's fast, cheap, and good enough.

Thousands of other filmmakers and writers around the country are operating with the same loose standards, racing to produce the 4,000 videos and articles that Demand Media publishes every day. The company's ambitions are so enormous as to be almost surreal: to predict any question anyone might ask and generate an answer that will show up at the top of Google's search results. To get there, Demand is using an army of Muñoz-Donosos to feverishly crank out articles and videos. They shoot slapdash instructional videos with titles like "How To Draw a Greek Helmet" and "Dog Whistle Training Techniques." They write guides about lunch meat safety and nonprofit administration. They pump out an endless stream of bulleted lists and tutorials about the most esoteric of subjects.

Plenty of other companies—About.com, Mahalo, Answers.com—have tried to corner the market in arcane online advice. But none has gone about it as aggressively, scientifically, and single-mindedly as Demand. Pieces are not dreamed up by trained editors nor commissioned based on submitted questions. Instead they are assigned by an algorithm, which mines nearly a terabyte of search data, Internet traffic patterns, and keyword rates to determine what users want to know and how much advertisers will pay to appear next to the answers.

The process is automatic, random, and endless, a Stirling engine fueled by the world's unceasing desire to know how to grow avocado trees from pits or how to throw an Atlanta Braves–themed birthday party. It is a database of human needs, and if you haven't stumbled on a Demand video or article yet, you soon will. By next summer, according to founder and CEO Richard Rosenblatt, Demand will be publishing 1 million items a month, the equivalent of four English-language Wikipedias a year. Demand is already one of the largest suppliers of content to YouTube, where its 170,000 videos make up more than twice the content of CBS, the Associated Press, Al Jazeera English, Universal Music Group, CollegeHumor, and Soulja Boy combined. Demand also posts its material to its network of 45 B-list sites—ranging from eHow and Livestrong.com to the little-known doggy-photo site TheDailyPuppy.com—that manage to pull in more traffic than ESPN, NBC Universal, and Time Warner's online properties (excluding AOL) put together. To appreciate the impact Demand is poised to have on the Web, imagine a classroom where one kid raises his hand after every question and screams out the answer. He may not be smart or even right, but he makes it difficult to hear anybody else.

The result is a factory stamping out moneymaking content. "I call them the Henry Ford of online video," says Jordan Hoffner, director of content partnerships at YouTube. Media companies like The Atlanta Journal-Constitution, AOL, and USA Today have either hired Demand or studied its innovations. This year, the privately held Demand is expected to bring in about $200 million in revenue; its most recent round of financing by blue-chip investors valued the company at $1 billion.

In this industrial model of content creation, Muñoz-Donoso is working the conveyor belt—being paid very little for cranking out an endless supply of material. He admits that the results are not particularly rewarding, but work is work, and Demand's is steady and pays on time. Plus, he says, "this is the future." He has shot more than 40,000 videos for Demand, filming yo-yo whizzes, pole dancers, and fly fishermen. But ask him to pick a favorite and he's stumped. "I can't really remember most of them," he says.

In an era overwhelmed by FlickrYouTubeWikipedia–BloggerFacebookTwitter–borne logorrhea, it's hard to argue that the world needs another massive online content company. But what Demand has realized is that the Internet gets only half of the simplest economic formula right: It has the supply part down but ignores demand. Give a million monkeys a million WordPress accounts and you still might never get a seven-point tutorial on how to keep wasps away from a swimming pool. Yet that's what people want to know. Ask Byron Reese.

Reese is a tall Texan who serves as Demand's chief innovation officer and who created the idea-spawning algorithm that lies at the heart of Demand's process. To determine what articles to assign, his formula analyzes three chunks of information. First, to find out what terms users are searching for, it parses bulk data purchased from search engines, ISPs, and Internet marketing firms (as well as Demand's own traffic logs). Then the algorithm crunches keyword rates to calculate how much advertisers will pay to appear on pages that include those terms. (A portion of Demand's revenue comes from Google, which allows businesses to bid on phrases that they would like to advertise against.) Third, the formula checks to see how many Web pages already include those terms. It doesn't make sense to commission an article that will be buried on the fifth page of Google results. Finally, the algorithm, like a drunken prophet, starts spitting out phrase after phrase: "butterfly cake," "shin splints," "Harley-Davidson belt buckles."

But that's just the start. Armed with those key words, another algorithm, called the Knowledge Engine, dives back into the data to figure out exactly what people want to know about the term. If the original algorithm divines "2009 Chevy Corvette" as a profitable title, the Knowledge Engine will return with "cost of 2009 Corvette"; for "shin splint" it might come back with "equine treatment shin splints." The second algorithm also looks at how well past titles with similar words have performed in terms of ad revenue. Demand has learned, for instance, that "best" and "how to" bring in traffic or high clickthrough rates, while "history of" is ad poison. At the end of the process, the company has a topic and a dollar amount— the term's "lifetime value," or LTV—that Demand expects to generate from any resulting content.

The focus on LTV keeps Demand away from any kind of breaking news coverage or investigative work, neither of which tends to hold its value. It does, however, produce the kind of evergreen stories typically seen in newspaper features sections. *The Atlanta Journal-Constitution* recently commissioned Demand to produce some travel articles that ran online and in print.

The algorithm's endless ramblings—a collection of cacophonous phrases and esoteric subjects—seem haphazard and chaotic. But Reese knows there is logic at work. When asked for the most valuable topic in Demand's arsenal, he replies instantly: "'Where can I donate a car in Dallas?' One, you have a certain number of people searching for it. Two, the bid term 'donate a car' is in the double-digit dollars, like $15 or $20 per click. People have a propensity—17 percent—to click on an ad when they see the word car. There's very little competition. And the article will retain its value for a long time." So why Dallas? He has no idea: "Dallas just happens to be the location where we know people are searching for how to donate a car."

That's not to say there isn't any room for humans in Demand's process. They just aren't worth very much. First, a crowdsourced team of freelance "title proofers" turn the algorithm's often awkward or nonsensical phrases into something people will understand: "How to make a church-pew breakfast nook," for example, becomes "How to make a breakfast nook out of a church pew." Approved headlines get fed into a password-protected section of Demand's Web site called Demand Studios, where any Demand freelancer can see what jobs are available. It's the online equivalent of day laborers waiting in front of Home Depot. Writers can typically select 10 articles at a time; videographers can hoard 40.

Nearly every freelancer scrambles to load their assignment queue with titles they can produce quickly and with the least amount of effort—because pay for individual stories is so lousy, only a high-speed, high-volume approach will work. The average writer earns $15 per article for pieces that top out at a few hundred words, and the average filmmaker about $20 per clip, paid weekly via PayPal. Demand also offers revenue sharing on some articles, though it can take months to reach even $15 in such payments. Other freelancers sign up for the chance to copyedit ($2.50 an article), fact-check ($1 an article), approve the quality of a film (25 to 50 cents a video), transcribe ($1 to $2 per video), or offer up their expertise to be quoted or filmed (free). Title proofers get 8 cents a headline. Coming soon: photographers and photo editors. So far, the company has paid out more than $17 million to Demand Studios workers; if the enterprise reaches Rosenblatt's goal of producing 1 million pieces of content a month, the payouts could easily hit $200 million a year, less than a third of what *The New York*

Times shells out in wages and benefits to produce its roughly 5,000 articles a month.

Before Reese came up with his formula, Demand Media operated in the traditional way. Contributors suggested articles or videos they wanted to create. Editors, trained in the ways of search engine optimization, would approve or deny each while also coming up with their own ideas. The process worked fine. But once it was automated, every algorithm-generated piece of content produced 4.9 times the revenue of the human-created ideas. So Rosenblatt got rid of the editors. Suddenly, profit on each piece was 20 to 25 times what it had been. It turned out that gut instinct and experience were less effective at predicting what readers and viewers wanted—and worse for the company—than a formula.

The humans also couldn't produce ideas at the scale of the algorithm. On a recent day, Demand Studios had nearly 62,000 freelance assignments ready to be filled; coming up with that many ideas takes more than a white board and a conference room jammed with editors. And to Demand, scale is essential. One outside search engine marketer estimates that Demand earns a mere 15 to 60 cents per ad clicked. It takes millions of clicks to build a real business out of that.

Volume is also crucial to Demand's top distribution partner, Google. The search engine has struggled to make money from the 19 billion videos on YouTube, only about 10 percent of which carry ads. Advertisers don't want to pay to appear next to videos that hijack copyrighted material or that contain swear words, but YouTube doesn't have the personnel to comb through every user-generated clip. Last year, though, YouTube executives noticed that Demand was uploading hundreds of videos every day—pre-scrubbed by Demand's own editors, explicitly designed to appeal to advertisers, and cheap enough to benefit from Google's revenue-sharing business model. YouTube executives approached Demand, asked the company to join its revenue-sharing program, and encouraged it to produce as many videos as possible.

Since then, the two companies have grown even closer. When YouTube's sales team bemoaned the tiny supply of Spanish-language videos for it to run advertisements against, YouTube's Hoffner called up Demand. Within weeks, Demand Studios started issuing Spanish-language assignments. Soon it had uploaded a few hundred clips to YouTube— everything from how to be "un buen DJ" to how to fix a bathroom towel bar. "I know we do deals with the ESPNs and ABCs of the world, but Demand is incredibly important to us," says Hoffner (who is married to wired's executive director of communications). "They fill up a lot of content across the site."

And they do it by taking what used to be a deeply human and intuitive endeavor and turning it into a purely mathematical and rational one. This, Reese says, is the ultimate promise of his algorithm: "You can take something that is thought of as a creative process and turn it into a manufacturing process."

Richard Rosenblatt was born and raised in Southern California's San Fernando Valley and has rarely ventured far from Hollywood's orbit in spirit or in geography. He is 40 and wiry, with carefully tousled brown hair, a bright-white, ever-present smile, and a long, pinched nose. One day this spring, Rosenblatt was in the foyer of Demand's Santa Monica, California, headquarters, casually chatting with Brooke Burke—the bikini model, former TV host, and *Dancing With the Stars* winner—and her fiancé, a Baywatch actor. Rosenblatt is also friends with cyclist (and Demand investor) Lance Armstrong, a fact that he mentions frequently. ("I'm supposed to go to France Wednesday with Lance, but I just can't," he confided, sighing. "It's a lot of travel.") He is particularly fond of the exhortation "Go big or go home," a phrase that he includes in his email signature and has commemorated in the naming of Demand's Go Big conference room. Numerous executives told me that when they first met Rosenblatt, they were immediately repulsed: He was too slick and seemed to be missing the geek edge. "Then in five minutes you're like, 'Holy cow, this guy has it all to back it up,'" says Quincy Smith, CEO of CBS Interactive.

Demand is just the latest of Rosenblatt's run of startups, nearly all of which hewed to his "go big" mantra. After graduating from USC law school in 1994, he saw that companies were growing curious about the Internet, so he set up a company that offered a $3,000 Web-design seminar that came with a custom-built Web site. The startup, which was later called iMall, went public at $18 a share, shot up to $112, then plummeted when the Federal Trade Commission investigated the firm's claim that its clients' sites were earning $11,000 a month. They weren't, it turned out. Rosenblatt was forced to kill the seminar division, losing 95 percent of his company's $16 million in annual revenue. He quickly refocused on iMall's other business of providing an ecommerce platform for small and medium-sized companies and sold the company in 1999 to Excite@Home for $565 million in stock. Rosenblatt bought a Ferrari. Excite@Home soon went bust.

In 2000, Rosenblatt took over the ailing drkoop.com, an online site tied to C. Everett Koop. Where others saw just another ad-dependent disease-information site, Rosenblatt saw a chance to turn the bearded former surgeon general into a brand, the next "Martha Stewart or Walt Disney—but for health," as he told *BusinessWeek* at the time. He created a line of Dr. Koop Men's Prostate Formula pills. The company went under.

Perhaps weary of going big, Rosenblatt went home, where he derived some comfort from the millions he had earned. He bought and sold a domain registrar company. He started a site called Superdudes, where users could create superhero-like avatars. He invested in a nightclub in San Diego.

But with the birth of Web 2.0, big was back. In 2004 a group of investors tapped Rosenblatt to run eUniverse (later renamed Intermix Media), a struggling Internet conglomerate that happened to own MySpace. Soon after Rosenblatt started, New York attorney general Eliot Spitzer charged Intermix with bundling adware and spyware with its free games and screensavers. Rosenblatt settled almost immediately, handing over $7.5 million—the entire cash holdings of Intermix. "It was the worst, most miserable time in my life," he says. Still, he could be consoled by the fact that his company had survived and still had MySpace, which was exploding into the Internet's dominant social media site. AOL, Viacom, and News Corp. were all sniffing around, and Rosenblatt began to play them off each other. Not long after settling with Spitzer, he sold Intermix to News Corp. for $650 million, of which he earned $23 million. Then he left the company.

Although Rosenblatt had been at MySpace for only 18 months, he had seen enough to come up with a theory: The social network was doing it wrong. It had built a supersite, aggregating millions of users and encouraging them to root around. But they had difficulty finding information about specific subjects. "I kept thinking about gardening," he says. "People wanted to talk about gardening, but they didn't want to do it on MySpace." Instead they went to Google, which was its own kind of aggregator, collecting everyone who searched for specific terms and directing them to appropriate sites. If he could collect enough tiny sites and sell Google ads against them, he could potentially build a more successful business than he could with one supersite.

On the strength of this plan, Rosenblatt raised $355 million from funders like Goldman Sachs, Oak Investment Partners, and legendary investor Gordon Crawford. Then he went looking for acquisitions. He bought eNom, one of the largest domain registrars, and Pluck, a company that handles commenting and social networks for Web sites, along with dozens of amateur-content sites that could catch lowly keyword ads. Among them: eHow, Trails.com, GolfLink.com, and Cracked .com. Rosenblatt now had three revenue sources: domain sales; services; and video, banner, and Google ads.

Demand Media was born. But it wasn't until 2007, when the company bought ExpertVillage.com, Byron Reese's how-to site (reportedly for roughly $20 million), that it began to realize its potential. Reese and Rosenblatt soon began working on an idea that Reese had long struggled with: Millions of visitors were coming to ExpertVillage and generating reams of data, but his editors didn't do anything with it. What if they used that information to determine what content to create?

Here is the thing that Rosenblatt has since discovered: Online content is not worth very much. This may be a truism, but Rosenblatt has the hard, mathematical proof. It's right there in black and white, in the Demand Media database—the lifetime value of every story, algorithmically derived, and very, very small. Most media companies are trying hard to increase those numbers, to boost the value of their online content until it matches the amount of money it costs to produce. But Rosenblatt thinks they have it exactly backward. Instead of trying to raise the market value of online content to match the cost of producing it—perhaps an impossible proposition— the secret is to cut costs until they match the market value.

Not everybody agrees with him. Howcast, one of Demand's largest competitors, also produces explainer videos and how-tos. Unlike Demand, the company employs a staff of editors and writers and gets freelance voice-over pros. Filmmakers can earn a couple thousand dollars shooting the videos, and the difference is noticeable. (Howcast's "How to Make Friends at a New School" includes such useful tidbits as "sit in the middle of the classroom to surround yourself with as many potential new friends as possible." Demand-owned eHow's "How to Be Popular in School" video, in contrast, offers such vague guidance as "be nice to everybody.") "We believe that quality holds long-term value," Howcast CEO Jason Liebman says. He emphasizes that his team comes up with titles the old-fashioned way: deciding what people want to learn based on their own instincts, what holidays and events are coming up, and from general research. Yet Howcast pulls a tiny—and getting tinier—fraction of the traffic that eHow does, and Liebman hesitantly acknowledges that he's working on an algorithm to compete with Demand.

Liebman isn't the only one ready to mimic Demand's approach. CBS Interactive—which owns CNET, UrbanBaby, GameSpot, and other sites—also deploys an algorithm that helps guide what its sites cover. AOL is working on one as well. Smaller sites like Helium and Associated Content are trying to bring their own flood of freelancer-written work to the Net, using many of the same contributors as Demand.

The fact is, the Demand way may be inescapable. A senior executive at a major media company likened Demand's algorithmic-based content-creation factory to what he saw in the advertising industry in the past decade. Experience, relationships, and gut checks started losing out to raw data. "To customers, advertising may not look that different, but the systems to deliver the right ads to the right consumer at the right time have changed dramatically," he says. "The content systems are going through the early, early stages of that right now."

Still, Rosenblatt says he is trying to place a new emphasis on quality. "There's a constant debate internally," he says. "This might sound crazy, but I'd rather spend more and put more quality into the process. Long term, we'll make more money by increasing quality."

But when he gets into the details, it's clear that he's not moving far from his Henry Ford model. "We're not talking about $1,000 videos, so a couple dollars here or there can make a serious difference. For instance, pay an extra dollar for fact-checking."

How can anyone survive on that? Good question. Google it. If the answer isn't out there, it soon will be.

Hearth Surgery

The quest for a stove that can save the world.

Two men walked into a bar called the Axe and Fiddle. It was a Thursday night in early August, in the town of Cottage Grove, Oregon, and the house was full. The men ordered drinks and a vegetarian Reuben and made their way to the only seats left, near a small stage at the back. The taller of the two, Dale Andreatta, had clear blue eyes and a long, columnar head crowned with gray hair. He was wearing a pleated kilt, festooned with pockets and loops for power tools, and spoke in a loud, unmodulated voice, like a clever robot. His friend, Peter Scott, was thinner and more dishevelled, with a vaguely Biblical look. He had long brown hair and sandalled feet, sun-baked skin and piercing eyes.

None of the locals paid them any mind. Cottage Grove, like much of Oregon, is home to hippies and hillbillies in equal measure. At the Axe and Fiddle, lumbermen from the local Weyerhaeuser and Starfire mills sat side by side with former Hoedads—free-living tree planters who'd reforested large tracts of the Bitterroot and Cascade Mountains. The bar was flanked by a bookstore and, a few doors down Main Street, a store that specializes in machine guns. "I can't imagine that his market's that big," the bookstore's owner told me. "I mean, how many machine guns does a guy need?"

The featured act at the bar that night was a burlesque troupe from New York called Nice Jewish Girls Gone Bad. Just how they'd landed in the Oregon woods wasn't clear, but they stuck stubbornly to their set list. They sang a song about gefilte fish ("Fear Factor for Jews") and danced suggestively to Yiddish hip-hop. They promised to put the whore back in hora, and when that met with only polite applause—"Look it up on Wikipedia"—they asked for a show of hands from local Jews. There were five. Finally, near the end of the show, one of the performers—a spindly comedian with thick black glasses and a T-shirt that said "Freak"—peered out from under the spotlight and fixed her eyes, a little desperately, on Peter Scott. "Do you have a job?" she said, almost to herself.

Scott said no, then yes.

"That sounds fishy. What is it you do?"

Scott fidgeted for a second, then mumbled, "I make stoves for Africa."

"You what?"

"I make stoves for Africa."

Scott was being modest. In the small but fanatical world of stovemakers he is something of a celebrity. ("Peter is our rock star," another stovemaker told me.) For the past seven years, under the auspices of the German aid agency GTZ, Scott has designed or built some four hundred thousand stoves in thirteen African countries. He has made them out of mud, brick, sheet metal, clay, ceramic, and discarded oil drums. He has made them in villages without electricity or liquid fuel, where meals are still cooked over open fires, where burns are among the most common injuries and smoke is the sixth leading cause of death. In the places where Scott works, a good stove can save your life.

He and Andreatta were in Cottage Grove for Stove

Camp. A mile or two from the Axe and Fiddle, a few dozen engineers, anthropologists, inventors, foreign-aid workers, and rogue academics had set up tents in a meadow along a willowy bend in a fork of the Willamette River. They spent their days designing and testing wood-burning stoves, their nights cooking under the stars and debating thermodynamics. Stove Camp was a weeklong event hosted by the Aprovecho Research Center—the engineering offshoot of a local institute, education center, and environmental collective. Now in its tenth year, the camp had become a kind of hippie Manhattan Project. It brought together the best minds in the field to solve a single, intractable problem: How do you build cheap, durable, clean-burning stoves for three billion people?

A map of the world's poor is easy to make, Jacob Moss, a Stove Camper who works for the Environmental Protection Agency and started its Partnership for Clean Indoor Air, told me. Just follow the smoke. About half the world's population cooks with gas, kerosene, or electricity, while the other half burns wood, coal, dung, or other solid fuels. To the first group, a roaring hearth has become a luxury—a thing for camping trips and Christmas parties. To the second group, it's a necessity. To the first group, a kitchen is an arsenal of specialized appliances. To the second, it's just a place to build a fire.

Clean air, according to the E.P.A., contains less than fifteen micrograms of fine particles per cubic metre. Five times that amount will set off a smoke alarm. Three hundred times as much—roughly what an open fire produces—will slowly kill you. Wood smoke, as sweet as it smells, is a caustic swirl of chemical agents, including benzene, butadiene, styrene, formaldehyde, dioxin, and methylene chloride. Every leaf or husk adds its own compounds to the fire, producing a fume so corrosive that it can consume a piece of untreated steel in less than a year. The effect on the body is similar. Indoor smoke kills a million and a half people annually, according to the World Health Organization. It causes or compounds a long list of debilities—pneumonia, bronchitis, emphysema, cataracts, cancers, heart disease, high blood pressure, and low birth weight—and has been implicated in a number of others, including tuberculosis, low I.Q., and cleft palate, among other deformities.

A well-made stove can easily clear the air, by piping the smoke out through a chimney or burning the fuel more efficiently. Yet most appliance manufacturers see no profit in making products for people who can't pay for them. And most aid agencies have found easier ways to help the poor—by administering vaccines, for instance. Stovemakers are a chronically underfunded bunch, used to toiling in the dusty margins of international development. Aside from a few national programs in Asia and the Americas, their projects have tended to be small and scattershot, funded a few thousand stoves at a time by volunteers and N.G.O.s. "We've been watering this rock for a long time," Dean Still, the head of Aprovecho, told me.

Lately, though, the rules have changed. As global temperatures have risen, the smoke from Third World kitchens has been upgraded from a local to a universal threat. The average cooking fire produces about as much carbon dioxide as a car, and a great deal more soot, or black carbon—a substance seven hundred times as warming. Black carbon absorbs sunlight. A single gram warms the atmosphere as much as a fifteen-hundred-watt space heater running for a week. Given that cooking fires each release one or two thousand grams of soot in a year, and that three billion people rely on them, cleaning up those emissions may be the fastest, cheapest way to cool the planet.

In June, the sweeping Waxman-Markey climate bill was passed by the U.S. House of Representatives. Hidden among its fourteen hundred pages was a short section calling on the E.P.A. to identify ways to provide stoves to twenty million households in five years. The bill made no mention of how or where the stoves might be built, or who might pay for them. But there was talk of carbon-credit subsidies, international co-financing, and major-appliance manufacturers entering the fray.

The engineers of Stove Camp, in other words, found themselves suddenly blinking in the spotlight—like a band of raccoons caught digging through a scrap heap. "Kill a million and a half people and nobody gives a damn," one government official told me. "But become part of this big climate thing and everyone comes knocking at your door."

The entrance to Stove Camp was marked by a piece of weathered plywood, hung on a rusty railroad trestle, with the words "Fred's Island" spray-painted on it. The place wasn't technically an island—it was bordered by the river on two sides and the railroad on the third—but it did belong to a retired carpenter named Fred Colgan. When I arrived on a Sunday evening, he and Aprovecho's Dean Still showed me an old trailer where I could sleep, a few yards from the tracks. "Wait till that timber train comes through at four in the morning," Colgan said. He gripped an imaginary bedstead and rattled his head up and down. "If you see giant rats in the middle of the night, you haven't had too much to drink. We're infested with nutria."

Still laughed. "A nutria is a rodent," he said. "Entirely harmless."

"It's a rat the size of a cocker spaniel."

Before Colgan and his wife, Lise, bought the island, four years ago, it had belonged to a slaughterhouse and meatpacking operation, which left its buildings scattered across the grounds. Colgan offered the use of them to Still in 2006, after the stove program outgrew its original facilities a few miles up the road. The research center now has seven employees and a rotating cast of volunteers, who spend their time testing and developing stoves for projects worldwide. Their offices occupy a ramshackle complex along the river, with a wooden corral to one side and a labyrinth of labs, workshops, and storage rooms in back. Still holds his stove meetings in the meat locker, where the carcasses used to hang.

"Here's the deal," he told us one morning. "The world is absolutely littered with failed stoves. At the U.N., they laugh at us when we say that we have another project. So if we keep on blowing it we're in trouble." He peered at the bleary-eyed campers, about thirty strong, gathered around mismatched Formica tables. Jacob Moss, the E.P.A. official, sat next to a pulmonologist from the National Institutes of Health; Peter Scott had recently returned from Uganda, and others had worked on projects in Haiti, Honduras, Mexico, Malawi, Peru, India, and China. "It ain't easy," Still told them. "But it ain't impossible. We're going to be offered opportunities. But if there's going to be money for twenty million stoves we have to be ready. And we have to not screw this up."

Still, who is fifty-seven, is one of the presiding spirits of the stove community. He has a large ruddy face and a mop of white hair, a wide walrus mustache, and dark eyebrows that curve high above his eyes, giving him a look of perpetual, delighted surprise. Decades of living and working in hardscrabble villages have instilled an improbable ebullience in him, and a correlative roundness of form. I once compared him to Buddha when I was talking to Scott, who quickly corrected me. "Dean's a mystic Episcopalian," he said. "The only thing Buddhist about him is his girth." It's true that Still keeps plastic statues of St. Francis, the Virgin Mary, and the Archangel Michael glued to the dashboard of his truck. (Michael's flaming sword, he says, reminds him that "sometimes to make something good happen you have to kick people in the ass.") But when I was with him they were joined by well-foxed copies of William James and a book of Mad Libs. When it comes to stoves, he said, any spiritual guidance will do.

Earlier that summer, Still had flown to London to accept an Ashden Award for Sustainable Energy, presented by Prince Charles. To prepare for the ceremony and press interviews, he'd had to buy his first suit since his wedding twelve years ago, and the Ashden foundation had given him a week's worth of elocution lessons. ("The English, geez, they're so unconsciously imperialist.") Still has a clear but indecorous way of talking, with an old hippie's loitering rhythms and self-questioning asides. Although he has trained a generation of stove designers and built one of the world's premier stove-testing labs, his science is mostly self-taught and he's uncomfortable playing the expert. "I'm just the mouth," he told us, waving his hands at the engineers in the room. "These guys are the brains." They just needed a little prodding now and then.

He turned to the whiteboard behind him and scrawled out some bullet points with a pink marker. "This is now the definition of a good stove, according to Waxman-Markey," he said: "1. Reduces fuel use by more than fifty per cent. 2. Reduces black carbon by more than sixty per cent. 3. Reduces childhood pneumonia by more than thirty per cent. 4. Affordable ($10 retail or less). 5. Cooks love it. 6. Gets funded." The last three weren't in the bill, Still admitted, but no stove could succeed without them. And none had ever met all six criteria at once.

"So this is what we have to do this week, my dears," he said. "Save the damn world." He grinned. "I mean, you didn't want an easy problem, did you?"

Building a stove is simple. Building a good stove is hard. Building a good, cheap stove can drive an engineer crazy. The devices at Aprovecho looked straightforward enough. Most were about the size and shape of a stockpot, with a cylindrical combustion chamber and a cooking grate on top. You stuck some twigs in the chamber, set them on fire, and put your pot on the grate—nothing to it. Yet one stove used a pound of wood to boil a gallon of water, and another used two. Fire is a fickle, nonlinear thing, and seems to be affected by every millimetre of a stove's design—the size of the opening, the shape and material of the chamber, the thickness of the grate—each variable amplifying the next and being amplified in turn, in a complex series of feedback loops. "You've heard of the butterfly effect?" one engineer told me. "Well, these stoves are full of butterflies."

Like science and religion, stove design is riven into sects and disciplines. Some engineers use only low-cost materials like mud or brick; others dabble in thermoelectric generators and built-in fans—cleaner and more efficient, but also more expensive. Most stoves are built for combustion: they consume the wood and reduce it to ash. But a few are designed for gasification instead. These stoves heat the wood until it releases its volatile compounds, which are ignited in the air. (All that's left of the wood afterward is its carbon skeleton, which can be burned separately as charcoal or used as a fertilizer.) Gasifiers can be remarkably clean-burning, but they're also finicky. Because the fire burns at the top of the stove, rather than rising up from a bed of coals at the bottom, its flames are easily stifled when new fuel is added, turning the stove into a smoke bomb.

In the vestibule of the Aprovecho building, Still had set up a small "Museum of Stoves" on facing wall racks. Its contents came from more than a dozen countries, in an odd menagerie of shapes and sizes: an elegant clay chulha from India, a squat steel Jiko from Kenya, a painted coal burner from China, like an Easy-Bake oven. Most were better than an open fire, yet all had failed the test in some way—too flimsy or inefficient or expensive or unstable or unclean or hard to use. "We still haven't cracked the nut," Peter Scott said.

Scott had come to Stove Camp to build a better injera stove. Injera is the spongy pancake that Ethiopians eat with almost every meal. The batter is usually made of an ancient grain called teff, and fermented until it's bubbly and tart. It's poured onto a ceramic griddle, or mitad, then set over an open fire or a concrete hearth. In Ethiopia, injera is often cooked by women's coöperatives, in kitchens that may have forty or fifty smoky, inefficient stoves running simultaneously—one reason that the country has lost more than ninety per cent of its forests since the early sixties. "In the north, people will travel hundreds of kilometres to get wood, then double back to bring it to market," Scott told me. A good stove, he figured, could cut that fuel use in half.

For the past several months, Scott and his kilt-wearing friend Dale Andreatta—a mechanical engineer from Columbus, Ohio, who often did stove projects pro bono—had been collaborating on a prototype. It had an efficient ceramic combustion chamber, shaped like a miniature fireplace, with a round griddle perched above it like a tabletop. Scott had tried using a traditional mitad, since local cooks would much prefer it, but the ceramic wouldn't heat evenly, so he'd switched to steel instead. Steel conducts heat much more efficiently than ceramic, and it's often used for the plancha griddles in tortilla stoves. Injera, though, is an unforgiving dish. Its batter is thin and watery, so it can't be moved around like a tortilla, and any hot spots in the griddle will burn it. "The Ethiopians are unbelievably particular," Scott said. "If the injera doesn't have the exact size of bubble in the batter, they'll say it's garbage."

Luckily, Scott was used to improvising under much rougher conditions. His years in the African bush had left him, at forty, as sober and sinewy as Still was gregarious and stout. Scott had lived in mud huts in Swaziland, battled intestinal infections in Zambia, and been robbed by bandits in Uganda. When he first went to Africa for a stove project, in 2002, he was taken hostage on his third day, in an Internet café in Pretoria. "They tied us up, laid us on the ground, a gun at the back of the head," he told me. "I had a strong premonition that I was going to die. But I didn't die. So after that I didn't worry too much about my own safety." He went on to build stoves for refugees in the Congo, tobacco-curing barns in Malawi and Tanzania, and institutional stoves throughout eastern and southern Africa. In 2006, he became the first Aprovecho member to receive an Ashden Award. (As a Canadian, he told me, he was excused from the elocution lessons.)

Over the next few days, I'd periodically find Scott and Andreatta skulking around the Aprovecho workshops and laboratories, looking for tools or discussing metallurgy. Their preliminary tests had not been encouraging: the griddle was two hundred degrees hotter at the center than at the edge. When I asked Andreatta how it was going, he lifted an eyebrow. "The optimist thinks the glass is half full," he said. "The pessimist thinks the glass is half empty. The engineer knows the real truth: that the glass is twice as large as it should be for optimum utilization of resources."

When Aprovecho was founded, in the late nineteen-seventies, building stoves was a good deal less complicated. "Appropriate technology" was the byword then. Grounded in the teachings of Gandhi and the economist E. F. Schumacher, the philosophy held that poor countries are best served by low-cost, low-tech, local development. Better to teach villagers to make a stove than to give them stoves that they can't afford to repair or replace.

Aprovecho took the idea a step further. "We wanted to work as an inverse Peace Corps," Ianto Evans, one of the founding members, told me. Evans was an architect and ecologist who'd done research and volunteer work in Guatemala and was then teaching at Oregon State. Instead of exporting American know-how to the Third World, he and a small group of artists and academics decided, they would try to teach Americans to live more sustainably. "We would bring in villagers from Kenya or Lesotho, have them stay with us, and teach us what they knew—everything from cooking to growing things to assessing how much is too much." They would build a model Third World village in the Oregon woods.

In 1981, with the help of a Canadian foundation, the group bought forty acres of second-growth timber five miles west of Cottage Grove. The land lay on a south-facing slope at the end of a logging road. It was rough, marginally fertile ground, wet year-round and often freezing in the winter. But the new owners spared no effort in improving it. They deep-tilled the soil and enriched it with compost. They planted pear, apple, and quince trees, a grape arbor, and a bamboo grove. They built a library, a workshop, an adobe hut, and passive solar cabins, and, to top it all, a giant tree house thirty feet above the ground. To neighbors or passersby they might have seemed like squatters, yet they were ambitious, industrious, self-serious folk. *Aprovecho,* in Spanish, means "I make good use of."

Deforestation was the issue of the moment, and Evans believed that stoves were an ideal solution. A few years earlier, at a research center in Quetzaltenango, Guatemala, he and a team of local craftsmen had tested a variety of designs and materials and brought in cooks to try them out. "Any fool can do technical things," he told me. "But if people don't want it, don't bother." The team eventually hit upon a mixture of sand, clay, and pumice that was stable and freely available. They cast it into a massive hearth, about waist-high, carved out a firebox, burners, and interior channels to direct the heat, then added a chimney for the smoke. They dubbed it Lorena, after the Spanish words for mud and sand, *lodo* and *arena*.

The Lorena never made many inroads to American kitchens, but it was an immediate hit internationally. While Evans was still testing it, a United Nations representative saw the stove and persuaded him to publish the design. "The facts are stunning," Evans wrote, in a 1979 book on the Lorena. "Data from several sources indicate that improved stoves— and of these the Lorena stove appears to have advantages over the others—can save one-half to three-quarters or more of the wood normally used in cooking." Projects for the Peace Corps, World Bank, USAID, and the governments of Senegal and Lesotho followed, often inspiring others in turn. In some areas, the Lorena was so popular that its name became a generic term: it simply meant "improved stove."

In one sense, though, it was no improvement at all. The Lorena was good at removing smoke and preventing burns (no small things). It was handsome, easy to use, and helped warm the house. What it didn't do was save fuel—at least compared with a well-tended open fire. Its thick walls, rather than concentrating the heat, absorbed it: the stove warmed the room because it wasn't warming the food. Studies later found that the Lorena used up to twice as much wood as an open fire and needed up to three times as long to boil a pot of water. "It sounds funny, but there are still people making Lorenas today," Dean Still says. "They don't understand the difference between insulation and a heat sink."

By the time Still arrived at Aprovecho, in the summer of 1989, funding for stoves had dried up. The Lorena, as it turned out, was only one of hundreds of well-meaning but misconceived projects worldwide. There were mud stoves that dissolved in the rain, designer stoves that worked only with a certain pot, portable stoves that fell over when you stirred cornmeal mush on them. In 1983, the Indian government launched a national program that distributed some thirty-five million stoves across the subcontinent. The units came in various designs from local manufacturers; most were neither sturdy nor especially efficient. Several years later, when a doctoral student from Berkeley surveyed the results in Andhra Pradesh, she found a single stove still in use—as a bin for grain.

"They were good-hearted people," Still says of his predecessors at Aprovecho. "But they were idealistic artists. They were farmers and architects and artisans more than they were engineers." Still didn't seem, on the face of it, much better qualified. Before coming to Aprovecho, he'd worked in a trauma ward in Illinois, lived in a trapper's cabin in Colorado, and served as a security guard on an ocean freighter. He had owned a gas station, worked as a janitor in a synagogue, earned a master's degree in clinical psychology but never used it professionally—"Not one day," he says. Instead, he built a seagoing catamaran with two friends and crisscrossed the Pacific in it. Then he sold the boat, moved to Baja, built a thatched hut by the Sea of Cortez, and stayed there for nine years. "My idea was this," he says. "Can Dean learn to sit under a tree and be contented?"

The answer was no. But his wanderings left him oddly suited to building stoves. He was a skilled carpenter and designer, used to improvising with cheap materials. He was intimately familiar with the needs and hazards of life in developing countries. And he was a born community organizer. His parents, Douglas and Hanna Still, were political activists in the heroic sixties mold. They'd worked with César Chávez in California, the Black Panthers in Chicago, and Martin Luther King, Jr., in the South. (King and Still's father, who was a Presbyterian minister, spent a night in jail together in Albany, Georgia, after a protest.) By the age of thirteen, Dean was tagging along to a civil-rights rally in Milwaukee, wearing a "Black Power" T-shirt among crowds of bellowing racists. At sixteen, he was among the rioters at the 1968 Democratic National Convention in Chicago, narrowly escaping arrest. His parents always encouraged him to be a freethinker, he says. "So when I was in seventh or eighth grade I told them, 'You're right. School is just a training ground for cogs. I'm going to quit and have adventures.'"

Still was first drawn to Aprovecho by its work in sustainable agriculture and forestry. But it was the stoves that kept him there. Not long after he arrived, in 1989, he met a local inventor named Larry Winiarski—a mild, bespectacled, dumpling-shaped man in his forties, perennially clad in overalls. Winiarski had a doctorate in engineering from Oregon State and had worked for the E.P.A. for thirteen years, analyzing the heat discharge from power plants. It didn't take him long to spot the Lorena's inadequacies.

Working as a volunteer, Winiarski sketched out ten principles of stove design and began to build prototypes with Evans and other Aprovecho members. The new devices, which they called rocket stoves, for the powerful roar of their draft, were the physical opposite of the Lorena. They were small and lightweight, so that little heat was wasted on warming the stove itself. They had vertical combustion chambers that acted as chimneys, mixing the wood's volatile gases with air so that the rockets burned more efficiently. And they had well-insulated walls that forced the hot gases through narrow gaps around the pot, heating it as quickly as possible.

"Larry is one of those rare people in my life, when you ask him a question about stoves he's almost always right," Still says. "He just really, really understands fire." Aprovecho went on to build a number of rocket stoves and to publicize them in books and newsletters, but the group's loyalty still lay with the Lorena. "People were basically ignoring Larry when I showed up," Still told me. "Hippies love earthen structures." The community's open-air kitchen, for instance, was dominated by a clay bread oven that took hours to heat up and consumed great quantities of firewood. With Winiarski's guidance, Still conducted an experiment. Next to the bread oven, he built a simple rocket stove. It was made of a fifty-five-gallon drum, laid horizontally, with a thirty-three-gallon drum inside it and a rocket combustion chamber below. The new stove looked nothing like a traditional bread oven, yet it was hot within fourteen minutes on the strength of a few twigs. An hour later, when the bread was done, the clay oven was still warming up. "That's what won people over," Still says.

Over the next few years, Still and Winiarski built ever more elaborate devices for the community: room heaters, water heaters, jet-pulse engines, wood-fired refrigerators. They were just tinkering, mostly, in the absence of funding for more ambitious work. Aprovecho, by then, was in turmoil. Evans was evicted from the property in the early nineties, after a dispute over the community's finances. Then county inspectors declared the tree house and other structures illegal, and everything had to be torn down, rebuilt, and reorganized. "It was a hippie nightmare," Still says.

To Peter Scott, who came to Aprovecho in 1997, the situation seems not uncommon. "People in environmental communities tend to be escaping from normal society," he told me. "If things were great where they came from, they wouldn't have left. And that sort of opens us up to the pain of the world and what's happening to it. We're all a little crazy, maybe." Scott was twenty-eight when he showed up in Oregon and already a veteran activist. In British Columbia, where he was born, he had stood in front of bulldozers on logging roads, climbed old-growth trees to spare them the axe, and acted in an environmental-theatre troupe. An article on solar cookers in *Mother Jones* first led him to Aprovecho, he says—that and memories of a trip to the Congo and the denuded landscapes there. "I'm here to save the forests of Africa by building stoves!" he remembers declaring on his first day. Dean Still just laughed and told him to go pick some vegetables.

Even more than new designs, Still began to realize, stove-makers needed data—to win back their credibility with reliable laboratory and field research. In 2000, when the stove lab was just a toolshed in the woods, Aprovecho built its first emissions detector and began testing Winiarski's designs. By 2004, Still had grants from the E.P.A. and the Shell Foundation to test stoves from other programs. By 2006, when the lab moved to Fred's Island, it had half a million dollars in funding and a staff of scrappy young engineers. (Nordica Mac-Carty, the lab manager, runs her jury-rigged Datsun on French-fry oil from a local diner. Karl Walter, the electronics designer, once built an airplane by hand and flew it to New York.) The research center now supports itself, in good part, with sales of microprocessor-controlled portable emissions detectors, designed and built in-house. The hippie commune has become a quality-control center.

Early in October, Still and I flew to Guatemala to visit the world's longest-running stove study. The village of San Lorenzo, where it's based, is in the remote western highlands, close to nine thousand feet above sea level. It feels like one of the world's forgotten places—its houses, made of mud and straw, cling to terraces that look out over plunging valleys and volcanic peaks—yet its cooks are among the most closely observed in the world. Walk into many local kitchens, and you'll find, attached to the walls or in the children's clothes, an array of electronic sensors and transmitters. Some measure particle emissions; others are motion detectors or carbon-monoxide monitors. Next to the chimney, on top of the stove, is a piece of black duct tape with a small silver disk beneath it. Plug the disk into a Palm Pilot, and it will tell you exactly when and for how long that stove was used in the previous month.

In seventeenth-century England, when a stovemaker wanted to test a new design, he'd soak a piece of coal in cat's urine and throw it into the fire. If the stench went up the chimney with the smoke, the design was deemed a success. Stove-testing is more of a numbers game now: minutes to boil, grams of fuel, milligrams of black carbon. Yet the practical effects of those numbers aren't always clear—especially on the emissions side. "We have no idea how low you have to go before you get the majority of the health benefits," Jacob Moss told me. "Is it peak exposures you want to get rid of, or is pollution a steady-state thing? Rocket stoves still have a whole slew of emissions that are an order of magnitude higher than E.P.A. standards." Cutting them in half, or even by two-thirds, may not be enough, he said.

The study that Still and I observed was aimed squarely at such uncertainties. Its detectors were the work of Kirk Smith, a professor of global environmental health at Berkeley and one of the world's leading authorities on indoor air pollution. Seven years ago, Smith and a team of students, researchers, and Guatemalan collaborators began tracking more than five hundred local families, all with pregnant mothers or infants less than four months old. The families were divided, at random, into two groups. Half were given plancha stoves with chimneys; the other half continued to cook over open fires. (After two years, when the first phase of the study was over, the second group got stoves as well.) Every week, Smith's team would give the families a medical checkup and download the data from its sensors. In this way, they could track their pollution exposure and its effects in real time. "My wife likes to say that most men spend their lives watching women cook," Smith says. "Her husband has managed to make a career of it."

Smith is a rumpled sixty-two-year-old with tousled gray

hair and eyelids as heavy as a basset hound's—he seems both tireless and perpetually short of sleep. When Still and I drove up to his site with him from Guatemala City, he spoke absorbingly, and almost continuously, for six hours about public health. (Last June, for a vacation, he took his wife and daughter to Chernobyl.) San Lorenzo is a six-hour flight plus layover on the red-eye from San Francisco, followed by a vertiginous trek, by truck or multicolored bus, up whipsawing mountain roads. For three years, Smith made the trip every month. His funders left him little choice, he told us.

"I'd go to an air-pollution conference and show them my measurements, and they'd say, 'Good Lord, these are orders of magnitude higher than in our cities! And these are the most vulnerable populations in the world. Just go out and fix it!'" Instead of funding stove projects, though, they'd pass him along to the next agency. "So I'd go across the street, to the international health meeting," Smith went on, "and they'd say, 'Well, Mr. Smith, you have a pretty convincing problem, but we have seven dollars a year per capita. Do you really expect us to take a dollar out of our budget for vaccines? We need to be damn certain that we can make a difference.'" The pharmaceutical companies had dozens of randomized trials to back up their claims. What did Smith have?

San Lorenzo is his answer. The study, which was funded by the N.I.H. in 2001, now generates so much information that Smith needs two full-time workers to enter it into computers. On the morning after we arrived, Still and I joined the team on their rounds through the village. While Still scrutinized the stoves and suggested ways to improve them (he and Smith were hatching plans for a more efficient "hyper plancha"), I sat and watched the women cook. Diminutive and shy, in their bright embroidered blouses and tapestry skirts, they quietly answered questions as their children clutched their legs or peeked out from behind doorframes. The houses were low-ceilinged and bare, with earthen floors, corrugated roofs, and a tree stump or two for furniture. Some had sheaves of Indian corn drying from the rafters, or raised eaves that allowed a little light to leak in. A field hand in San Lorenzo makes about twenty dollars a week, Smith said—"Truth be told, they haven't recovered since Cortez." But in most of the houses with stoves at least the air was clear. In those with open fires it hung so thick and noxious that the walls were blackened, the joists and beams shaggy with creosote. It was like sitting inside a smoker's lung.

Near the end of our rounds, we paid a visit to Angela Jiménez, a small, sharp-featured woman who was part of Smith's original control group. Jiménez is thirty-five and has five children, including four-month-old twins. When we walked in, she was simmering a pot of corn for tortillas and sautéing a *recado de pescado*—a thin brown sauce made with dried fish and cornmeal, ground together on a slab of volcanic rock. Smith's team had given her a stove six years earlier, but she hadn't bothered to maintain it. The clay tiles and steel griddle were pocked with holes, and smoke was billowing into the room. On the wall behind the stove, the team had hung a poster explaining the dangers of carbon monoxide, but the words were too covered in soot to be legible.

We were getting ready to leave when Jiménez's nine-year-old son, Wilder, lurched in with his baby sister, Milvia, in his arms. She was tightly bundled in blankets, with a blue-and-white knit cap on. Her face was covered in dried phlegm and she was crying hard, with a steady, wheezing cough. Jiménez lifted her up and laid her against her shoulder. Her daughter had been sick for eight days, she told us, and was running a fever. "You should take her to the clinic," Smith said. "Eight days is a long time at that age." Jiménez looked at him with hooded eyes and turned back to the stove. If she went to the clinic, they'd just send her to the hospital, she said. "And that's where people go to die."

Smith later prevailed upon Jiménez to let his team drive her to his clinic, where a physician gave both infants a diagnosis of severe pneumonia. Milvia was hypoxic: her lungs were so full of fluid that they couldn't get enough oxygen into her blood. Her twin brother, Selby, was even sicker: his blood was only eighty-two per cent oxygenated, and his lungs made crackling noises under a stethoscope. "He could pass away tonight," Smith said. Pneumonia is the leading killer of children worldwide, and San Lorenzans are especially susceptible to it. They're so malnourished that their height, at eighteen months, is already two standard deviations below the norm. And their immune systems are further weakened by the toxins in wood smoke. On average, Smith has found, the children in the village get pneumonia every other year.

"So this is the bottom line," he told me that night, bringing up a graph on his laptop. "This is seventeen years of applying for grants, seven years of research, three and a half million dollars, and me coming down here for a week of every month." Thanks to his electronic sensors, Smith knew his subjects' cooking habits in microscopic detail. He knew when they lit the stove but left the room while it was burning. He knew how much smoke was in the air when they were cooking and how much carbon monoxide was in their breath. And by combining such data with their weekly medical records he could show, for the first time, how the risk of disease increased with exposure—what epidemiologists call a dose-response curve.

"For groups like the Gates Foundation and USAID, the metric is cost-effectiveness," Moss had told me. "How many people are you going to save with a hundred million dollars? That's what they want from this field, and they don't have it yet." Until now. Smith had data on half a dozen diseases that a decent stove could help prevent (it could lower blood pressure about as much as a low-salt diet, for instance). But the most dramatic numbers were for pneumonia. The graph on his laptop had an x-axis for exposure and a y-axis for disease. In between, the data followed a steeply rising curve. The children who inhaled the least smoke were between sixty-five and eighty-five per cent less likely to contract severe pneumonia than those who inhaled the most.

"Those numbers are as good as for any vaccine," Smith said. The plancha stoves cost about a hundred dollars each, yet they were a bargain in public-health terms. "In our country, we pay forty thousand dollars per year of life saved," Smith said. "Even if you take the lower end of the benefit, this would cost at most a few hundred dollars per life-year. It's a no-brainer." In a country like India, he and a team of co-authors later estimated, in an article in *The Lancet,* stoves could save more than two million lives in ten years.

Smith's data may be good enough for the Gates Foundation, but the harder part will be convincing local villagers. Most of the San Lorenzans liked their stoves, and maintained them well enough. But they considered the smoke from cooking more of an annoyance than a threat. (In Africa, some even welcome it as a defense against flies and mosquitoes.) "These kinds of correlations just aren't that easy to make," Smith said. "Think of cigarettes. They kill one out of two smokers prematurely—no war has ever had that effect. Yet famous scientists have died saying there is no connection." To imagine cooking as harmful is an even greater leap. "It's not cyanide," Still said. "They can always think of an eighty-nine-year-old who's been cooking over an open fire all her life. And Grandma's doing just fine."

The best examples of this insouciance, in San Lorenzo, were the wood-fired saunas that most of the villagers used.

The tradition dated back to the ancient Mayans, who would heat rocks over an outdoor fire and carry them into a stone bathhouse. The modern version, known as a *chuj,* was just a mud-caked hut about the size of a large doghouse. It had an open fire inside, a pallet to lie on, and a blanket to seal the door. A *chuj* was essentially a human smokehouse, yet the same villagers who swore by their plancha stoves—including Vincente Tema, one of Smith's Guatemalan staff—took sauna baths once or twice a week for half an hour. (The baths were especially good for pregnant women, they said.) When I asked Tema if I could try his *chuj,* Smith shrugged. I might want to take a carbon-monoxide monitor with me, he said.

The experience wasn't altogether unpleasant—there are worse things, apparently, than becoming a giant slab of bacon. But by the time I stumbled out, sixteen minutes later, my head was swimming. When Smith later downloaded the monitor's data at his office, it showed the carbon monoxide in the *chuj* spiking to five hundred parts per million, then abruptly levelling off. The program wasn't designed to show levels any higher than that, he explained. "Oh, buddy," Still said, staring at the screen. "If you'd gone to a thousand for ten minutes, you'd be in a coma now."

Stories like these were a source of endless frustration to stovemakers. The trouble with tradition, they'd found, is that it can be remarkably thickheaded. Ignore it, and your shiny new stove may get turned into a flowerpot. Cater to it, and you may end up with a new version of the same old problem. The campers in Cottage Grove spent half their time agonizing over cultural sensitivity ("We're highly dominated by elderly white engineering types," a stovemaker who'd worked in Uganda told me. "So you get a lot of preposterous ideas that'll never fly in the kitchen") and the other half grousing about "design drift." Too many stoves start out as marvels of efficiency, they said, and are gradually modified into obsolescence. Once the engineer is gone, the local builder may widen the stove's mouth so it can burn larger sticks, only to draw in too much cold air. Or he'll make the stove out of denser bricks, not realizing that the air pockets in the clay are its best insulation. The better the stove, the tighter its tolerances, the easier it is to ruin.

"When we first got into this, we had this utopian vision of working with local communities to build locally grown stoves," the E.P.A.'s Jacob Moss told me. "We've moved away from that—I won't say a hundred and eighty degrees, but maybe a hundred and sixty. I don't really listen to small stove projects anymore. When I hear Dean say that one millimetre can make a non-trivial difference, it's inconceivable to me that all these local stovemakers can make all these stoves efficiently. You have to work in a different way."

Three years ago, on a taxi ride in southern China, Still had a glimpse of the future. He was working as a consultant for the E.P.A. at the time, passing through the city of Kunming, when he spotted some odd little stoves for sale on a street corner. He shouted for the driver to stop and stepped outside to examine one. "It was like Shangri-La," he told me. The stove was meant for burning coal, so its design was all wrong for wood, but it was sturdy, compact, and cleanly manufactured. More important, its combustion chamber was made of a hard yet miraculously light and porous clay—a combination that stovemakers had been scouring the earth to find. "There, in this two-dollar coal burner, was everything needed to make the world's perfect rocket stove," Still says.

The stove had a telephone number printed on it, so Still called it on his cell phone. Two months later, he was visiting the factory where the stove was built, in eastern China. Within two years, the factory was producing a stove to Aprovecho's specifications. Sold under the name StoveTec, it isn't much to look at: a hollow clay tube, clad in green sheet metal, with an opening in front and a pot support on top. But it incorporates all ten rocket-design principles with a consistency that only mass production can offer. The StoveTec uses about half as much wood as an open fire, produces less than half as much smoke, and sells for eight dollars wholesale. In the United States, where it retails for five times as much, it has been especially popular among Mormons and survivalists.

Still's stove is a kind of proof of principle. It shows that an efficient, user-friendly stove can be mass-produced at a cost that even the very poor can afford. But it also shows what's missing. The StoveTec isn't suited to some dishes—tortillas, chapatis, heavy porridges—and its life expectancy is less than two years. While it's much less smoky than an open fire, it can't quite meet the Waxman-Markey standards.

The search for the perfect stove continues, in other words. Not long before Stove Camp, I visited a company called Envirofit, in Fort Collins, Colorado. Envirofit's laboratories are housed at Colorado State University, in a converted power plant from the nineteen-thirties. On the morning of my tour, half a dozen experiments were going on simultaneously. One glass case held nine stoves, all furiously burning pellets fed to them by an automatic hopper. Across the room, the smoke was being parsed into its chemical components by a rack of blinking machinery. (Wood smoke may not be cyanide, as Still put it, but hydrogen cyanide turns out to be one of its trace elements.) On a catwalk upstairs, a programmer was modelling green and yellow flames on his computer, while a biologist down the hall was subjecting live human lung cells to wood smoke. "We grow them in the basement, but they're fully functional," I was told. "They even produce phlegm."

Envirofit's C.E.O., Ron Bills, is a former executive of Segway, Yamaha, and Bombardier. His new company is technically a non-profit, yet Bills believes that stovemakers, for too long, have treated the developing world as a charity ward instead of a business opportunity. "A lot of the poor—call them emerging consumers—get inundated with crummy stuff," he told me. "So we're going back to Henry Ford." Envirofit's first new product was essentially a rebranded version of Aprovecho's stove, made by the same Chinese factory with a few improvements in durability and design. In July, however, the company unveiled a new model. It was shaped like an ordinary rocket stove, though much more stylish, and had a major innovation at its core: a durable metal combustion chamber. Made of an alloy developed together with Oak Ridge National Laboratory, in Tennessee, it could withstand the caustic fumes of a wood fire for more than five years, yet cost only three dollars a unit to produce. The Envirofit combustion chamber could be shipped for a fraction of the cost of a fully built stove, and adapted to local designs and cooking traditions. It was mass production and appropriate technology rolled into one.

"That's the goose that laid the golden egg right there," Bills told me. "That's the Intel inside." He had nothing against groups like Aprovecho, he said. They could continue to hold their Stove Camps and sell their stoves made out of clay. "But Henry Ford didn't stop with the Model T. If we are going to make an impact in my lifetime, it has to be done at scale. And when you have a three-billion-product opportunity, what is enough scale? One million, two million, five million? I like to dream big." Thanks, hippies, he seemed to be saying. Now, please step aside.

On the last day of Stove Camp, I stumbled out of bed late, in search of coffee—the timber train having catapulted me awake, as usual, four hours earlier. Aprovecho was as busy as a science fair. The pulmonologist from N.I.H. was putting the finishing touches on a rocket stove made from an oil drum. A Norwegian designer was running emissions tests on a little tin gasifier. And another camper was watching emission measurements unspool across a laptop. "Look at that!" he shouted. "It's flat-lining! There's almost no particulate matter!" On the whiteboard next door, the words "Save the World" had long since been erased and replaced with mathematical equations.

Scott and Andreatta were in the far corner of the workshop, probing their injera stove with an infrared thermometer. Their week had been a succession of setbacks and breakthroughs. When their first prototype, with its steel griddle, had too many hot spots, Scott had suggested that they try aluminum. It conducted heat even better than steel and was considerably cheaper. A few e-mails to Ethiopia had confirmed that the metal could be locally cast from recycled engine blocks. By the next morning, Andreatta had roughed out a plywood mold for the griddle and they'd taken it to a foundry in Eugene. But the design proved too complicated to cast—it had radiating fins along the bottom to distribute the heat. So they'd settled on something simpler.

The new griddle was a third of an inch thick and flat on both sides. Andreatta had put a ceramic baffle beneath it to temper and diffuse the flames, but he still had his doubts. The melting point of aluminum is twelve hundred and twenty degrees Fahrenheit—about half as high as the peak temperature inside a rocket stove. If they weren't careful, the griddle would dissolve before their eyes. Andreatta switched on his L.E.D. headlamp and peered at the infrared thermometer. For now, the griddle was holding steady at four hundred and thirty-three degrees—just five degrees short of the target temperature. Better yet, the center was less than twenty-five degrees hotter than the outer edge. "Even Ethiopian women don't get it in that range," Scott said.

Still strolled by, wearing a T-shirt with a giant longhorn beetle on it. He had a groggy grin on his face, as if he'd just woken up to a redeemed and revitalized world. Sometimes he saw the stove community more as Ron Bills seemed to see it—as a gathering of undisciplined hobbyists, engaged in the equivalent of building iPods out of toothpicks and aluminum foil. But this wasn't one of those days. Earlier that summer, a research group under Vijay Modi, a professor of mechanical engineering at Columbia, had surveyed cooks in Uganda and Tanzania who had tested a variety of improved stoves. In both studies, the StoveTec/Envirofit design had won the highest rating, beating out the most recent Envirofit stove in the Tanzanian study. "My people, they aren't always very smart," Still had told me. But they were inventive, resourceful, and doggedly resilient. And, after thirty years of trial and error and endless field research, they understood fire very, very well.

The injera stove was the kind of project that might always fall to them. "What is the market for an improved cookstove, really?" Still said. "People hope that it's big, but we have an eight-dollar stove and it's not easy to sell. Everyone forgets that poor people are really poor." In Africa, where less than a quarter of the population has electricity and the most efficient technologies are beyond reach, an open fire can still seem hard to beat, if only because it's free. "But you know what? We're going to do it," Still said. "A lot of people think that if you don't make a whole lot of money at something it can't be good. I think those people are wrong. If you want to do what poor people need, and you really don't stop, you're not going to be rich. Not unless you're a lot smarter than I am."

Just before we broke camp the next morning, Scott came to find me in the meat locker: the prototype was ready for its first pancake. He and Andreatta had hoped to cook true injera bread for the occasion, but they couldn't find the time—or the teff—to make a proper sourdough. So they'd settled for Aunt Jemima. "This is our first test," Scott said, holding up a pitcher of pancake batter. "People of the world, cut us some slack." Then he poured it onto the hot griddle.

Over the next three months, the stove would go through more rounds of fiddling and redesign. The aluminum would prove too conductive for real injera and get swapped out for a traditional mitad. To get the ceramic to heat evenly, the baffles beneath it would have to be removed. At one point, in Addis Ababa, Scott would nearly abandon the project, only to have an Ethiopian cook make some key suggestions. Yet the result would be even better than it seemed on this sunny August morning: the world's first successful rocket injera stove— twice as efficient and many times more durable than those it was meant to replace.

As the batter hit the griddle, it spread into a circle that nearly reached the edge. Within a minute, it was bubbling up evenly across its surface. "Yeah, baby!" Scott said. "If we'd tried that last Friday, it would be blackened char in the middle." He slid a spatula under the batter and tried to flip it, leaving half on the griddle but the rest well browned. He stared at the pancake. "We can't really fucking believe it," he said. "I mean, these designs usually take months and you're still scratching your head." The stove was almost ready, he thought. Now they just had to convince a few million Ethiopians.

Adam Higginbotham

The Inkjet Counterfeiter

Albert Talton was one of the most prolific counter-
feiters in U.S. history, printing more than seven
million dollars in phony currency—with supplies
purchased from Staples.

Behind an anonymous-looking door on the fifth floor of the
United States Secret Service headquarters, on H Street in
Washington DC, is a small, windowless room known by the
agents who work there as "the specimen vault." Lining the
walls are dozens of filing cabinets filled with narrow steel
drawers, containing scores of transparent plastic sleeves. In
each sleeve is an individual note of US currency—a single,
five, ten, 20, 50 or 100. The face value of the cash runs to millions of dollars. But the money in the drawers is worthless.

The specimen vault is the reference library of the Secret
Service's counterfeit investigators. It holds an example of every
fake US tender confiscated since the end of the 19th century.
Most of the bills spent—or "passed," in the law-enforcement
jargon—were created decades ago by skilled artists familiar
with the fine engraving techniques and heavy machinery of
the printing industry, career criminals who churned out thousands of dollars at a time. But the advent of desktop publishing has changed the forger's profile, giving almost anyone

with a copy of Photoshop and a scanner the means to print money. And if opportunistic bedroom forgers have made the crime more widespread, their operations are often small-scale and easy to detect; few ever produce more than $10,000.

But in January 2005, the Secret Service field office in Los Angeles discovered a fake $100 bill of remarkably high quality. Four years later in the specimen vault Kelley Harris, counterfeit specialist with the Criminal Investigative Division, hands me a Ziploc bag containing 14 bills which appear genuine. "Not bad," he concedes. Despite the best efforts of the Secret Service, the printer of these notes evaded capture for more than three years. By then Albert Edward Talton, of Lawndale, California, was responsible for putting more than $7 million in phony currency into circulation; he made much of it using kit bought at his local Staples office-supplies store. Albert Talton, 46, is charming and soft-spoken, a big, fastidious man with a taste for expensive cars and high-end audio equipment. Born and raised in southern California, he has been a criminal for most of his life. For ten years he was in and out of jail, and in 2001 he was convicted of bank fraud and sentenced to five years. Yet he also studied electrical engineering at California State University and is a man of considerable ingenuity. In 1987, when Bose was manufacturing a new type of speaker system, Talton wanted to know how it worked. "I was amazed," he says from the Federal Correctional Institution in Lompoc, California. "How could they get that much bass out of a speaker the size of a shoe box?" So he bought himself a Bose set-up for $2,500, went home, and took it apart. He figured out what the company's technicians had done and built his own version. This would not be his last experiment in reverse engineering.

In June 2004 he was released from prison, eventually finding work at a car-repair garage in Inglewood, California. A few months later his boss showed him a fake $50 note someone had passed to him. Talton examined it and thought: "I could do better than that."

There are few criminals pursued with more vigour than those who make their own money. Counterfeiting is considered such a threat to the fabric of the United States that, along with treason, it is one of only two criminal offences named in the Constitution. Although now better known for its role in presidential security, the Secret Service was actually founded by the Treasury in 1865 to combat currency counterfeiting.

Fake bills make up a tiny fraction of the cash in circulation at any time—the Service puts it at less than 0.1 per cent—but this still amounts to some $780 million in the US alone. And its impact can be significant: losses incurred by accepting counterfeit currency are not covered by insurance, and a run of fake bills will shake international confidence in the dollar. In the UK, where known fake notes made up approximately 0.03% of all sterling in circulation, £13.7 million worth of counterfeit notes were removed from circulation last year. The vast majority (98 per cent) were £20 notes.

Almost every physical attribute of the money in your wallet was conceived with the intention of making it hard to duplicate. UK notes are printed on paper made from a mixture of cotton fibre and linen rag; euro notes are printed on 100 per cent cotton; and US notes are printed on paper composed of 75 per cent cotton and 25 per cent linen, giving it a feel that's easily distinguished from the smooth wood-pulp paper commonly used in copiers.

In 1996, US currency underwent a significant redesign, specifically to combat the growing use of colour copiers and computer scanners by counterfeiters as the technology became more sophisticated and widespread. The US Treasury has since introduced three further series of notes, each employing more complex security features: the most recent of which includes coloured backgrounds, intricate patterns of microprinting, water-marks, embedded security threads visible when the bill is held to the light and ink that appears to change colour, depending on the viewing angle.

Security features of UK notes are similar and include raised print (eg on the words "Bank of England"); watermarks; embedded metallic thread; holograms; and fluorescent ink visible only under UV lamps. There are three printing processes involved (offset litho, intaglio and letterpress) using a total of 85 specialised inks. Euro notes incorporate many of these features too, including watermarks, raised print, a metallic security strip, holograms, and colour-changing ink. But even the latest technology cannot thwart every forger. "The security features make it more difficult," says Special Agent Edwin Donovan, "but there's no such thing as 'uncounterfeitable.'"

When Talton set out to circumvent the US Treasury's security measures, he had no experience in counterfeiting, graphic design or printing, and he didn't even own a computer. His first attempts were made with a Hewlett-Packard all-in-one inkjet printer/scanner/fax/photocopier, which could be picked up at the time for less than $150. Early experiments, printed on regular paper, were fuzzy, so he cleaned up the original image on a computer. But there was a problem, Talton says: "It wouldn't take the mark." Counterfeit-detection pens mark yellow on genuine currency but brown or black on fake. Talton didn't know why. At first he thought the Treasury treated the paper, so he experimented with chemicals he found at the garage and even tried dipping his notes in fabric softener. Nothing worked. Frustrated, he began to take a detection pen everywhere he went, trying it on any paper he came across. He was about to give up when one day, in the toilet, he found himself staring at the roll of tissue. He took out the pen: the mark showed up yellow. Talton discovered that toilet paper,

Bibles, dictionaries and newsprint are all made from the same recycled paper pulp, and all take the yellow mark. Newsprint is strong, and it has an additional advantage for the large-scale buyer: as Talton puts it, "Newsprint is real cheap."

Every investigation that the US Secret Service conducts into counterfeiting has the same goal, says agent Donovan: "To stop the bleeding." In order to staunch the flow of fake bills, US Treasury agents must arrest the people who are passing them, trace the transactions back up the chain of distribution, catch the printer and seize his equipment. "Plant suppression," as the service calls it, is a painstaking process: wise printers insulate themselves so those who spend the money have no idea of its source.

Talton's counterfeit notes were first noticed early in 2005. All $100 bills, they were meticulously made. "It was key to his success," says Mack Jenkins, one of two US attorneys who prosecuted the case. "He didn't just make the easiest-to-produce counterfeit; he made the best he could." The simplest method of making counterfeit money is to scan both sides of a bill and print them on either side of a piece of paper. But in a real bill the security strip and watermark are embedded, so this kind of counterfeit is never convincing.

Talton realised he could solve the problem by using two sheets of tissue-thin newsprint: he printed imitation watermarks and security strips on the back of one, then glued the sheets together with the security features inside. Next he printed the front and back faces of the bills on either side of the sheets, which he hung from clothes-lines and coated with hairspray, creating a texture similar to that of genuine currency and a barrier that helped the paper take the mark of a counterfeit pen. Finally, he cut the notes to size. For all his scrupulousness, though, Talton used the same scan for every $100 bill he printed, so the alphanumeric codes to the left and right of the portrait of Benjamin Franklin never changed. These are the quadrant number and the face-plate number, which indicate which plate at the Bureau of Engraving and Printing was used to make the bill: Talton's $100 came from plate no 38, spot H, quadrant no 2, and so was marked H2 and H38.

Albert Talton says he did not have any grand plan in mind when he started his operation. It was just an experiment "to see if I could do it," he tells me in a letter from prison, a few months after our initial conversation. Once he had made 20 or 30 bills, he gave them to an acquaintance—"a street person"—to see what he could do with them. The acquaintance sold them and returned for more. The H2/H38 notes appeared slowly in southern California, logged by Secret Service officers one or two at a time early in 2005. For the next year they followed a similar pattern: $100 here, $200 there, always around Los Angeles. But in 2006, the bills began to spread across the country in large quantities: $11,500 in January; $57,600 in March; $115,100 in September. In 2005 and 2006, a total of $1,300,200 in H2/H38 notes were retrieved. Secret Service agents questioned anyone caught passing the notes in any volume, but they always told the same story: they had no idea that the money was counterfeit and they certainly didn't know where it had come from. By early 2007, the stream of notes had become a flood—$347,700 in March alone. Jenkins would later calculate that by the end of 2008, at least $127,000 in H2/H38 notes had been spent in Macy's stores, and $19,000 in Jack in the Box fast-food joints. But the Secret Service still had no leads.

In September 2007, Talton received a single order for $500,000 and began working day and night. He dedicated an upstairs room in his new house to a regimented counterfeiting process, with two Hewlett-Packard computers, nine inkjet and laser-jet printers, stacks of paper divided by type; it was a manufacturing routine based on production-line principles: "Probably the best organised office I've ever seen," Mack Jenkins says. Once a week, Talton drove to Staples in nearby Hawthorne to replenish his supply of printer cartridges, drop his empties in the store's recycling bin, and use a Staples rewards card to accrue points in his own name. In the last three months of the year, Secret Service offices logged the passing of another $1,297,500 in counterfeit $100 bills bearing the H2/H38 mark. Agents were no closer to finding the person who was printing them than they had been two years before.

On January 14, 2008, at an H&M store in LA, a former employee bought $1,000 worth of clothes with $100 bills that all bore the H2/H38 mark. The following day two women returned with the purchase and asked for a refund. Under interrogation, the three suspects not only admitted that they knew the notes were counterfeit but also revealed who they had come from: Troy Stroud, who was put under surveillance.

Two months later, Stroud was hawking Talton's latest product: a counterfeit $20. Because $20 bills are so easy to pass —few businesses check every one they receive—the investigation assumed a greater sense of urgency. Informants wearing wires met with Stroud and bought some of his H2/H38 bills; they also introduced him to two undercover Secret Service agents. The service got everything on tape and put a transponder (a receiver-transmitter tracking device) on Stroud's white Range Rover.

On April 10, Paul McCorry attended a meeting at which $2,500 in counterfeit hundreds was sold to another informant on the Secret Service payroll: he arrived in an orange Mercedes coupe bearing a licence plate that read "MCCORRY." On April 15, three agents tailed Stroud to a Popeyes fried-chicken franchise in Inglewood. While Stroud waited in the drive-through line, special agent Matthew Mayo entered the restaurant and watched him pay for his meal with a $20 bill. Naturally, it was a counterfeit.

On April 23, agents followed Stroud to the house in Lawndale. The following day, they searched the bins outside, turning up fragments of counterfeit bills, printer cartridges, and a name: Albert Talton.

Early in the morning of May 8, Stroud was arrested. Talton's house in Lawndale was raided later that day when the Secret Service entered using a battering ram and shotguns. They found Goldberg at work in the kitchen; McCorry was in the bathroom; Talton himself was upstairs. On a computer screen was the image of a $100 bill. The agents found $162,000 in finished notes, and almost $1.4 million in partially completed bills. "You can't get caught much more red-handed than that," Mack Jenkins says.

Between November 2008 and May 2009, Albert Talton and his three co-conspirators were convicted of "forging or selling counterfeit obligations of the United States." Talton was sentenced to nine years and two months in prison. The Secret Service put the total of all currency printed by Talton and successfully spent up to March 2009 at $6,798,900—though ultimately both Talton and the authorities acknowledged that the sum was higher. "They agreed to keep it under the seven million mark," Talton says. "I had bills out there after that—and those weren't even just the hundreds." By the time Talton was arrested, his money had been circulated in every state in the nation and in nine foreign countries. Of all the phony currency that was confiscated, four examples will be filed in the steel drawers of the specimen vault. The rest will be burned by the Secret Service—all but four further bills. In his office in the US courthouse in downtown Los Angeles, Mack Jenkins explains that he and his fellow prosecutor, Mark Williams, are awaiting delivery of two sets of examples of Talton's best work—a $20 and a $100. These will be mounted and framed as souvenirs.

"So we will have our own," Jenkins says. "It will be stamped 'counterfeit' on the back, but it will be up on our walls."

Williams smiles. "And if we ever want some Popeyes," he says, "we'll just crack the plaque open and go buy some chicken."

Anne Trubek

Handwriting Is History

*Writing words by hand is a technology that's just
too slow for our times, and our minds.*

At 11 p.m. on Dec. 27, I checked my inbox out of habit. I had
581 new e-mails. All had been sent between 8 and 11 p.m. The
days between Christmas and New Year's are not usually a
busy time for e-mailing. What was going on?

It turns out that the home page for msn.com had linked to
a short article I had published a year earlier. In the article, I
argue that we should stop teaching cursive in primary schools
and provide some background on the history of handwriting
to back up my claims.

The comments on my piece were hostile, insulting and ve-
hemently opposed to my argument. The onslaught continued
for a few more days: Some 2,000 comments were submitted,
and editors took down about 700 of the worst. If you check
this article online today, you will find more than 1,300 comments. For some reason, people are very invested in handwriting.

If we define writing as a system of marks to record information (and discount petroglyphs, say), handwriting has been
around for just 6,000 of humanity's some 200,000 years. Its

effects have been enormous, of course: It alters the brain, changes with civilizations, cultures and factions, and plays a role in religious and political battles. Throughout the even smaller slice of time that is American history, handwriting has reflected national aspirations. The comments posted on my article about handwriting were teeming with moralism. ("I'm sorry, but when I see messy handwriting it tells me something about the person; maybe carelessness? Impatience? . . . Penmanship is everything. . . . Good penmanship shows the world we are civilized.") One might consider handwriting as a technology—a way to make letters—and conclude that the way of making them is of little moment. But handwriting is bound up with a host of associations and connotations that propel it beyond simply a fine-motor skill. We connect it to personal identity (handwriting signals something unique about each of us), intelligence (good handwriting reflects good thinking) and virtue (a civilized culture requires handwriting).

Most of us know, but often forget, that handwriting is not natural. We are not born to do it. There is no genetic basis for writing. Writing is not like seeing or talking, which are innate. Writing must be taught.

About 6,000 years ago, the Sumerians created the first schools, called tablet houses, to teach writing. They trained children in Sumerian cuneiform by having them copy the symbols on one half of a soft clay tablet onto the other half, using a stylus. When children did this—and when the Sumerians invented a system of representation, a way to make one thing symbolize another—their brains changed. In *Proust and the Squid: The Story and Science of the Reading Brain,* Maryanne Wolf explains the neurological developments writing wrought: "The brain became a beehive of activity. A network of processes went to work: The visual and visual association areas responded to visual patterns (or representations);

frontal, temporal, and parietal areas provided information about the smallest sounds in words . . . ; and finally areas in the temporal and parietal lobes processed meaning, function and connections."

The Sumerians did not have an alphabet—nor did the Egyptians, who may have gotten to writing earlier. Which alphabet came first is debated; many consider it to be the Greek version, a system based upon Phoenician. Alphabets created even more neural pathways, allowing us to think in new ways (neither better nor worse than non-alphabetic systems, like Chinese, yet different nonetheless).

When we think of handwriting, we often assume a script, a regularized way to make letters, to which all writers adhere in order to aid communication. A famous early script is Roman square capital, which looks exactly as you imagine it: monumental u's in the shape of our modern v's and no spacing between words. It was written with a stylus and chiseled onto the sides of buildings.

Proclaiming the virtuousness of one way of forming a "j" over others is a trope that occurs throughout handwriting's history. For instance, early Christians jettisoned Roman scripts they deemed decadent and pagan. In their scriptoria, monks developed Uncial to replace Roman scripts. An internecine battle ensued when Irish monks developed a variation on Uncial that traditionalists deemed an upstart, quasi-heretical script.

Puritans in England and America also developed a script to distance themselves from the seeming Catholicism of the elaborate scripts popular in the 18th century. They adopted the plainer copperplate, or round hand. The Declaration of Independence is written in copperplate.

In the American colonies, a "good hand" became a sign of class and intelligence as well as moral righteousness. Benjamin Franklin was a proponent of proper handwriting, and when he founded the Academy of Philadelphia (which became the University of Pennsylvania), those seeking entrance were required to "write a legible hand." But very few Americans were eligible to enter Franklin's academy. First, to do so, you had to be male. Second, you had to have been taught to write; many women and non-wealthy men were taught to read, but not write. Only wealthy men and businessmen learned to write. Even when public schooling began, writing was not always included in the curriculum, so many colonists could read but not write. It was not until the beginning of the 19th century—a scant 200 years ago—that schooling became universal. Then, handwriting was finally taught to American schoolchildren.

For many, the prospect of handwriting dying out would signal the end of individualism and the entree to some robotic techno-future. (As one comment on my article put it, "What's next, putting programming chips in our brains?") But when we worry about losing our individuality, we are likely misremembering our schooling, which included rote, rigid lessons in handwriting. We have long been taught the "right" way to form letters. The history of American penmanship is dominated by two true believers, Platt Rogers Spencer and A. N. Palmer, whose fiercely moral and economic attachments to their scripts nicely sum up much of what we consider essential to American identity.

Spencer, "the father of American handwriting," was a fanatic who was obsessed with script even as a child. He made it big when he established a chain of business schools—the slogan was "Education For Real Life"—to teach his script, Spencerian, which he based on natural forms: leaves, trees, etc. Spencerian was the standard script taught from the 1860s to the 1920s. This transcendentalist move toward a script that better followed the human body's movements is belied by his insistence on rigor and standardization. He advised his students to practice six to 12 hours a day. Mastering his script would, Spencer believed, make someone refined, genteel, upstanding.

Later in the 19th century, Palmer invented a script that would better suit the industrial age. The Palmer Method stresses a "plain and rapid style." He rejected the slightly fey Spencerian for a muscular, rugged script better suited to a commercial culture. By 1912, Palmer was a household word, and a million copies of his (printed) writing manuals had sold. Educators taught his method, and millions of Americans were "Palmerized."

The Palmer Method was gradually supplanted when educators decided to teach children manuscript (or printing) first, and cursive later, to get them started writing younger. Handwriting enthusiasts consider the end of the Palmer Method to be the end of good handwriting in America.

It took the printing press to create a notion of handwriting as a sign of self. For monks, whose illuminated manuscripts we now venerate as beautiful works of art (as they most certainly are), script was not self-expressive but formulaic, and rightly so. When the printing press was invented, the monks were worried about this new capricious technology, which was too liable to foibles and the idiosyncratic mark of the man helming the press. A hand-copied manuscript was for them then the authoritative, exact, regularized text. In his treatise, *In Praise of Copying,* the 15th-century monk Trithemius argued that "printed books will never be the equivalent of handwritten codices, especially since printed books are often deficient in spelling and appearance."

Handwriting slowly became a form of self-expression when it ceased to be the primary mode of written communication. When a new writing technology develops, we tend to romanticize the older one. The supplanted technology is vaunted as more authentic because it is no longer ubiquitous or official. Thus for monks, print was capricious and script reliable. So too today: Conventional wisdom holds that computers are devoid of emotion and personality, and handwriting is the province of intimacy, originality and authenticity.

This transition, and the associations we make with old and new technologies, played out while millions of Americans were being Palmerized in school, and the Palmer Method is inextricably linked to a new writing technology that was starting to compete with handwriting: the typewriter.

In post–Civil War America, the Remington Arms Company needed a new product to boost sales (rifles were moving more slowly). The company unveiled the first typewriter in 1874. It was heavy and loud and looked like a big metal sewing machine, as it was set on a table with a treadle at the bottom. The machine was cumbersome, the noise it made cacophonous. Worse, you had to write blind: the keys hit the underside of the paper. It did not sell. Businesses wouldn't accept documents written on it because they were not penned. Remington sold only a few of that first model, but Mark Twain bought one. In his autobiography, he claimed to be the "first person in the world to apply the type-machine to literature" when he submitted a typed manuscript of *The Adventures of Tom Sawyer* to his publisher.

Twain hated blind typing, though, and he gave his Remington away to his friend William Dean Howells, the eminent *Atlantic* editor and novelist. Howells returned it, uninterested, six months later. But as with personal computers and cell phones, early adopters of a good technology will eventually persuade the rest of us we need it, too. In the 1890s, the typewriter gained a carriage return, and the new models allowed you to see the page while typing. By 1905, it was a curiosity *not* to own a typewriter.

That first Remington introduced the QWERTY keyboard, which separates common letter pairs to prevent bars from sticking when struck sequentially. Although others have developed more efficient, user-friendly and ergonomic keyboards, none has caught on. We seem stubbornly wed to QWERTY, as our thirst for the new new thing accompanies a stubborn grip on the familiar.

When Kitty Burns Florey's *Script and Scribble: The Rise and Fall of Handwriting,* a nostalgic look at handwriting's history and call to revive it in schools, came out early in 2009, the reviews tended to follow a pattern: The reviewer begins by admitting he or she never handwrites anymore, but thinks that is a shame. He or she goes on to laud Florey's book and ends by promising to do more handwriting in the future. Michael Dirda writes, "After reading *Script and Scribble,* I feel like digging out my beat-up calligraphy manuals. . . . Of course, I also need to clean out the dried ink from my italic pen. But before you know it, even Ludovico Arrighi—the great Renaissance master of italic —will be envying my p's and q's." Florey wrote her own version of this genre in an article on the writing of her book. She tells how she always writes on the computer, never longhand: "My last eight books are children of Microsoft Word, and virtually everything I write, from a long book to a short e-mail, is done on the computer." While researching the book, she learned how to do italic script, and became enamored of it. She ends her piece by advising all of us to do more handwriting: "I suggest you set aside half an hour, grab a piece of paper and a pen, and, in your best script (be it Italic, Palmer, or a cleaned-up version of your usual scrawl), write a poem, start a diary, send a note to a friend, or . . . compose a love letter."

I doubt whether the critics or Florey have followed up on their pledges to handwrite more. Nevertheless, people seem to think that school kids should be spending more time honing their mastery of the capital G. A 2007 U.S. Department of Education study found that 90 percent of teachers spend 10 minutes a day on handwriting. Zaner-Bloser, the most popular handwriting curriculum used today, deems that too little and is encouraging schools to up that amount to at least 15 minutes a day.

But typing in school has a democratizing effect, as did the typewriter. It levels the look of prose to allow expression of ideas, not the rendering of letters, to take center stage. Florey is aware of this but does not take the time to unpack the assumptions contained in her reason why we should continue to teach handwriting: "Children are judged by their handwriting; if they produce indecipherable chicken-scratching, a teacher will not be sympathetic." Florey mentions that when she was asked to judge handwritten applications for writing positions, she was "drawn to those with legible handwriting and prejudiced against the scrawlers."

Does having good handwriting signal intelligence? No, not any more than it reveals one's religiosity. But many teachers make this correlation: It is called the "handwriting effect." Steve Graham, a professor at Vanderbilt University who studies handwriting acquisition, says that "teachers form judgments, positive or negative, about the literary merit of text based on its overall legibility." Graham's studies show that "[w]hen teachers rate multiple versions of the same paper differing only in terms of legibility, they assign higher grades to neatly written versions of the paper than the same versions with poorer penmanship." This is particularly problematic for boys, whose fine-motor skills develop later than do girls. Yet all children are taught at the same time—usually printing in first grade and cursive in third. If you don't have cursive down by the end of third grade, you may never become proficient at it.

While we once judged handwriting as religiously tinted, now secular, we transpose our prejudices to intelligence. The new SAT Writing Exam, instituted in 2006, requires test takers to write their essays in No. 2 pencil. Not only will those with messy handwriting be graded lower than ones written more legibly, but those who write in cursive—15 percent of test takers in 2006—received higher scores than those who printed.

As of 2002, public schools had one computer for every four students, and since then, the number has risen. Despite talk of the digital divide, most high school students, even in low-income schools, are required to type and print out their essays, and they are able to find the means to do so. So assuming access, a standard font and printer paper, typing levels the playing field. Is this egalitarianism not a key value that, like the alphabet, goes all the way back to the Greeks?

When my son was in second grade, he had to stay in for recess almost every day because he could not properly form his letters. I was called in for "interventions," warned that he would fail the Ohio Proficiency Tests if scanners could not read his test answers. (No Child Left Behind leaves teachers with less time to teach handwriting and fewer means to teach it, yet more tests students must take to prove they have mastered it.) For Simon, homework was always stressful. He would stare at a blank page for an hour. Then he would write one word and then stop; write a few letters and then stop. Soon, he began to fear taking up a pencil at all, and we had nightly battles over his language arts worksheets. Then he began to worry about not having anything to say, not knowing how to say it, or he would come up with ideas that he would not write down because they would take too long and thus write nothing. Perennially being told his handwriting was bad transmuted in his mind into proof that he was a bad writer—a poor student incapable of expressing ideas. He simply hated the physical process of writing. And since handwriting dominated his education in grades 1, 2 and 3, he hated school, too.

I transferred him to a private school where he was allowed

to dictate his writing assignments. For his fourth-grade assignments, I sat at the computer, my laptop on the dining room table, as he paced the dining room, wildly gesticulating, sometimes stopping to put his hand on his chin in thought, but mainly speaking without stopping. I am a fast typist, but I could not keep up; I had to break his train of words. He spoke aloud in full clauses and paragraphs. What would have taken him about three or four hours (I am not exaggerating) by hand took him about four minutes by mouth.

The moral of this story is not that typing is superior to handwriting, that parents should have to transcribe the stories of their offspring or that private schools are superior to public ones. The moral of the story is that what we want from writing—what Simon wants and what the Sumerians wanted—is cognitive automaticity, the ability to think as fast as possible, freed as much as can be from the strictures of whichever technology we must use to record our thoughts. As Wolf writes: "A system that can become streamlined through specialization and automaticity has more time to think. This is the miraculous gift of the reading brain." This is what Palmer wanted for his students—speed. This is what the typewriter promised Twain. This is what typing does for millions. It allows us to go faster, not because we want everything faster in our hyped-up age, but for the opposite reason: We want more time to think.

This is how Simon describes why he hates to handwrite: "I have it all in my memory bank, and then I stop, and my memory bank gets wiped out."

Whatever we use to write, there will be a shortfall between conception and execution, between the ideas in our heads and the words we produce. We often insert nostalgia into this gap. Today, writing a novel with a BIC pen and a legal pad is considered as sweetly funny as William Dean Howells composing his first short story in a compositor's stick, upside down and backwards (his father was a printer) or Gay Talese's habit of writing on shirt boards (those cardboard panels they put in your shirts at the dry cleaners). Toni Morrison, Jim Harrison, John Updike and others write (or, unfortunately, have written) by hand.

We also make up stories to romanticize the mundane. The Sumerians used writing for accounting—they developed tokens to count sheep. But the Sumerians made up a better story for the invention of writing: "A messenger from the lord of Kulab arrived at a distant kingdom, too exhausted to deliver an important oral message. So as not to be frustrated by mortal failings, the lord of Kulab had also 'patted some clay and set down the words as on a tablet . . . and verily it was so.'" (As Wolf points out, this tale "sidestep[s] the awkward matter of who was able to read the lord of Kulab's words.")

Handwriting does have a presence that can be absent in typed prose, I admit. I have a binder of notes my grandmother wrote shortly before she died. She scrawled her life story in thick black felt-tip on the backs of envelopes. I have been slowly typing up her notes to preserve them for the family, and as I squint to make out words, I sense the felt experience of her hand on paper. And I will admit that when I find a smooth expanse of sand or a bark-less tree trunk, I long to scratch my name in them.

I have no desire to lose the art of handwriting, to lose the knowledge retained in archives or to take pencils away from those who seek to wield them: Matthew McKinnon, a freelance writer, re-taught himself cursive at the age of 30 because he had forgotten it, found it useful for his work and wanted to "shake the cobwebs" out of the area of his brain it activates. Kitty Burns Florey is starting a "slow writing" movement, mimicking the slow food movement, to revive the art of handwriting. Each year, the Spencer Society holds a weeklong "saga" where you can learn to master Spencerian script. Handwriting has always been both a way to express thoughts and an art, and preserving the artistic aspects, be it through calligraphy or mastering comic book lettering, is worthy. In schools, we might transition to teaching handwriting as we do other arts, specifically as a fine-motor skill and encourage calligraphers as we should letter press printers or stained glass window makers. These arts have a life beyond nostalgia.

When people hear I am writing about the possible end of handwriting, many come up with examples of things we will always need handwriting for: endorsing checks (no longer needed at an ATM), grocery lists (smartphones have note-taking functions), signatures (not even needed to file taxes anymore). These will not be what we would lose. We may, however, forsake some neurological memory. I imagine some pathways in our brains will atrophy. Then again, I imagine my brain is developing new cognitive pathways each time I hit control C or double click Firefox. That I can touch-type, my fingers magically dancing on my keyboard, free of any conscious effort (much as you are looking at letters and making meaning in your head right now as you read), amazes me. Touch-typing is a glorious example of cognitive automaticity, the speed of execution keeping pace with the speed of cognition.

Do not worry. It will take a long time for handwriting to die, for us to have the interview with the "last handwriter" as we do today with the last living speakers of some languages. By 1600 B.C., all Sumerian speakers had died, but the writing system that replaced Sumerian, Akkadian, kept aspects of Sumerian alive. It would take another 1,000 years—until 600 B.C.—for Sumerian writing to disappear completely. Even the revolutionary Greeks took a long time to change habits. After they created the Greek alphabet, they spent 400 years doing nothing with it, preferring their extant oral culture. Handwriting is not going anywhere soon. But it is going.

Sam Anderson

In Defense of Distraction

Twitter, Adderall, lifehacking, mindful jogging,
power browsing, Obama's BlackBerry, and the
benefits of overstimulation.

I. THE POVERTY OF ATTENTION

I'm going to pause here, right at the beginning of my riveting article about attention, and ask you to please get all of your precious 21st-century distractions out of your system now. Check the score of the Mets game; text your sister that pun you just thought of about her roommate's new pet lizard ("iguana hold yr hand LOL get it like Beatles"); refresh your work e-mail, your home e-mail, your school e-mail; upload pictures of yourself reading this paragraph to your "me reading magazine articles" Flickr photostream; and alert the fellow citizens of whatever Twittertopia you happen to frequent that you will be suspending your digital presence for the next twenty minutes or so (I know that seems drastic: Tell them you're having an appendectomy or something and are about to lose consciousness). Good. Now: Count your breaths. Close your eyes. Do whatever it takes to get all of your neurons lined up in one direction. Above all, resist the urge to fixate on the picture, right over there, of that weird scrambled guy typing.

Do not speculate on his ethnicity (German-Venezuelan?) or his backstory (Witness Protection Program?) or the size of his monitor. Go ahead and cover him with your hand if you need to. There. Doesn't that feel better? Now it's just you and me, tucked like fourteenth-century Zen masters into this sweet little nook of pure mental focus. (Seriously, stop looking at him. I'm over here.)

Over the last several years, the problem of attention has migrated right into the center of our cultural attention. We hunt it in neurology labs, lament its decline on op-ed pages, fetishize it in grassroots quality-of-life movements, diagnose its absence in more and more of our children every year, cultivate it in yoga class twice a week, harness it as the engine of self-help empires, and pump it up to superhuman levels with drugs originally intended to treat Alzheimer's and narcolepsy. Everyone still pays some form of attention all the time, of course—it's basically impossible for humans not to—but the currency in which we pay it, and the goods we get in exchange, have changed dramatically.

Back in 1971, when the web was still twenty years off and the smallest computers were the size of delivery vans, before the founders of Google had even managed to get themselves born, the polymath economist Herbert A. Simon wrote maybe the most concise possible description of our modern struggle: "What information consumes is rather obvious: It consumes the attention of its recipients. Hence a wealth of information creates a poverty of attention, and a need to allocate that attention efficiently among the overabundance of information sources that might consume it." As beneficiaries of the greatest information boom in the history of the world, we are suffering, by Simon's logic, a correspondingly serious poverty of attention.

If the pundits clogging my RSS reader can be trusted (the ones I check up on occasionally when I don't have any new e-mail), our attention crisis is already chewing its hyperactive way through the very foundations of Western civilization. Google is making us stupid, multitasking is draining our souls, and the "dumbest generation" is leading us into a "dark age" of bookless "power browsing." Adopting the Internet as the hub of our work, play, and commerce has been the intellectual equivalent of adopting corn syrup as the center of our national diet, and we've all become mentally obese. Formerly well-rounded adults are forced to MacGyver worldviews out of telegraphic blog posts, bits of YouTube videos, and the first nine words of *Times* editorials. Schoolkids spread their attention across 30 different programs at once and interact with each other mainly as sweatless avatars. (One recent study found that American teenagers spend an average of 6.5 hours a day focused on the electronic world, which strikes me as a little low; in South Korea, the most wired nation on earth, young adults have actually died from exhaustion after multi-day online-gaming marathons.) We are, in short, terminally distracted. And *distracted,* the alarmists will remind you, was once a synonym for *insane.* (Shakespeare: "poverty hath distracted her.")

This doomsaying strikes me as silly for two reasons. First, conservative social critics have been blowing the apocalyptic bugle at every large-scale tech-driven social change since Socrates' famous complaint about the memory-destroying properties of that newfangled technology called "writing." (A complaint we remember, not incidentally, because it was written down.) And, more practically, the virtual horse has already left the digital barn. It's too late to just retreat to a quieter time. Our jobs depend on connectivity. Our pleasure-cycles—no trivial matter—are increasingly tied to it. Information rains down faster and thicker every day, and there are plenty of non-moronic reasons for it to do so. The question, now, is how successfully we can adapt.

Although attention is often described as an organ system, it's not the sort of thing you can pull out and study like a spleen. It's a complex process that shows up all over the brain, mingling inextricably with other quasi-mystical processes like emotion, memory, identity, will, motivation, and mood. Psychologists have always had to track attention secondhand. Before the sixties, they measured it through easy-to-monitor senses like vision and hearing (if you listen to one voice in your right ear and another in your left, how much information can you absorb from either side?), then eventually graduated to PET scans and EEGs and electrodes and monkey brains. Only in the last ten years—thanks to neuroscientists and their functional MRIs—have we been able to watch the attending human brain in action, with its coordinated storms of neural firing, rapid blood surges, and oxygen flows. This has yielded all kinds of fascinating insights—for instance, that when forced to multitask, the overloaded brain shifts its processing from the hippocampus (responsible for memory) to the striatum (responsible for rote tasks), making it hard to learn a task or even recall what you've been doing once you're done.

When I reach David Meyer, one of the world's reigning experts on multitasking, he is feeling alert against all reasonable odds. He has just returned from India, where he was discussing the nature of attention at a conference with the Dalai Lama (Meyer gave a keynote speech arguing that Buddhist monks multitask during meditation), and his trip home was hellish: a canceled flight, an overnight taxi on roads so rough it took thirteen hours to go 200 miles. This is his first full day back in his office at the University of Michigan, where he directs the Brain, Cognition, and Action Laboratory—a basement space in which finger-tapping, card-memorizing, tone-identifying subjects help Meyer pinpoint exactly how much information the human brain can handle at once. He's been up since 3 a.m. and has by now goosed his attention several times with liquid stimulants: a couple of cups of coffee, some tea. "It does wonders," he says.

My interaction with Meyer takes place entirely via the technology of distraction. We scheduled and rescheduled our appointment, several times, by e-mail. His voice is now projecting, tinnily, out of my cell phone's speaker and into the microphone of my digital recorder, from which I will download it, as soon as we're done, onto my laptop, which I currently have open on my desk in front of me, with several windows spread across the screen, each bearing nested tabs, on one of which I've been reading, before Meyer even had a chance to tell me about it, a blog all about his conference with the Dalai Lama, complete with RSS feed and audio commentary and embedded YouTube videos and pictures of His Holiness. As Meyer and I talk, the universe tests us with a small battery of distractions. A maximum-volume fleet of emergency vehicles passes just outside my window; my phone chirps to tell us that my mother is calling on the other line, then beeps again to let us know she's left a message. There is, occasionally, a slight delay in the connection. Meyer ignores it all, speaking deliberately and at length, managing to coordinate tricky subject-verb agreements over the course of multi-clause sentences. I begin, a little sheepishly, with a question that strikes me as sensationalistic, nonscientific, and probably unanswerable by someone who's been professionally trained in the discipline of cautious objectivity: Are we living through a crisis of attention?

Before I even have a chance to apologize, Meyer responds with the air of an Old Testament prophet. "Yes," he says. "And I think it's going to get a lot worse than people expect." He sees our distraction as a full-blown epidemic—a cognitive plague that has the potential to wipe out an entire generation of focused and productive thought. He compares it, in fact, to smoking. "People aren't aware what's happening to their mental processes," he says, "in the same way that people years ago couldn't look into their lungs and see the residual deposits."

I ask him if, as the world's foremost expert on multitasking and distraction, he has found his own life negatively affected by the new world order of multitasking and distraction.

"Yep," he says immediately, then adds, with admirable (although slightly hurtful) bluntness: "I get calls all the time from people like you. Because of the way the Internet works, once you become visible, you're approached from left and right by people wanting to have interactions in ways that are extremely time-consuming. I could spend my whole day, my whole night, just answering e-mails. I just can't deal with it all. None of this happened even ten years ago. It was a lot calmer. There was a lot of opportunity for getting steady work done."

Over the last twenty years, Meyer and a host of other researchers have proved again and again that multitasking, at least as our culture has come to know and love and institutionalize it, is a myth. When you think you're doing two things at once, you're almost always just switching rapidly between them, leaking a little mental efficiency with every switch. Meyer says that this is because, to put it simply, the brain processes different kinds of information on a variety of separate "channels"—a language channel, a visual channel, an auditory channel, and so on—each of which can process only one stream of information at a time. If you overburden a channel, the brain becomes inefficient and mistake-prone. The classic example is driving while talking on a cell phone, two tasks that conflict across a range of obvious channels: Steering and dialing are both manual tasks, looking out the windshield and reading a phone screen are both visual, etc. Even talking on a hands-free phone can be dangerous, Meyer says. If the person on the other end of the phone is describing a visual scene—say, the layout of a room full of furniture—that conversation can actually occupy your visual channel enough to impair your ability to see what's around you on the road.

The only time multitasking does work efficiently, Meyer says, is when multiple simple tasks operate on entirely separate channels—for example, folding laundry (a visual-manual task) while listening to a stock report (a verbal task). But real-world scenarios that fit those specifications are very rare.

This is troubling news, obviously, for a culture of Black-Berrys and news crawls and Firefox tabs—tools that, critics argue, force us all into a kind of elective ADHD. The tech theorist Linda Stone famously coined the phrase "continuous partial attention" to describe our newly frazzled state of mind. American office workers don't stick with any single task for more than a few minutes at a time; if left uninterrupted, they will most likely interrupt themselves. Since every interruption costs around 25 minutes of productivity, we spend nearly a third of our day recovering from them. We keep an average of eight windows open on our computer screens at one time and skip between them every twenty seconds. When we read online, we hardly even read at all—our eyes run down the page in an *F* pattern, scanning for keywords. When you add up all the leaks from these constant little switches, soon you're hemorrhaging a dangerous amount of mental power. People who frequently check their e-mail have tested as less intelligent than people who are actually high on marijuana. Meyer guesses that the damage will take decades to understand, let alone fix. If Einstein were alive today, he says, he'd probably be forced to multitask so relentlessly in the Swiss patent office that he'd never get a chance to work out the theory of relativity.

II. THE WAR ON THE POVERTY OF ATTENTION

For Winifred Gallagher, the author of *Rapt,* a new book about the power of attention, it all comes down to the problem of jackhammers. A few minutes before I called, she tells me, a construction crew started jackhammering outside her apartment window. The noise immediately captured what's called her bottom-up attention—the broad involuntary awareness that roams the world constantly looking for danger and rewards: shiny objects, sudden movements, pungent smells. Instead of letting this distract her, however, she made a conscious choice to go into the next room and summon her top-down attention—the narrow, voluntary focus that allows us to isolate and enhance some little slice of the world while ruthlessly suppressing everything else.

This attentional self-control, which psychologists call executive function, is at the very center of our struggle with attention. It's what allows us to invest our focus wisely or poorly. Some of us, of course, have an easier time with it than others.

Gallagher admits that she's been blessed with a naturally strong executive function. "It sounds funny," she tells me, "but I've always thought of paying attention as a kind of sexy, visceral activity. Even as a kid, I enjoyed focusing. I could feel it in almost a mentally muscular way. I took a lot of pleasure in concentrating on things. I'm the sort of irritating person who can sit down to work at nine o'clock and look up at two o'clock and say, 'Oh, I thought it was around 10:30.'"

Gallagher became obsessed with the problem of attention five years ago, when she was diagnosed with advanced and aggressive breast cancer. She was devastated, naturally, but then realized, on her way out of the hospital, that even the cancer could be seen largely as a problem of focus—a terrifying, deadly, internal jackhammer. It made her realize, she says, that attention was "not just a latent ability, it was something you could marshal and use as a tool." By the time she reached her subway station, Gallagher had come up with a strategy: She would make all the big pressing cancer-related decisions as quickly as possible, then, in order to maximize whatever time she had left, consciously shift her attention to more positive, productive things.

One of the projects Gallagher worked on during her recovery (she is now cancer free) was *Rapt,* which is both a survey of recent attention research and a testimonial to the power of top-down focus. The ability to positively wield your attention comes off, in the book, as something of a panacea; Gallagher describes it as "the sine qua non of the quality of life and the key to improving virtually every aspect of your experience." It is, in other words, the Holy Grail of self-help: the key to relationships and parenting and mood disorders and weight problems. (You can apparently lose seven pounds in a year through the sheer force of paying attention to your food.)

"You can't be happy all the time," Gallagher tells me, "but you can pretty much focus all the time. That's about as good as it gets."

The most promising solution to our attention problem, in Gallagher's mind, is also the most ancient: meditation. Neuroscientists have become obsessed, in recent years, with Buddhists, whose attentional discipline can apparently confer all kinds of benefits even on non-Buddhists. (Some psychologists predict that, in the same way we go out for a jog now, in the future we'll all do daily 20-to-30-minute "secular attentional workouts.") Meditation can make your attention less "sticky," able to notice images flashing by in such quick succession that regular brains would miss them. It has also been shown to elevate your mood, which can then recursively stoke your attention: Research shows that positive emotions cause your visual field to expand. The brains of Buddhist monks asked to meditate on "unconditional loving-kindness and compassion" show instant and remarkable changes: Their left prefrontal cortices (responsible for positive emotions) go into overdrive, they produce gamma waves 30 times more powerful than novice meditators, and their wave activity is coordinated in a way often seen in patients under anesthesia.

Gallagher stresses that because attention is a limited resource—one psychologist has calculated that we can attend to only 110 bits of information per second, or 173 billion bits in an average lifetime—our moment-by-moment choice of attentional targets determines, in a very real sense, the shape of our lives. *Rapt*'s epigraph comes from the psychologist and philosopher William James: "My experience is what I agree to attend to." For Gallagher, everything comes down to that one big choice: investing your attention wisely or not. The jackhammers are everywhere—iPhones, e-mail, cancer—and Western culture's attentional crisis is mainly a widespread failure to ignore them.

"Once you understand how attention works and how you can make the most productive use of it," she says, "if you continue to just jump in the air every time your phone rings or pounce on those buttons every time you get an instant message, that's not the machine's fault. That's your fault."

Making the responsible attention choice, however, is not always easy. Here is a partial list, because a complete one would fill the entire magazine, of the things I've been distracted by in the course of writing this article: my texting wife, a very loud seagull, my mother calling from Mexico to leave voice mails in terrible Spanish, a man shouting "Your weed-whacker fell off! Your weed-whacker fell off!" at a truck full of lawn equipment, my *Lost*-watching wife, another man singing some kind of Spanish ballad on the sidewalk under my window, streaming video of the NBA playoffs, dissertation-length blog breakdowns of the NBA playoffs, my toenail spontaneously detaching, my ice-cream-eating wife, the subtly shifting landscapes of my three different e-mail in-boxes, my Facebooking wife, infinite YouTube videos (a puffin attacking someone wearing a rubber boot, Paul McCartney talking about the death of John Lennon, a chimpanzee playing Pac-Man), and even more infinite, if that is possible, Wikipedia entries: puffins, *MacGyver*, Taylorism, the phrase "bleeding edge," the Boston Molasses Disaster. (If I were going to excuse you from reading this article for any single distraction, which I am not, it would be to read about the Boston Molasses Disaster.)

When the jackhammers fire up outside my window, in other words, I rarely ignore them—I throw the window open, watch for a while, bring the crew sandwiches on their lunch break, talk with them about the ins and outs of jackhammering, and then spend an hour or two trying to break up a little of the sidewalk myself. Some of my distractions were unavoidable. Some were necessary work-related evils that got out of hand. Others were pretty clearly inexcusable. (I consider it a victory for the integrity of pre-web human consciousness that I was able to successfully resist clicking on the first "related video" after the chimp, the evocatively titled "Guy shits himself in a judo exhibition.") In today's attentional landscape, it's hard to draw neat borders.

I'm not ready to blame my restless attention entirely on a faulty willpower. Some of it is pure impersonal behaviorism. The Internet is basically a Skinner box engineered to tap right into our deepest mechanisms of addiction. As B. F. Skinner's army of lever-pressing rats and pigeons taught us, the most irresistible reward schedule is not, counterintuitively, the one in which we're rewarded constantly but something called "variable ratio schedule," in which the rewards arrive at random. And that randomness is practically the Internet's defining feature: It dispenses its never-ending little shots of positivity—a life-changing e-mail here, a funny YouTube video there—in gloriously unpredictable cycles. It seems unrealistic to expect people to spend all day clicking reward bars—searching the web, scanning the relevant blogs, checking e-mail to see if a co-worker has updated a project—and then just leave those distractions behind, as soon as they're not strictly required, to engage in "healthy" things like books and ab crunches and undistracted deep conversations with neighbors. It would be like requiring employees to take a few hits of opium throughout the day, then being surprised when it becomes a problem. Last year, an editorial in the *American Journal of Psychiatry* raised the prospect of adding "Internet addiction" to the *DSM,* which would make it a disorder to be taken as seriously as schizophrenia.

A quintessentially Western solution to the attention problem—one that neatly circumvents the issue of willpower—is to simply dope our brains into focus. We've done so, over the centuries, with substances ranging from tea to tobacco to NoDoz to Benzedrine, and these days the tradition seems to be approaching some kind of zenith with the rise of neuro-enhancers: drugs designed to treat ADHD (Ritalin, Adderall), Alzheimer's (Aricept), and narcolepsy (Provigil) that can produce, in healthy people, superhuman states of attention. A grad-school friend tells me that Adderall allowed him to squeeze his mind "like a muscle." Joshua Foer, writing in *Slate* after a weeklong experiment with Adderall, said the drug made him feel like he'd "been bitten by a radioactive spider" —he beat his unbeatable brother at Ping-Pong, solved anagrams, devoured dense books. "The part of my brain that makes me curious about whether I have new e-mails in my in-box apparently shut down," he wrote.

Although neuroenhancers are currently illegal to use without a prescription, they're popular among college students (on some campuses, up to 25 percent of students admitted to taking them) and—if endless anecdotes can be believed— among a wide spectrum of other professional focusers: journalists on deadline, doctors performing high-stakes surgeries, competitors in poker tournaments, researchers suffering through the grind of grant-writing. There has been controversy in the chess world recently about drug testing at tournaments.

In December, a group of scientists published a paper in *Nature* that argued for the legalization and mainstream acceptance of neuroenhancers, suggesting that the drugs are really no different from more traditional "cognitive enhancers" such as laptops, exercise, nutrition, private tutoring, reading, and sleep. It's not quite that simple, of course. Adderall users frequently complain that the drug stifles their creativity—that it's best for doing ultrarational, structured tasks. (As Foer put it, "I had a nagging suspicion that I was thinking with blinders on.") One risk the scientists do acknowledge is the fascinating, horrifying prospect of "raising cognitive abilities beyond their species-typical upper bound." Ultimately, one might argue, neuroenhancers spring from the same source as the problem they're designed to correct: our lust for achievement in defiance of natural constraints. It's easy to imagine an endless attentional arms race in which new technologies colonize ever-bigger zones of our attention, new drugs expand the limits of that attention, and so on.

One of the most exciting—and confounding—solutions to the problem of attention lies right at the intersection of our willpower and our willpower-sapping technologies: the grassroots Internet movement known as "lifehacking." It began in 2003 when the British tech writer Danny O'Brien, frustrated by his own lack of focus, polled 70 of his most productive friends to see how they managed to get so much done; he found that they'd invented all kinds of clever little tricks— some high-tech, some very low-tech—to help shepherd their attention from moment to moment: ingenious script codes for to-do lists, software hacks for managing e-mail, rituals to avoid sinister time-wasting traps such as "yak shaving," the tendency to lose yourself in endless trivial tasks tangentially related to the one you really need to do. (O'Brien wrote a program that prompts him every ten minutes, when he's online, to ask if he's procrastinating.) Since then, lifehacking has snowballed into a massive self-help program, written and revised constantly by the online global hive mind, that seeks to help you allocate your attention efficiently. Tips range from time-management habits (the 90-second shower) to note-taking techniques (mind mapping) to software shortcuts (how to turn your Gmail into a to-do list) to delightfully retro tech solutions (turning an index card into a portable dry-erase board by covering it with packing tape).

When I call Merlin Mann, one of lifehacking's early adopters and breakout stars, he is running late, rushing back to his office, and yet he seems somehow to have attention to spare. He is by far the fastest-talking human I've ever interviewed, and it crosses my mind that this too might be a question of productivity—that maybe he's adopted a time-saving verbal lifehack from auctioneers. He talks in the snappy aphorisms of a professional speaker ("Priorities are like arms: If you have more than two of them, they're probably make-believe") and is always breaking ideas down into their atomic parts and reassessing the way they fit together: "What does it come down to?" "Here's the thing." "So why am I telling you this, and what does it have to do with lifehacks?"

Mann says he got into lifehacking at a moment of crisis, when he was "feeling really overwhelmed by the number of inputs in my life and managing it very badly." He founded one of the original lifehacking websites, 43folders.com (the name is a reference to David Allen's Getting Things Done, the legendarily complex productivity program in which Allen describes, among other things, how to build a kind of "three-dimensional calendar" out of 43 folders) and went on to invent such illustrious hacks as "in-box zero" (an e-mail-management technique) and the "hipster PDA" (a stack of three-by-five cards filled with jotted phone numbers and to-do lists, clipped together and tucked into your back pocket). Mann now makes a living speaking to companies as a kind of productivity guru. He Twitters, podcasts, and runs more than half a dozen websites.

Despite his robust web presence, Mann is skeptical about technology's impact on our lives. "Is it clear to you that the last fifteen years represent an enormous improvement in how everything operates?" he asks. "Picasso was somehow able to finish the *Demoiselles of Avignon* even though he didn't have an application that let him tag his to-dos. If John Lennon had a BlackBerry, do you think he would have done everything he did with the Beatles in less than ten years?"

One of the weaknesses of lifehacking as a weapon in the war against distraction, Mann admits, is that it tends to become extremely distracting. You can spend solid days reading reviews of filing techniques and organizational software. "On the web, there's a certain kind of encouragement to never ask yourself how much information you really need," he says. "But when I get to the point where I'm seeking advice twelve hours a day on how to take a nap, or what kind of notebook to buy, I'm so far off the idea of lifehacks that it's indistinguishable from where we started. There are a lot of people out there that find this a very sticky idea, and there's very little advice right now to tell them that the only thing to do is action, and everything else is horseshit. My wife reminds me sometimes: 'You have all the information you need to do *something* right now.'"

For Mann, many of our attention problems are symptoms of larger existential issues: motivation, happiness, neurochemistry. "I'm not a physician or a psychiatrist, but I'll tell you, I think a lot of it is some form of untreated ADHD or depression," he says. "Your mind is not getting the dopamine or the hugs that it needs to keep you focused on what you're doing. And any time your work gets a little bit too hard or a little bit too boring, you allow it to catch on to something that's more interesting to you." (Mann himself started getting treated for ADD a year ago; he says it's helped his focus quite a lot.)

Mann's advice can shade, occasionally, into Buddhist territory. "There's no shell script, there's no fancy pen, there's no notebook or nap or Firefox extension or hack that's gonna help you figure out why the fuck you're here," he tells me. "That's on you. This makes me sound like one of those people who swindled the Beatles, but if you are having attention problems, the best way to deal with it is by admitting it and then saying, 'From now on, I'm gonna be in the moment and more cognizant.' I said not long ago, I think on Twitter— God, I quote myself a lot, what an asshole—that really all self-help is Buddhism with a service mark.

"Where you allow your attention to go ultimately says more about you as a human being than anything that you put in your mission statement," he continues. "It's an indisputable receipt for your existence. And if you allow that to be squandered by other people who are as bored as you are, it's gonna say a lot about who you are as a person."

III. EMBRACING THE POVERTY OF ATTENTION

Sometimes I wonder if the time I'm wasting is actually being wasted. Isn't blowing a couple of hours on the Internet, in the end, just another way of following your attention? My life would be immeasurably poorer if I hadn't stumbled a few weeks ago across the Boston Molasses Disaster. (Okay, seriously, forget it: I hereby release you to go look up the Boston Molasses Disaster. A giant wave of molasses destroyed an entire Boston neighborhood 90 years ago, swallowing horses and throwing an elevated train off its track. It took months to scrub all the molasses out of the cobblestones! The harbor was brown until summer! The world is a stranger place than we will ever know.)

The prophets of total attentional meltdown sometimes invoke, as an example of the great culture we're going to lose as we succumb to e-thinking, the canonical French juggernaut Marcel Proust. And indeed, at seven volumes, several thousand pages, and 1.5 million words, *À la Recherche du Temps Perdu* is in many ways the anti-Twitter. (It would take, by the way, exactly 68,636 tweets to reproduce.) It's important to remember, however, that the most famous moment in all of Proust, the moment that launches the entire monumental project, is a moment of pure distraction: when the narrator, Marcel, eats a spoonful of tea-soaked madeleine and finds himself instantly transported back to the world of his childhood. Proust makes it clear that conscious focus could never have yielded such profound magic: Marcel has to abandon the constraints of what he calls "voluntary memory"—the kind of narrow, purpose-driven attention that Adderall, say, might have allowed him to harness—in order to get to the deeper truths available only by distraction. That famous cookie is a kind of hyperlink: a little blip that launches an associative cascade of a million other subjects. This sort of free-associative wandering is essential to the creative process; one moment of judicious unmindfulness can inspire thousands of hours of mindfulness.

My favorite focusing exercise comes from William James: Draw a dot on a piece of paper, then pay attention to it for as long as you can. (Sitting in my office one afternoon, with my monkey mind swinging busily across the lush rain forest of online distractions, I tried this with the closest dot in the vicinity: the bright-red mouse-nipple at the center of my laptop's keyboard. I managed to stare at it for 30 minutes, with mixed results.) James argued that the human mind can't actually focus on the dot, or any unchanging object, for more than a few seconds at a time: It's too hungry for variety, surprise, the adventure of the unknown. It has to refresh its attention by continually finding new aspects of the dot to focus on: subtleties of its shape, its relationship to the edges of the paper, metaphorical associations (a fly, an eye, a hole). The exercise becomes a question less of pure unwavering focus than of your ability to organize distractions around a central point. The dot, in other words, becomes only the hub of your total dot-related distraction.

This is what the web-threatened punditry often fails to recognize: Focus is a paradox—it has distraction built into it. The two are symbiotic; they're the systole and diastole of consciousness. Attention comes from the Latin "to stretch out" or "reach toward," distraction from "to pull apart." We need both. In their extreme forms, focus and attention may even circle back around and bleed into one other. Meyer says there's a subset of Buddhists who believe that the most advanced monks become essentially "world-class multitaskers"—that all those years of meditation might actually speed up their mental processes enough to handle the kind of information overload the rest of us find crippling.

The truly wise mind will harness, rather than abandon, the power of distraction. Unwavering focus—the inability to be distracted—can actually be just as problematic as ADHD. Trouble with "attentional shift" is a feature common to a handful of mental illnesses, including schizophrenia and OCD. It's been hypothesized that ADHD might even be an advantage in certain change-rich environments. Researchers have discovered, for instance, that a brain receptor associated with ADHD is unusually common among certain nomads in Kenya, and that members who have the receptor are the best nourished in the group. It's possible that we're all evolving toward a new techno-cognitive nomadism, a rapidly shifting environment in which restlessness will be an advantage again.

The deep focusers might even be hampered by having too much attention: Attention Surfeit Hypoactivity Disorder.

I keep returning to the parable of Einstein and Lennon— the great historical geniuses hypothetically ruined by modern distraction. What made both men's achievements so ground-breaking, though, was that they did something modern technology is getting increasingly better at allowing us to do: They very powerfully linked and synthesized things that had previously been unlinked—Newtonian gravity and particle physics, rock and blues and folk and doo-wop and bubblegum pop and psychedelia. If Einstein and Lennon were growing up today, their natural genius might be so pumped up on the possibilities of the new technology they'd be doing even more dazzling things. Surely Lennon would find a way to manipulate his BlackBerry to his own ends, just like he did with all the new technology of the sixties—he'd harvest spam and text messages and web snippets and build them into a new kind of absurd poetry. The Beatles would make the best viral videos of all time, simultaneously addictive and artful, disposable and forever. All of those canonical songs, let's remember, were created entirely within a newfangled mass genre that was widely considered to be an assault on civilization and the sanctity of deep human thought. Standards change. They change because of great creations in formerly suspect media.

Which brings me, finally, to the next generation of attenders, the so-called "net-gen" or "digital natives," kids who've grown up with the Internet and other time-slicing technologies. There's been lots of hand-wringing about all the skills they might lack, mainly the ability to concentrate on a complex task from beginning to end, but surely they can already do things their elders can't—like conduct 34 conversations simultaneously across six different media, or pay attention to switching between attentional targets in a way that's been considered impossible. More than any other organ, the brain is designed to change based on experience, a feature called neuroplasticity. London taxi drivers, for instance, have enlarged hippocampi (the brain region for memory and spatial processing)—a neural reward for paying attention to the tangle of the city's streets. As we become more skilled at the 21st-century task Meyer calls "flitting," the wiring of the brain will inevitably change to deal more efficiently with more information. The neuroscientist Gary Small speculates that the human brain might be changing faster today than it has since the prehistoric discovery of tools. Research suggests we're already picking up new skills: better peripheral vision, the ability to sift information rapidly. We recently elected the first-ever BlackBerry president, able to flit between sixteen national crises while focusing at a world-class level. Kids growing up now might have an associative genius we don't—a sense of the way ten projects all dovetail into something totally new. They might be able to engage in seeming contradictions: mindful web-surfing, mindful Twittering. Maybe, in flights of irresponsible responsibility, they'll even manage to attain the paradoxical, Zenlike state of focused distraction.

Mark Bowden

A Crime of Shadows

*After months of prowling Internet chat rooms, pos-
ing as the mother of two young daughters, Detective Michele Deery thought she had a live one:
"parafling," a married, middle-aged man who
claimed he wanted to have sex with her kids. But
was he just playing a twisted game of seduction?
Both the policewoman and her target give the
author their versions of the truth, in a case that
challenges the conventional wisdom about online
sexual predators, and blurs the lines among crime,
"intent," and enticement.*

Detective Michele Deery works in a cubicle in the basement
of the Delaware County courthouse, in Media, Pennsylvania.
The only window is high on the wall, over a tall filing cabinet,
and opens into a well, below ground level. The space feels like
a cave, which has always struck Deery as about right, because
her job is to talk dirty online to strange men.

Deery seems altogether too wholesome for the work. She
has athletic good looks, with tawny skin, big brown eyes, and
long straight brown hair that falls over her shoulders. Her parents sent her to Catholic schools, and her mother, a retired district judge, now jokes that she wants her money back. Her

daughter's beat is in the vilest corners of cyberspace, in chat rooms indicating "fetish" or various subgenres of flagrant peccancy. One of the many false identities Deery has assumed online is something truly rare, even in this polluted pond—that of a middle-aged mother of two pre-pubescent girls who is offering them up for sex. Baiting her hook with this forbidden fruit, she would cast the line and wait to see who bit.

It usually didn't take long. Men began vying for her attention the minute she logged on, night or day. Deery would begin a dialogue, dangling the illicit possibility, gauging how serious her mark was. There were "players," those who were just horny and despicable, and there were doers, or at least potential doers, the true bad guys. The goal was to identify the latter, hook them, and then reel them in, turn them into "travelers." Once a traveler took that all-important step out of fantasy and into the real world, his behavior went from the merely immoral to the overtly criminal. When they delivered themselves for the promised rendezvous, instead of meeting a mother and her young daughters they would find a team of well-armed, cheerfully disgusted Delaware County police officers. As a fantasy, her come-on seemed overbaked—not one daughter, but two! It is doubtful that such a woman exists anywhere, and yet men fell for it. Her unit had a near-100-percent conviction rate. The bulletin board over her desk displays mug shots of her catches, very ordinary-looking men, facing the camera wide-eyed with shock, staring at the fresh ruin of their lives.

Which leads to the case presented here. One of the stunned faces in that array belongs to a man I will call "J," who would spend a year in prison after taking Deery's bait. For this account, both Deery and J were willing to speak openly and at length; transcripts of online chats and police interrogations have also been made available. The story reflects what they said about themselves and their actions, and presents two very different points of view.

Shortly before six o'clock on the evening of Monday, September 19, 2005, Deery went to work in her cave, logging on to Yahoo and expertly navigating its public chat rooms. In one of the many rooms labeled "fetish," she logged on with the suggestive screen name "heatherscutiepies." At this time of day the weirdos were coming home from work, bellying up to their home computers.

She received three quick instant messages from someone using the name "parafling":

—hello
—may I ask what your into or looking for
—NOTHIG is taboo to me

Parafling had the detective's interest. She typed an answer:

—well why don't u tell me wht ur into

A MURKY REALM

Entrapment has long been a factor in the enforcement of vice laws, which seek to punish behavior that is furtive and widespread. Such ordinances answer society's quest for moral clarity, positing a direct parallel between right versus wrong and legal versus criminal. Police patrolling the precincts of sin do not often find the streets empty. How are they to tell the difference between the casual sinner and the criminal?

American courts have long recognized the right of police to invent ruses. Sting operations flourish in a climate of fear. Courts and lawmakers become less and less scrupulous about basic fairness. The more frightening and reprehensible the threat, the more license and latitude are given to the police.

For a variety of reasons, few of them valid, the child-molester has become the pre-eminent domestic villain of our time. Deery's work is part of a national effort. In 1998, in response to growing fears of sexual predation online, Congress provided funds for the Department of Justice to create the Internet Crimes Against Children (ICAC) task force, which among other things provides federal grants to local police departments for programs to find and apprehend online predators. In practice that means looking for people who potentially fit the mold—people who seem as if they might be poised to commit a crime even if they have not yet done so. This leads unavoidably into the gray area of thoughts, intentions, and predispositions—and into the equally murky realm of enticement and entrapment. It is a way of conducting police business that, without extreme care, can itself become a form of abuse—in which the pursuer and the pursued grow entangled in a transaction that takes on a gruesome life of its own. This is the terrain explored by Philip K. Dick in his classic short story "The Minority Report," and in the Steven Spielberg movie based on it, in which an official government department of "Precrime" identifies, charges, and jails people on the basis of anticipated actions.

As Jad, one of the policemen in the movie version, says, "We're more like clergy than cops."

POLITE NIBBLE

Bingo! A woman! The line popped up in a window at the top of J's screen as soon as he logged in to the chat room.

He had peeked into a number of active chats to see how many women were there, and logged on to the ones with a promising ratio. His screen name, parafling, was a nod to paraflying, the tiny parachute/tricycle flying machines he had once or twice enjoyed. It was the only really different, exciting thing about him. He imagined it was like a colorful lure on the surface of a pond.

He was excited to see on-screen that this woman, calling herself heatherscutiepies, lived in his state, Pennsylvania, and was 39 years old. He had immediately tapped her with three messages, and she had responded:

—well why don't u tell me wht ur into

The sun blazed in from the window to his back porch. J had about an hour before his wife would be home from work. She knew nothing of his cybersex life, or if she did, she ignored it. A burly, round-faced man of 42, with a thickly muscled neck and shoulders, thinning hair, and a goatee, he was seated before the computer in their living room in a small, two-story town house in suburban Philadelphia. J had just finished a long day repairing copy machines, driving from one job to the next. This was his time, a quiet interlude before his wife came in the door from her job at the local hospital. He would have to deal with her until about eight p.m., which is when she usually retired upstairs.

J didn't sleep much. The steroids he was injecting to help him bulk up made his heart race and filled him with explosive energy and lust. He felt like a walking hard-on. The Internet was his only outlet, and it had become a compulsion. He would open up three or four windows into sexually oriented chat rooms, looking for a woman to talk dirty to him. If he got lucky in one of these early-evening sessions, he would arrange to continue with her later that night after his wife went upstairs. Then they would play, cooking up together an erotic stew. He would enjoy an extended period of arousal and then masturbate. This was his routine. This was his sex life.

In the years he had been dipping into these chat rooms, he had learned a few things about the women who entered them. They were skittish. J was convinced that everyone, down deep, had twisted sexual desires, and he had reasons in his own life for believing this—his first sexual relationship, as a teenager, which had lasted five years, was with a slightly older girl who liked sadomasochistic play. In this sense, women were no different from men, except they were more reluctant to show themselves. The ones who entered the fetish rooms had desires that were very specific. Men were eager and up for whatever—that certainly defined J—but women were looking to scratch a particular itch. He knew that if he answered the query from heatherscutiepies wrongly, she would simply stop responding. Her question was a polite nibble. The response was critical. He had chatted about this online with other men, comparing notes on opening moves, and the safest approach seemed to be simply to announce that you were into "everything," right off the bat.

He typed:

—I am into bondage s/m breeding incest young rape spanking you name it

Nine seconds later came her response.

—cool.

Hooked! Then she asked another question:

—where in pa?
—west of philly , you
—oh no kiddin im in philly burbs.. just moved outside city not 2 long ago.

This carried a jolt of erotic possibility. J often had no idea where the person he chatted with was. Proximity spiced the game with a chance at something real. His chats had led only once before to a real encounter, three years earlier. Acting out the online scenario for real had felt awkward. He did as she asked, and they had sex, but he left knowing he would never do it again. Reality was stark and messy—it had texture and odor and harsh lighting. Acting out the roles felt phony and wrong. It lacked the purity of the idea. The episode had taught him to stay on his side of the line.

That was before he had started injecting steroids, however. Now the sheer weight of lust was straining him to his limits. One of his co-workers, a former Marine, had counseled him that women were drawn to thickly muscled men, so he had thrown himself headlong into bodybuilding—pumping iron, ingesting growth supplements, and ignoring even the modest dosage restraints urged by experienced gym rats. The results were striking and obvious: his neck, shoulders, and arms were bursting out of his shirts. But this had no effect whatever on women. It only redoubled his desire. The news that this woman was nearby—a real woman!—came with the exquisite thrill, all but forgotten, of potential.

Heatherscutiepies wrote him another message. Both used the slapdash vernacular of Internet chat, with its shorthand spelling, frequent abbreviation, and minimal punctuation, which often led to confusion. She explained why she had left Philadelphia for the suburbs.

—wage tax was kickin my ass

Then she added, sardonically, the online acronym for amusement:

—lol [laugh out loud]
—damn so very close.

She asked:

—ever try any of ur taboo's or just fantasy?
—yes I have had sex with cousin and about 10 years ago
    i did breed a married woman because hubby did not
    want too, so I did,lol nd never heard from hr after
    that

None of this was true. He had learned from earlier chats that if he said he had never tried a thing the woman would stop responding. It was best to claim to have done everything. Besides, making these things up came easily to him. In the years he had been chatting sexually online, J had learned to ease fluidly into a realm of complete make-believe. Already he had covered two of the categories of taboo he had listed at the outset, incest and "breeding"—having sex with a woman to get her pregnant. Neither had seemed to click. All he knew was her screen name, that she lived nearby, and that she was 39. If he was going to line up some serious sex talk with her later, he would need to quickly find what enticed her. Even in this shameless arena there was courtship. So he asked for some sexual direction, and then followed immediately with two more ordinary conversational queries, showing a willingness to talk about anything she wished.

—what are you into,,,,,,,,,,,,are you married,,,,kids???

She responded:

—no kiddin

This was meant as a humorous lament, but J took it as a question. He thought she was asking if he really wanted to know.

—yep no kiddng.
—im divorced 2 girls
—WOW age??
—im 39
—no sorry girls,lol
—8 11

J wrote three lines in rapid succession:

—I saw your age
—yummmmmmmmmmm—tell me what do you look like??

He followed this immediately with a request for a picture, and she responded:

—if I get 2 know u a little bettr ill send
—are you looking for a man to be daddy and take you and the girls???
—no just 4 sum fun
—ok can you just describe yourself then to me,and I respect that too
—dont want any permanent feature here
—cool

J was zeroing in. She had two little girls and her screen name was heatherscutiepies. The cutiepies were apparently her girls. If this was her turn-on, he was neither shocked nor repulsed. Years of immersion in chat rooms had inured him to strangeness. Words were J's game. Perverse ideas. He had never been aroused by images. He was not a porn addict. What gripped him was a woman limning her darkest dreams—for him.

This was the essence of his personal fetish, a woman baring all, not the private parts of her body but the private parts of her mind, her unique sexuality, her heart's most peculiar desire. It drove him wild. He was after heatherscutiepies' singular taboo. The key to her erotic zone, the thing J sought to provide in return, was complete acceptance. His chatting partner had to feel free to go anywhere with him. That was now his goal. To get her there without turning her off or scaring her away, he would become whatever heatherscutiepies wished. The idea was to turn her on. Then he could work gently toward some of the things that pleased *him*.

He typed two messages:

—would you like to be like side lovers doing you and the girls??
—maybe breeding you and the oldest or anything like that?

That clicked. He received four responses from heatherscutiepies in quick succession:

—yea
—no breedin as of now
—good god
—im strapped for money as it is

A PACKAGE DEAL?

Down in her cave, Deery decided that she had a live one. When they were finished chatting, she would type a request on the courthouse's internal network for a warrant to obtain his I.P. (Internet Protocol) address. Then she could get private information from his Internet provider.

He had mentioned "young" right off the bat. That was important. The rules against entrapment forbade her from suggesting the criminal act, but he had brought it up himself. Then he had asked about the "girls," her imaginary children. When she gave him their ages, he had replied, "yummmmmm-mmmmm."

Except, on closer examination, the import of that expression of appetite was less clear. Sometimes as two people typed out a conversation, with the slight delay that entailed, dialogue overlapped. When she told him she had two girls, he had initially asked, "WOW age??" She had immediately responded, "im 39," thinking he was asking about her. That line was typed at 5:57:07 p.m. Eight seconds later he corrected her, "no sorry girls,lol" and then typed two more messages in the next 11 seconds, "I saw your age," and "yummmmmmmmmmm." Between those responses, at 5:57:20, she had typed, "8 11." His comment "I saw your age" came one second after she had given the ages of her girls, so they had been typing those lines at virtually the same time, and parafling's "yummmmmmmmmmm" had come just five seconds later. Was he reacting to her, or to the ages of her girls? On the screen, and eventually on the printout, the sequence made it look as if he was reacting to the ages of the girls, when in fact it was hard to tell.

It became more clear 13 seconds later, when he asked what she looked like and for her picture. His focus seemed to be primarily on her. But then, when he asked if she wanted him to "take" her, he had included the girls. Was he asking if she wanted him to have sex with her and the girls, or was he asking if she was looking for a sugar daddy, someone to take care of her and the girls? The abbreviated, highly colloquial syntax left plenty of room for interpretation. The detective played it safe and assumed he had meant the latter. But then right away he had mentioned, on his own, "doing you and the girls." That was evidence. Parafling was soliciting sex with two minors.

J next sent her a description of himself, including the size of his penis—"7." (Why did they all exaggerate?, Deery wondered. It was so lame.) He pushed for more information— asking for her "measurements."

Deery typed that she did not know them.

To J, that seemed odd, but then, in this Internet space, who wasn't? She kept deflecting his interest in her. Was she just being coy, or was she really more into the idea of his having sex with her girls? He wrote:

—LOL so tell me if and when we meet when and how
   you would like this

Again she did not spell out exactly what she craved, so J continued to make conversation. He asked her about her two jobs—she had told him she cut hair at home and worked as a bartender at night—and then tried to reassure her that he was honest, candid, and serious. He explained his screen name, and then urged her to make clear if she was serious about wanting to meet with him in the real world:

—if you want cyber then say so, want real say so

He began to entertain for the first time in years the possibility of meeting a real woman and having real sex.

—I am looking for exaclty what you are offering, no strings noperment be there when ever you want I will please you and the girs

She wrote:

—u ever playd w yung?

This heather wanted him to talk about having sex with little girls. It could not be clearer that it was a package deal. She came with her cutiepies or not at all.

"PROSTITUTION" OF THE LAW

The first entrapment defense upheld by the U.S. Supreme Court was in 1932, during Prohibition, when the defendant, a paper-mill worker named Randall Sorrells, was convicted of selling whiskey during a social encounter at his home in Clyde, North Carolina. Sorrells had received several longtime friends who brought along a visitor from nearby Charlotte. The men were World War I veterans, and the newcomer, who was actually a Prohibition agent, had served in France in the same infantry division. Convivial conversation ensued, and at one point the agent asked his host if he could get him some whiskey. Sorrells told him that he "did not fool with whisky." The agent was persistent. Again he was rebuffed. After more talk, the agent appealed to Sorrells's old comradeship and again pleaded for help. Sorrells relented. He left the house and returned with a jug. When he handed it over and took the agent's five dollars, he was arrested.

Convicted at trial, Sorrells appealed, finally winning his case in the country's highest court. Writing for the other justices, Chief Justice Charles Evans Hughes called the methods used in his case a "prostitution of the criminal law." He noted that the crime for which Sorrells was prosecuted by the government was "the product of the creative activity of its own officials."

Since that ruling, the issue of entrapment has come before the Supreme Court several times, and arguments have traditionally turned on what has become known as the "subjective" and the "objective" tests. The subjective test for entrapment considered primarily the defendant's state of mind: was the subject inclined to commit the crime anyway? The objective test centered more on the action of the investigators: were their methods sufficient to induce an otherwise law-abiding citizen to commit a crime? If a defendant had a history to suggest he was predisposed to committing a crime, it was very hard to show that police efforts alone were responsible. Both rules left much room for interpretation, and neither was likely to help someone accused of a particularly repellent crime.

The most recent Supreme Court ruling on entrapment, in 1992, went a way toward knocking down the subjective test. In 1987, a Nebraska man named Keith Jacobson ordered a magazine called *Boys Who Love Boys,* which was described as a publication containing pictures of "11- and 14-year-old boys engaged in sexual activity." The magazine didn't exist: it was the invention of the U.S. Postal Service. Federal agents arrested Jacobson after he went to the post office to pick up his order.

His conviction was overturned by the Supreme Court. In the majority opinion, Justice Byron White wrote: "In their zeal to enforce the law . . . Government agents may not originate a criminal design, implant in an innocent person's mind the disposition to commit a criminal act, and then induce commission of the crime so that the Government may prosecute." The justices did not address either the subjective or objective tests directly, but they made it clear that predisposition alone did not mean guilt, particularly if the crime was suggested by police to begin with.

IMAGINARY NUMBERS

During the past 15 years, as the Internet has made inroads into every facet of modern life, the fear of online child predation has grown far out of proportion to the actual problem. The belief that sexual deviants by the tens of thousands are prowling the Internet in search of children to entice and corrupt, and that their ranks are increasing rapidly, has won broad popular acceptance. The most widely cited statistic is "one in five," as in the number of children who have supposedly been approached by a sexual predator on the Internet. The origin of this figure is the Department of Justice's National Center for Missing & Exploited Children, which first reported it in 2001. Five years later the center amended the result to one in seven, but by either measure the figure suggests nothing less than an epidemic.

Until you look closer. The actual question posed in the department's "Youth Internet Safety" survey asked teenagers under 17 if they had received an "unwanted sexual solicitation," which was defined as follows: "a request to engage in sexual activities or sexual talk or give personal sexual information that was unwanted or, whether wanted or not, made by an adult." Since "adult" in this case was defined as anyone 17 or older, the definition included many would-be high-school Romeos, predators of a highly conventional and not particularly dangerous sort, and also took in a strain of intimate gossip familiar to all teenage girls. As the study's authors themselves noted, half the solicitations came from other teenagers. Not a single solicitation led to actual sexual contact. Violent sexual predators hunting children are out there, as they have always been, yet they remain blessedly rare, and most young people flee such strangeness instinctively. Only 3 percent of the contacts reported in the survey resembled the one most feared by parents, the adult stranger attempting to seduce a child.

Benjamin Radford, the managing editor of *Skeptical Inquirer* magazine, has noted instance after instance of the "one in five" figure and other kinds of misinformation on network broadcasts. On April 18, 2005, CBS reporter Jim Acosta declared on the evening news, "When a child is missing, chances are good it was a convicted sex offender." Radford responds, "Acosta is incorrect: if a child goes missing, a convicted sex offender is actually among the *least* likely explanations, far behind runaways, family abductions, and the child being lost or injured."

Yet NBC reporter Chris Hansen has warned Americans that "the scope of the problem is immense" and "growing." For several years Hansen hosted a popular series called "To Catch a Predator" on *Dateline NBC*. The show turned the moment of an alleged predator's confrontation and arrest into lurid home entertainment. In the opening episodes he reported that there were "50,000" sexual predators preying on children through the Internet at any given moment. There was no good basis for the "50,000" figure, and Hansen eventually stopped citing it. His source turned out to be an F.B.I. agent named Ken Lanning, who told NPR's Brooke Gladstone that he didn't really know where the number came from but that it was familiar to him from another context. "In the early 1980s," he explained, chuckling, "this was the number that was most often used to estimate how many children were kidnapped or abducted by strangers every year. But the research that was done in the early 1990s found that somewhere in the neighborhood of two to three hundred children every year were abducted in this manner." Lanning called 50,000 "a Goldilocks number." "It wasn't a real small number—it wasn't like 100, 200—and it wasn't a ridiculously large number, like 10 million. . . . [It was] not too hot, not too cold."

Like other popular delusions, fear of the Internet child-molester contains a trace of logic. It is reasonable to ask if the explosion of Internet pornography, including child pornography, might lead more troubled souls down a path to criminal depravity. But the Internet has been with us since the mid-1990s. If it were going to cause a sudden increase in molestation, wouldn't we have seen it by now? In fact, the trend lines go the opposite way. For instance, sexual assaults on teens fell dramatically—by 52 percent—between 1993 and 2005, according to the Justice Department's National Crime Victimization Survey.

Despite numbers like these, people are ready to believe there is an epidemic because they are repulsed by child pornography and assume that anyone who would look at it or think about it is not just perverted but dangerous. Those who take pictures of children engaged in sex acts and distribute them are criminals, and their actions have real victims. They are the most appropriate targets for law enforcement. There is no evidence that their sordid practices have bred an army of Internet predators.

GRAPHIC SCENARIOS

Heather had asked J a question:

—u ever playd w yung?

J was ready to play that game with her, to engage her fantasy in order to set her up for what *he* wanted: a chance to meet and have sex with her alone. To make that happen, he would become the perfect answer to her dark wish. So he lied to her. He told her he had once licked the vagina of a nine-year-old girl. She responded:

—k

After reassuring her on that count, J immediately came back with the scenario he preferred.

—I am looking to have you first then you and the girls or any way you feel comfortable. We would go as far as you want on any level
—so ur not new 2 this
—been 10 years or more but i will get back in the groove, lol
—lol

She asked about his marriage, and J told her, "she is into NOTHING at all I mean NOTHING. she knows nothing about me like this."
He wrote:

—so all we do willbe between you and I baby
—cool w me
—OH I will get out I drive all day long I could meet you during the day too even if girls were not there
—they get hm by 3 school is rite dwn the street

J saw the pattern. Every time he mentioned having sex with her alone, she would bring back the girls—"they get hm by 3." He could work with that:

—then at evening or weekend can please you and girls, shades drawn . . . could do you in AM then back for them, lol I can be flexaable darling
—ur pretty creative

If he could get her alone, they could play and he would be long gone by the time she came home with the girls. That could work. Real sex! He was tremendously excited by the idea.

—I have thought about this for so long baby
—yea its been a while for them

"Them." O.K., he thought, I get it. At this point J plunged in, inventing a sexual encounter with her and the girls, giving heather exactly what he thought she was after. The details are graphic and sickening, and cannot be printed. This kind of sex talk was not completely new to him. He had engaged other women online within the last few weeks with highly descriptive talk about sex with their children. So he asked specific questions about how physically able the girls were to have sex, and then slid back onto his own erotic turf, asking her if she liked to be tied up or to have clamps applied to her nipples. She wrote three successive lines:

—not so much no
—depends i guess
—how did u get into yung? u grow up in it too?

Back to the girls. Clearly this was a fixation with her. This was the itch she wanted scratched, no doubt about it. J ran with it. In his fantasies, there were no boundaries he was unwilling to cross. He would play her game because the prospect of meeting her in real life and having real sex had suddenly become the compelling drive of his life. He conjured an especially lurid scenario that involved his deflowering a child. She responded:

—nice
—I know you cannot but I love the idea of breeding a
    mom, and in time doing my own daugter with you
—u seem like a for real dude

J set about trying again to arrange a rendezvous with her alone, suggesting mornings, when the girls were in school. She balked. She reminded him they did not get off school until three o'clock, writing:

—IM SO not a am person lol. im a night owl

J pushed:

—maybe you will want your lover to yourself some times, lol

She brushed aside the idea:

—lol

When he persisted with the idea of a morning romp, just the two of them, she grew adamant:

—im NOT A MORNING PERSON DEAR not my thing

And J backed off:

—ok as you wish

She asked him again to describe what he wanted, and he unfolded a scene where he would watch the three of them, mother and children, playing sexually with one another.

—so ur more into watchin?

Uh-oh. He could lose her with this.

—NO want to see that and as you all are doing things i wil be doing things too but love to see that
—ok

He heard his wife opening the front door, and quickly shut down the computer. He didn't have time to sign off. Four times later that night he wrote lines to heather, whenever he would see her name on the list of active participants on his screen. He apologized for signing off without saying goodbye, explained, and reiterated his interest. At 10:36 that night he wrote a "HI baby," but there was no response. He tried once more at 1:01 a.m. with a hopeful, "HI baby hope we can talk agin::"

No answer.

HIS EYES, HER EYES

The Justice Department program that supports Michele Deery's work consists today of 59 investigative units throughout the country. Last year alone they arrested more than 3,100 people like those on Deery's bulletin board. The Web site for Deery's unit carries a curiously worded warning that is actually a tacit admission that there is no evidence for its claim. It says that the problem of online child predation "is growing so exponentially as to be impossible to track."

In a 2006 speech at the National Center for Missing and Exploited Children, then attorney general Alberto Gonzales managed to strike both of this hysteria's most notorious false notes, citing the "one-in-five" ratio and the "Goldilocks number" 50,000. He concluded, "It is simply astonishing how many predators there are, and how aggressive they act."

Yet the more numerous aggressors may be the police. Three researchers at the University of New Hampshire reported earlier this year that during the period between 2000 and 2006, when Internet use by juveniles grew between 73 and 93 percent, the number of people arrested for soliciting sex online from them grew only 21 percent, from 508 to 615. The number of people arrested for soliciting sex from undercover police like Deery, however, rose 381 percent during the same period. In other words, alleged child-molesters like J are many, many times more likely to be locked up for approaching detectives than children. And despite this full-court press on Internet child predation, those arrested for it represent only 1 percent of all arrests for sex crimes against children and adolescents.

Some of those 3,100 people are genuine predators. But others are just troubled men with poor judgment and over-sexed imaginations. A lawyer defending an accused predator is understandably hesitant to try an entrapment defense. Judges and juries have little sympathy for anyone who would entertain sex with a child, even as a fantasy, and detectives such as Deery are well schooled in the rules. After only his first conversation, J's legal case for entrapment was weak. In his opening line he listed "young" among his other sexual interests without any prompting. All Deery had asked was "why don't u tell me wht ur into?" And if you read this initial conversation looking for evidence of predisposition, it was there aplenty. It would take a careful parsing of the dialogue, and a subtle understanding of the context, to conclude anything other than J's guilt.

In real life, however, the detective and the copy-machine repairman were coming from entirely different places.

As J tells it, theirs was a no-holds-barred erotic negotiation, something that had started as a game but that rapidly evolved into the possibility of a real-world assignation. J had read heather quickly and correctly: she was primarily interested in arranging for him to have sex with her girls. He wanted the sex with her, not with the daughters, but picked up quickly that the former could not be had without promises of the latter. So he was prepared to pledge the one thing in order to get the other.

As Deery saw it, there were people who preyed sexually on children, and people who did not. It was her job to help protect children from the former. To find those people, she had to visit some very ugly virtual places, adopt some awful personas, and engage in highly distasteful conversations. The bad guys revealed themselves to her in her disguise. All she did was create an opportunity. She had not suggested having sex with her "daughters"—J had. His graphic scenarios were disgusting and damning, and sounded like the comments of someone intimately familiar with child rape. They had spilled out after only general prompting, such as "is there something u want to try that u haven't?" From her perspective, this parafling asshole could be a dangerous predator. His insistence on meeting her alone before being introduced to the girls was, she believed, a ploy. Sexual predators had become more and more wary. They had seen the TV shows and knew all about police methods. He wanted to see her alone to make sure she wasn't a cop before proceeding further.

The challenge would now be to get him to act on his stated desires—to lure him into the open.

NEGOTIATIONS

J's plaintive "HI baby hope we can talk agin::," entered just after one in the morning, hung there on the screen until he gave up and finally went to bed. He found her reassuring answer in the morning.

—no biggie.. just lemme know when ur around

J pounced on the response immediately, in a froth of desire.

—I want you so fucking badly PLEASE hold

His wife was on her way out the door. J left the screen for a few minutes and then came raging back with a graphic description of the various sexual acts he would like to perform with heather alone. Her response was skeptical:

—o?

J regrouped:

> —you dont want that darling BUT you know what I
> really want?????
> —what?
> —to please you and please your daughters

He offered to come by and see her that day, and launched again into a litany of sexual acts he was eager to perform with her. He suggested that when they had finished she might show him pictures of her daughters. This prompted a complaint:

> —ur flip floppin its confusing me . . . i mean it just
> seems like ur more into me then all of us..thats all

There it was, the deal again. J backtracked fast.

> —NO NO,,,,,,, want to please you first and get the ball
> rolling that is all it will be hard to be with you and
> them all, for the first time that is all i am saying
> would like to have you first then i will have the girls
> over and over YUMMMMMMMMMMMMM

And so the negotiation proceeded for the next month. She would back off whenever he talked about having sex with her alone, so he would indulge her, conjure up more graphic scenes of sex with her and the girls, but always he would return to his preferred plan for their real-world rendezvous. And consistently she would steer him right back to the daughters.

> —what should i tell the girls is what i really wanna
> know?

When he persisted in asking her to describe herself, she complained:

> —your annoying me now

After weeks of this, down in her basement cubicle at the court-house, Deery was at an impasse. It wouldn't do to arrange a meeting with parafling without her "girls." There was no crime in arranging a kinky sex session with an adult woman. The meeting had to be on his terms, and if what he wanted was just to have sex with her, all he had to do was admit it and she would drop her investigation. She kept offering him the door out.

> —ok i understand i think .. whatever u want .. its up to you
> —well I would LIKE to meet you make love to you, then return to take your girls, with you there. like the senerio we spoke about,,,,, that is what I would like,,,,, just need you to be ok with that
> —ill think about it .. that just seems kinda weird to me ill let u know . . . just seems odd to me that you woudl want to come here to do me .. then come back to do them .. seems shady

She had put her finger precisely on J's game. He intended to show up, have sex with Heather, and then split, but if she thought that, his opportunity would disappear. He poured cold water all over that suggestion:

> —shady?? really,,, WOW well it is NOT NOT at all,,, just a comfort level thing NOTHING shady at all
> ,,,,,,,,,

Heather drifted away. The next day she gave him a series of one-word responses. Then she was gone for days. On Wednesday of the following week they again began trying to work out a rendezvous, and again got hung up over his desire to meet with her alone. She complained:

—u say ur not really just into me, but it is still odd to
me that you just wanna meet ME..
—ok allow me to explain, ok,,,, as i told you before it
was only a comfort level,,,,, all 3 hot woman all new,
might me overwhelming and way HOT, lol so I only
SUGGESTED< to meet you first for a comfort level
thing,,,,,,,,,,,

Whenever he went back to talking about sex with her daughters, heather would warm to the dialogue. After outlining one
such imaginary encounter, he asked her:

—and you will like that too???, me playing with you
and them???

Heather wrote:

—when they r happy i am too that's why i said it
seemed lk u were into me n not them.. if that's the
case thats cool.. just say that no biggie
—NO into ALL want ALL
—k
—but if I can meet and play sometimes when the goirls
are NOT home, we can still play right, I want all
when ever I can, you, you and the girl, just the girls,
what ever
—ok thats fair

They made plans to meet the next day, and then J
launched into another explicit fantasy of how sex between her
and the girls together would go. Heather encouraged him to
continue, interjecting:

—I like how creative u r

and

—tell me

and, referring to an explicitly described sex act with her 11-year-old,

>—she will like that

and

>—then what

Except that, revealingly, she noticed that the fantasy he was spinning did not include him. He was the watcher, as she played sexually with the girls. She complained:

>—here is a tidbit of info . . . i can do all that w out you
>here . . . so clearly you are more into me then all of us
>whch is fine but u should be upfront about that from
>the get go

J tried to recover, but she retreated, complaining:

>—just sounds kinda off to me i gotta go .. tt u later

She was gone.

ARRANGING A RENDEZVOUS

Through October, heather would disappear for days at a time, then emerge just for a perfunctory exchange, and disappear again. For J, the breakthrough came on Monday afternoon, October 24, when for the first time she agreed to his scenario of meeting her alone for sex first. His proposal had not changed:

>—I was just thinking maybe you and I could meet ear-
>lier,,,,, play, I will wait in your bed as you leave and
>get the girl and then send in the oldest, when i will be
>in bed naked you close the door wait outside with
>youngest
>—thats cool

After more detailing of the various sexual acts planned with both her and the girls, again rendered in explicit detail, J reiterated:

> — . . . so we will play fast then if i get there at 2 since you need to pich the gorls up at 3 wow ok, fast one I see that is cool
> —why do u keep askin me that? to come here then leave then come back? seems odd
> —NO I am just trying to make it easy on ALL nothing sneaking at all
> —huh?
> —I am coolith whatever you ewant
> —well what do you want? im open after 2 .. i told u that a million times
> —ok cool
> —seems like ur really not into the girls, if not just say that .. its all good either way

Again J assured her that he was interested in her and her girls, but once more he made it clear that he was coming to meet her alone first. They would have sex and then she would leave to get the girls. After weeks of wrangling, she finally agreed to what he wanted.

They arranged to rendezvous on the afternoon of Friday, October 28, in the parking lot of a Wendy's on MacDade Boulevard just outside Media. She asked J to bring condoms, and he promised to do so.

On the morning of their meeting, J wrote heather:

> —I had a fucked up dream last night, lol
> —do tell?
> —that you set me up like you were the cops, I walked in and you arrested me for this and I needed to kill my-self, because I will never go to jaillol

—good god! are u serious

—I know fraked me out freaked me out

Before they signed off that morning, J made sure one more time that the plan was the way he wanted it. He would meet her, they would have sex, and then she would leave to pick up her girls and come back with them.

"GET OUT OF THE CAR!"

It was a short drive along Interstate 476, the Blue Route, to MacDade Boulevard. Before heading for their rendezvous J showered and changed into casual slacks, dress shoes, and a clean gray pullover shirt. He was excited. He had purchased the condoms she requested at a Rite Aid, a three-pack, the smallest item on the rack. He had the condoms in a bag with the sex toys he hoped to use in the short time they had before she would leave for her daughters. In the bag was a set of handcuffs, the play kind with no locks on them, some dildos, and some rope, in case she wanted to be tied up. He wanted to be right on time, because there would be only an hour for them to get to her house and have sex before she had to leave to get her daughters—and then he would flee.

He turned into the restaurant parking lot and started backing into a space. A car startled him, pulling up fast, right behind him, cutting him off. It made him angry, but then he saw another had pulled in front of him. They had nearly hit his car! Then men rushed toward him with handguns drawn. They were shouting, "Get out of the car! Get out of the car!"

His first thought: holdup! He was being robbed, hijacked. But then one of the men told him he was under arrest. These were cops. He stepped out and was immediately pushed against the side of his car and frisked, handcuffed, and placed in the back of a sport-utility vehicle.

J moved like someone in shock. Lieutenant David Peifer, Deery's boss and head of the ICAC unit, got behind the wheel. He was about J's age, a sturdy man with a crew cut and a handgun on his belt. J flung questions at him. Why was he being arrested? Because he had come there to meet with a woman? The lieutenant told him, in so many words, that he was under arrest for "soliciting" sex with children.

"I would never have touched those kids!," J protested. "I wasn't interested in them!"

"That's what they all say," Peifer replied.

J kept trying to explain himself, and the lieutenant instructed him, patiently, that he had to wait until they got back to his office, where they could talk at length. First he had to be fully advised of his rights.

His rights! J was angry, bewildered, and frightened. He knew that the scenario he had described to heather online was criminal, and he had seen busts like this on TV, but somehow his knowledge that the fantasies he described were untrue, that he never intended for them to actually happen, had convinced him he was safe. How could meeting an adult woman alone make him vulnerable to arrest?

He met Deery for the first time at the police station. He was sitting on a bench in Peifer's office, feeling vulnerable and foolish, his thick arms resting in his lap, handcuffed to a chair. When the detective entered and sat down, J didn't know who she was until the lieutenant introduced her as heather. She seemed timid. Peifer did most of the talking. J was frightened but also angry. He tried to stay calm as he explained to them both that he had no intention, despite whatever he had written, of sticking around for sex with the girls. Deery said, "You brought three condoms, one for me and one for each of the girls."

"They come in packs of three," he told her. "You can't buy just one."

Still, that looked bad.

Peifer and Deery gave J a transcript of the chats he had had with heatherscutiepies, and started reading to him some of the more explicit things he had said about having sex with children. J was frantic to explain himself. "The conversations were based on just to keep the woman interested and to just be erotic and aroused, and that was it," he said. They were not buying it. Peifer read him line after embarrassing, incriminating line.

"I, honest to God . . ." said J, exasperated. "I don't want them [the girls]. I never been into it, ever with anybody, anywhere, at any time!"

"And that's easy to say now that we've arrested you, and you're sitting here talking to the police," said Peifer.

"Even if I wasn't arrested, I wouldn't be interested in kids. It was just, I wanted . . . the woman to be excited. I wanted me to be excited. And that was it. I know how it looks. I know what you're reading, but—"

"When you bring kids into this whole thing, why would you even go there?" asked Peifer.

"I know," J said, defeated, but still trying to make them see, running phrases together in his panic. "The idea was only to keep her interested. I, in my mind, my mind, was working differently, I guess, than most people's because I just wanted to be with a real woman, not the kids, but I wanted, I didn't want to lose my opportunity to, to, have some real passion, and I, I was wrong in stating that. I know you're telling me it's solicitation, in your definition, but I, I can tell you that when I was doing it, it's not solicit—I wasn't trying to solicit because I know in my heart and in my mind, I would not under any circumstances be with a child and nor have I ever, ever, ever in any way shape or form, been with a child. I never want to."

"But you'd never know that by reading this chat," said Peifer.

"I understand that," said J.

It went on like this. He could see how they viewed what he had written, and it was obvious that it looked very bad. Criminal.

He still did not understand the seriousness of his predicament. When they were finished, J asked Peifer when he could go home. "No," the lieutenant explained in that calm, patient way of his. "You're being arrested and you are going to jail tonight."

FLASH FORWARD

J ended up serving a year in prison. His lawyer negotiated a plea that reduced what might have been a much longer stay, and that allowed him to serve his time in a relatively unthreatening county prison. He was charged with 16 counts, starting with "criminal attempt—rape forcible compulsion" and ending with "criminal solicitation—corruption of minors." He was given one year of parole and sentenced to 10 years of probation, during which time he must attend counseling weekly for his alleged sexual desire for children. His wife left him. He lost his job. His face, name, address, and criminal conviction for "Attempted Involuntary Sexual Deviate Intercourse" with a minor appear on the Pennsylvania Web site for "sexual offenders."

He is deeply ashamed, and bitter. He wanted to fight the charge. Indeed, he is still furious with the lawyer who persuaded him to take a plea, but it would appear that the copy-machine repairman received wise counsel. Because he didn't have a prayer of getting off. The array of charges against him could have sent him away to prison for up to eight years. At the trial, he would have been painted as an all-too-familiar monster. This was the interpretation of Deery and the Delaware County district attorney, and they were not particularly interested in any other. They might have been able to find out for sure on the day they arrested him. Deery could have worn a wire, and if he had been as determined as she believed he was to have sex with her daughters, she could have presented him with that exact opportunity, telling him, for example, that her girls were home at that moment and she was going to take him directly there, bypassing the prospect of his having sex with her. It might have unequivocally sorted out his interests. But it was clear that, to her, such a consideration was moot. "I had enough already to convict him," she said. "There was no need for a wire."

J was guilty of some things, serious things. He was guilty of saying he wanted to have sex with two imaginary children. He was guilty of being a troubled soul in a bad marriage, of abusing steroids, of a lifelong inability to establish a healthy intimacy with a woman, and of being morally adrift in a netherworld of illicit sexual desire. He was guilty of lacking moral boundaries and good sense. There is a chance that without treatment of some kind J would have evolved into someone dangerous. I asked him, "What if you found yourself, after all of that talk on the Internet, consumed with your steroidal lust, in a room with this woman and her children? Is it possible that you might have gone ahead with it?"

J bowed his head and thought about it for a long time.

"I don't know," he said. "I know I have no sexual interest in children at all. I pray that I would never have gone that far. I certainly had no intention of doing it. I intended to have sex with her and then leave. Period."

There is no evidence that J has ever made a sexual overture to a child. Deery told me that she couldn't remember ever arresting a child-molester who did not have child porn on his computer. It is all too easy to obtain. J had no images that were obviously child porn. His appalled parents paid for a battery of psychosexual testing, the kind where involuntary responses to images are measured. The tests showed exactly what J claimed, that he had no sexual interest in children.

J is off steroids. His body has slipped back into a normal shape, slightly pudgy. His manner is subdued, submissive, earnest, eagerly friendly, and polite. He helped several inmates earn high-school diplomas when he was in jail, and he is proud of that. He no longer owns a computer. He lives alone in his suburban town house with his dogs. He has joined a church. He says the pastor there has embraced him, forgiven him, and provided him with support and direction. After his arrest he went to every neighbor in his suburban cul-de-sac, knocking on doors to tell each of them his story. He did not want them to know only what they learned from the police. He says they believe him, and he feels accepted. He recently found a new job, after telling his whole story to the man who hired him. He sees the years he spent obsessed with cybersex as an illness, or a lapse into sinfulness, that drew him deeper and deeper into depravity. He is embarrassed. He has been humiliated.

But he has stayed angry. The classes he attends as a condition of his probation demand that he admit a sexual desire for children. It is considered an essential step toward recovery. J told his instructor that he has no such desire. He never did. He was told that if he persists in this denial he will jeopardize his probation and could be sent back to jail.

So he pretends to be something he is not. He is good at it.

Alex Hutchinson

Global Impositioning Systems

Is GPS technology actually harming our sense of direction?

When Alison Kendall's boss told her in 2007 that her civil service job was being transferred to a different building in another part of Vancouver, she panicked. Commuting to a new office would be no big deal for most people, she knew. But Kendall might well have the worst sense of direction in the world. For as long as she can remember, she has been unable to perform even the simplest navigational tasks. She needed a family member to escort her to and from school right through the end of grade twelve, and is still able to produce only a highly distorted, detail-free sketch map of her own house. After five years of careful training, she had mastered the bus trip to and from her office, but the slightest deviation left her hopelessly lost. When that happened, the forty-three-year-old had to phone her father to come and pick her up, even if she was just a few blocks from home, in the neighbourhood where she had lived most of her life.

Kendall (not her real name) decided to ask a neuropsychologist if she had medical grounds for turning down the transfer. He referred her to a neuro-ophthalmology clinic at the University of British Columbia, where a young post-doc from Italy named Giuseppe Iaria was studying the neuro-science of orientation and navigation. After a battery of tests, Iaria concluded that Kendall was perfectly normal. She had average intelligence, memory, and mental imaging abilities, and her brain was completely undamaged. She was simply unable to form a "cognitive map," the mind's way of representing spatial relationships. When he put her in a brain scanner and asked her to explore the streets of a computer-generated virtual town, her hippocampus—the brain region responsible for cognitive maps—remained inactive, even though basic memory tests had shown that it was functional. Earlier this year, a paper by Iaria, neuro-ophthalmologist Jason Barton, and their colleagues appeared in the journal *Neuropsychologia,* describing a new disorder called "developmental topographical disorientation," or dtd. Kendall was "Patient 1."

Like any other human trait, navigational skill varies widely—some people crow about their abilities, while others lament their ineptitude. So in a way, Kendall's condition came as no surprise. ("I was expecting to find someone like that eventually," Iaria says.) But the brain's navigational wiring doesn't just reflect our talent at getting from A to B; it also reflects the ways in which we perceive and interact with the world around us. As our surroundings have evolved over the centuries, so too have our navigational strategies and conceptions, shaped most recently by urbanization and the advent of high-speed travel.

We're now on the cusp of an even more dramatic change, as we enter the age of the global positioning system, which is well on its way to being a standard feature in every car and on every cellphone. At the same time, neuroscientists are starting to uncover a two-way street: our brains determine how we navigate, but our navigational efforts also shape our brains. The experts are picking up some worrying signs about the changes that will occur as we grow accustomed to the brain-

free navigation of the gps era. Once we lose the habit of forming cognitive maps, we may find ourselves becoming more
and more like Patient 1.

It was the flower shop that messed me up. I was navigating
through the virtual town Iaria had built within a video game
platform, trying to learn the locations of four landmarks: a
Wendy's, a Days Inn, a flower shop, and a movie theatre
showing Hugh Grant's *Love Actually*. It took me three tries
to place all of them in the correct positions on a map; typical
scores range from two to five. "You're average," Iaria (who
has since taken a faculty position at the University of Calgary)
said cheerfully, crushing my hopes of being a super-outlier.
That morning, as I'd walked the three kilometres from my
downtown hotel to Vancouver General Hospital, I'd oriented
myself by marking the cues provided by an unfamiliar city:
glancing at a few key street names I'd jotted on a piece of
paper; keeping the mountains on my left once I'd crossed the
Granville Street Bridge; and more or less ignoring the shore-
lines, which seemed to point in different directions every time
I looked at the water.

Iaria and McGill University researcher Véronique Bohbot
demonstrated in a widely cited 2003 study that our mapping
strategies fall into two basic categories. One is a spatial strategy that involves learning the relationships between various
landmarks—creating a cognitive map in your head, in other
words, that shows where the flower shop and other destinations sit on the street grid. The other is a stimulus-response
approach that encodes specific routes by memorizing a series
of cues, as in: get off the bus when you see the glass skyscraper,
then walk toward the big park. For their study, Iaria and Bohbot created a virtual maze that tested both methods; they
found that about half of us prefer spatial strategies, while the
other half prefer stimulus-response.

Most of us can use both, depending on the circumstances, but we have a bias toward one or the other. (Kendall was relying solely on cues, in the absence of cognitive mapping skills.) Stimulus-response navigators tend to complete the task more quickly and make fewer errors. "Cognitive mapping is difficult, it's complicated, it's tedious," Bohbot says. The spatial approach does have one major advantage, though: versatility. If I memorize the routes from the flower shop to the movie theatre, and from the movie theatre to the Wendy's, I can whip back and forth along those routes very quickly. But what if I want to go from the flower shop straight to the Wendy's? Without a cognitive map, I have no way of figuring out shortcuts or exploring new routes to different destinations. I can only go where my stimulus-driven mind has already left a trail of bread crumbs.

The idea that we carry maps in our heads is relatively new. An experimental psychologist at the University of California, Berkeley, Edward C. Tolman, coined the term "cognitive map" in a 1948 paper showing that rats in certain types of mazes were able to figure out shortcuts to a destination—a clear sign that they weren't simply learning a sequence of left and right turns. Amazingly, a series of experiments in the 1970s suggested that cognitive maps are more than metaphorical. Certain neurons in the hippocampus, called "place cells," were observed activating only when the rat was in a specific place. Let the animal wander through a maze, and you could watch a chain of neurons fire in a spatial pattern that exactly matched its path, at a smaller scale.

Whether the same picture can be extended to humans remains a matter of considerable controversy. We don't know whether the firing patterns of neurons in our hippocampus would trace out the patterns of our neighbourhood, because researchers aren't allowed to implant arrays of electrodes in our brains. We do know, though, that the human hippocampus stores the same kind of information as the rat hippocampus does, thanks in part to a remarkable series of experiments on a group of truly gifted navigators.

For those of us who have grown up in the reassuring embrace of grid-patterned streets that run straight and don't change names every two blocks, Old World cities like London—recently declared the most confusing city in the world by a 12,500-person Nokia Maps survey—present huge challenges. So pity the cabbies. Before getting behind the wheel of a black cab, would-be drivers have to pass a test called the Knowledge, which requires them to memorize some 25,000 streets and thousands of landmarks, a task that takes two to four years.

A cognitive map featuring that level of detail, as you might imagine, requires a fair amount of storage space, and, sure enough, University College London neuroscientist Eleanor Maguire found that the back part of the hippocampus in London taxi drivers is enlarged compared with that of the general population. The longer they've been driving, the bigger the gap. Maguire also found, though, that the front part of the hippocampus gets correspondingly smaller. "So there is a price to pay for their expertise," she says. This difference showed up in tests of visuo-spatial memory, including one in which the drivers were asked to memorize the position of sixteen objects on a table, then put them back in place after they'd been removed. "They were incredibly poor at doing that," she says. While it isn't yet clear whether this happens because the requirements of storing a map of London take over other parts of the brain or because of some other process, what these studies do make clear is the brain's plasticity: its very structure is shaped by the demands we place on it.

It follows, then, that the shape of our hippocampus, and the organization of our brain, must depend on when and where we've lived. If a few years in a taxi can produce noticeable differences in our brains, imagine what a lifetime of roaming the featureless Arctic or sailing between remote Polynesian islands would do. Similarly, determining whether someone like Alison Kendall has a genuine disorder, or simply lies at the extreme edge of a normal range of navigational skill, is not straightforward. "If you hear her story, you think, 'That's really out there,'" says Jason Barton. "But there's variation in every human ability, and this, I'm sure, is one of them."

Since Kendall's story was published, 450 more people have contacted Iaria. About fifty of them display some signs of brain damage, but the other 400 share three key characteristics. "First, they have no other neurological conditions. They function normally, in a range of jobs," he says. "Second, they get lost every day. And third, they've been getting lost since they were children." Over the summer, he posted nine tests on a website called *gettinglost.ca*. They are designed to test orientation, spatial memory, and a series of other cognitive skills. The goal is to identify more dtd sufferers, and eventually to bring them in and run more detailed tests to find out what they have in common. But he also wants people with normal navigation skills to take the tests—as many as possible. "If you do a study with ten, twenty, fifty subjects, you make kind of a speculation," he says. "If you have 50,000, there's no variability that can affect your data."

That number isn't as far fetched as it sounds. Researchers studying face blindness, a cognitive condition with key similarities to dtd, managed to get some 60,000 people to take their online tests. A data set that large would allow Iaria to get a snapshot of what is normal for the population as a whole, along with insight into how navigational abilities depend on factors like age and gender. Mind you, this approach does have one significant blind spot: if something is altering the navigational skills of the entire population, it won't be detected.

In June, Al Byrd's three-bedroom home, built by his father on the western outskirts of Atlanta, was mistakenly torn down by a demolition company. "I said, 'Don't you have an address?'" a distraught Byrd later recounted. "He said, 'Yes, my gps coordinates led me right to this address here.'" The incident joined a long list of satellite-guided blunders, including one last year in which a driver in Bedford Hills, New York, obeyed instructions from his gps to turn right onto a set of train tracks, where he got stuck and had to abandon his car to a collision with a commuter train. Incredibly, the same thing happened to someone else at exactly the same intersection nine months later. In Europe, narrow village roads and country lanes have turned into deadly traps for truckers blindly following gps instructions, and an insurance company survey found that 300,000 British drivers have either crashed or nearly crashed because of the systems.

More subtly, the increase in gps use has meant that people spend less time learning details about their neighbourhoods. British researchers testing cognitive map formation in drivers found that those using gps formed less detailed and accurate maps of their routes than those using paper maps. Similarly, a University of Tokyo study found that pedestrians using gps-enabled cellphones had a harder time figuring out where they were and where they had come from. Their navigational aids, in other words, had allowed them to turn off their hippocampi.

To many, the beauty of the devices is precisely that we no longer have any need to painstakingly assemble those cognitive maps. But Cornell University human-computer interaction researcher Gilly Leshed argues that knowledge of an area means more than just finding your way around. Navigation underlies the transformation of an abstract "space" to a "place" that has meaning and value to an individual. For the gps users Leshed and her colleagues observed in an ethnographic study, the virtual world on the screens of their devices seemed to blur and sometimes take over from the real world that whizzed by outside. "Instead of experiencing physical locations, you end up with a more abstract representation of the world," she says.

On a snowmobile trip of over 500 kilometres across the Arctic, this blurring of the real and the virtual became obvious to Carleton University anthropologist Claudio Aporta. Returning from Repulse Bay to Igloolik, a village west of Baffin Island where he was conducting fieldwork, he and an Inuit hunter became engulfed in fog. The hunter had been leading the way along traditional routes, guided by the winds, water currents, animal behaviour, and features such as the *uqalurait,* snowdrifts shaped by prevailing winds from the west by northwest. Like London taxi drivers, Inuit hunters spend years acquiring the knowledge needed to find their way in their environment, part of a culture in which "the idea of being lost or unable to find one's way is without basis in experience, language, or understanding—that is, until recently," as Aporta and Eric Higgs wrote in a 2005 paper on "satellite culture" and the rise of gps use in Igloolik.

Heavy fog is the one condition that stymies even the most expert Inuit navigators. The traditional response is to wait until the fog lifts, but, knowing that Aporta had mapped the outbound journey on his gps, his guide asked him to lead the way on his snowmobile. "It was an incredible experience, because I could see absolutely nothing," he recalls. "I didn't know if there was a cliff ahead; I was just following the gps track for five kilometres, blind, really." This was the extreme version of the city driver blankly turning left and right at the command of his gps, and it required a leap of faith. "Believe me," he says, chuckling, "I was sweating like crazy."

The demonstrable benefits of gps have, however, removed much of the incentive for the younger generation in Igloolik to undertake the arduous process of learning traditional navigation techniques. Elders worry about this loss of knowledge, for reasons that go beyond the cultural—a straight line across an empty icefield plotted by gps doesn't warn about the thin ice traditional trails would have skirted. Dead batteries and frozen screens, both common occurrences in the harsh Arctic conditions, would also be disastrous for anyone guided solely by technology.

Aporta notes, though, that gps is just one element of an "ecology of technologies" in Inuit life, stretching back to the rifle and the snowmobile, and encompassing even broader trends like the establishment of permanent settlements. "It's also the first technology in the history of navigation that gives you an answer to a spatial question without you needing to be engaged at all," he says. The net result is an increasing disconnection for young Inuit from the rhythms of their environment. And though the stakes are high in the harsh conditions of the Arctic, similar changes are taking place everywhere. "I like to ask my students questions about the Rideau River, which is right here," he says, gesturing to a window overlooking the Carleton campus. "Where is the river flowing? How did people use it before? And people born in Ottawa have really struggled to give me environmental information about a feature they see on a daily basis."

Across the hall from Véronique Bohbot's tiny office on the ground floor of Douglas Hospital, on the south shore of the island of Montreal, a mock mri machine is set up, complete with a glass-panelled control room and an electric platform that slides the patient into a cylindrical imaging chamber at the touch of a button. Here, experimental subjects practise navigating through a virtual maze on a screen they can only see through a series of mirrors. They must learn to keep their heads perfectly immobile in order for Bohbot to be able to peer inside their brains once they've graduated to the "functional" mri machine off-site. fmri tracks the flow of blood to different parts of the brain, allowing near-real-time monitoring of which areas light up during different tasks. Iaria and Bohbot used the technology to confirm that spatial navigators use the hippocampus, while stimulus-response learners use another region of the brain called the caudate nucleus.

Another mri technique called "voxel-based morphometry" maps brains of different sizes onto a standard template, so the relative size of their subunits can be compared. In 2007, as a follow-up to the first study, Bohbot and her collaborators showed that the half of the population that prefer to use spatial strategies have bigger hippocampi, while the half that prefer stimulus-response navigation have bigger caudate nuclei —a predictable result, given the plasticity demonstrated by London taxi drivers. But that leaves an unresolved chicken-and-egg question: does using spatial strategies make your hippocampus bigger, or does having a bigger hippocampus make you more inclined to use spatial strategies?

To probe more deeply, Bohbot teamed with Jason Lerch, a researcher at the mouse imaging centre at Toronto's Hospital for Sick Children. He trained a group of mice on a standard challenge called the Morris water maze, tweaking it so half the mice were forced to use spatial strategy and the other half stimulus-response. "Lo and behold, after only five days of training he scanned them on a seven-tesla mri and found grey matter differences in the hippocampus and caudate nucleus," Bohbot says, "just like we did in humans." Then they dissected the brains (a luxury they don't have with human subjects) and found that the increased volume came from "dendritic arborization"—an increase in the number of connections to and from each neuron. "Instead of having a skimpy tree with one branch," she says, "it's going to have a dozen branches."

Though the data can only be extrapolated so far, Lerch's

mouse studies suggest that human brains begin to reorganize very quickly in response to the way we use them. The implications of this concern Bohbot. She fears that overreliance on gps, which demands a hyper-pure form of stimulus-response behaviour, will result in our using the spatial capabilities of the hippocampus less, and that it will in turn get smaller. Other studies have tied atrophy of the hippocampus to increased risk of dementia. "We can only draw an inference," Bohbot acknowledges. "But there's a logical conclusion that people could increase their risk of atrophy if they stop paying attention to where they are and where they go."

Of course, we do still navigate the local environments where we spend most of our time—our homes, our offices, our immediate neighbourhoods—without gps, so a change in brain structure is perhaps unlikely. And we also use the hippocampus to store autobiographical memories and to imagine the future. But Bohbot sees the decline in spatial thinking as part of a broader shift toward stimulus-response, reward-linked behaviour. The demand for instant gratification, for efficiency at all costs and productivity as the only measure of value—these sound like the laments of the nostalgist in the Age of the Caudate Nucleus. But here, they're based on neuroscience. "Society is geared in many ways toward shrinking the hippocampus," she says. "In the next twenty years, I think we're going to see dementia occurring earlier and earlier."

This was the point at which I started feeling guilty for giving my parents a gps system for Christmas last year. But of course gps has many positives. For patients suffering from disorders like Alison Kendall's, satellite navigation has provided a crucial lifeline. Among the Inuit, gps is helping to map and preserve traditional routes, and the technology is actually spurring interest in navigational heritage among younger people. Cornell's Gilly Leshed, too, saw benefits in her ethnographic study of gps users. Those with a poor sense of direction were able to explore more freely and were more likely to venture to new places, since directions home were always available at the press of a button. "Still, it doesn't force them to be attuned to their environment," she admits. "They're freed, but they're not challenged." Leshed and others hope gps will eventually be designed so as to spur engagement with the landscape without sacrificing convenience—for instance by pointing to landmarks ("Turn left after the gas station") rather than location-agnostic instructions ("Turn left in three blocks").

When I was a kid, I had an old *Mad* magazine from the 1960s that bemoaned the advent of the electric scooter and predicted that by the end of the century North Americans would look like oversized bowling pins with tiny, vestigial legs, ripe for knocking over by lean Communist invaders. Rather than forgetting how to walk, however, 4.5 million Canadians now pay to join health clubs where they can spin their legs on treadmills and exercise bikes to make up the miles they no longer travel in their daily lives. Many others choose to forsake "efficiency" by biking to work or walking to the supermarket, because they've realized that letting technology do too much leaves their bodies worse off. We may soon take the same approach with our brains.

In her basement lab in Montreal, Bohbot gave me a foretaste of the spatial memory training program she and her students have been developing for the past four years. Donning the requisite 3-D glasses, I navigated around an eerily accurate virtual version of the Douglas Hospital campus, projected onto an enormous three-metre-wide screen that divided the otherwise uniformly black room in two. Bohbot's group has created forty-six different virtual environments, each designed to force people to employ spatial memory rather than stimulus-response strategies. The proposed structure is an eight-week, sixteen-hour program featuring exercises that can run on a typical computer screen—though Bohbot isn't sure how successful an at-home program would be. "It's boring!" she admits. "And really, we have to be there administering it and telling people it's supposed to be hard."

For Kendall's part, she was able, after six weeks of working with Iaria for an hour a week, to shorten the time she needed to form a cognitive map in a simple virtual environment from thirty-two minutes to five. Her success offered further evidence that her inability to form cognitive maps isn't the result of hidden brain damage. She can do it; she's just very bad at it. The precise combination of genetic and environmental factors responsible for this shortcoming remains unclear, but the results of her training are heartening. They suggest that, as with any cognitive task, we may differ in our natural endowments, but we can always improve.

Of course, they also suggest that we can decline, and that's why Iaria, too, has reservations about gps. "It's an amazing tool, and I'm so grateful we have this kind of technology for people that need it," he says. "At the same time, I don't think it's a tool that we may want to use every day for fun. Because then you don't think about your environment, you don't look at it, you don't care about it." He often encounters people who believe they have terrible navigation skills but who turn out to perform perfectly well on his tests. It may be, for example, that their spouses always drive, so they have no reason to pay attention to their routes and consequently never know where they are. That's an attention problem, not a navigation problem.

Iaria himself, after years of studying the vagaries of human navigation, has become a good man to have at your side on a trip to points unknown. When he encounters new places, he knows which features to seek out to get oriented. He'll find the tallest building or landmark, and remember what it looks like from different perspectives. And he can give people good directions in whatever navigational language they happen to speak, whether by referring to landmarks, compass directions, distances, or street names. But that doesn't mean finding his bearings is an obsession. "You know, I lived in Paris, and to me one of the most beautiful things was just getting lost sometimes in these very small streets, and having a coffee and a cigarette with strangers, and going back trying to find your way," he says. "These days, there are very few moments you actually have the freedom to get lost."

Plugged In

Can Elon Musk lead the way to an electric-car future?

In a dressing room above the *Late Show with David Letterman* stage, the electric-car magnate Elon Musk sat on a sofa, eating cookies. Three of his employees hovered around him anxiously. Musk, thirty-eight, is the chairman, C.E.O., and product architect of Tesla Motors, and he was appearing on Letterman to show off the company's newest design: a sleek sedan called the Model S. Tesla plans to have the vehicle in production by 2011—at which point, if you believe Musk, gasoline-powered cars will suddenly look like oxcarts.

On this April day, he was wearing black half-boots and a gray hacking jacket. The curious apparel, together with his Pee-wee haircut, glowing blue-green eyes, South African accent (he was born in Pretoria), and manifest determination to save the world—single-handedly, if necessary—conspires to make him seem somewhat alien. He's the mysterious visitor who skims down the ramp, eager to help.

After co-founding the Internet start-ups Zip2 and Pay-Pal, when he was in his twenties, in 2002 Musk launched the Space Exploration Technologies Corporation (SpaceX), with the ultimate goal of colonizing Mars; the company recently won a $1.6-billion contract with NASA to resupply the Space Station. He is also the leading investor in and chairman of SolarCity, a solar-panel-installation company run by two of his cousins. And in 2004 he provided Tesla with its initial funding, in the belief that electric vehicles, or E.V.s, together with solar power, will help wean the world off oil, buying us time to address global warming (and colonize Mars). "The likelihood of humanity gaining a true understanding of the universe is greater if we expand the scope and scale of civilization, and have more time to think about it," he told me. "We're like a giant parallel supercomputer, and each of our brains runs a piece of the software."

Musk's goal for the Letterman show was to demystify electric cars, and to explain how he's going to fix Detroit from his headquarters, in Silicon Valley. His employees were with him to make sure he didn't come across as a total geek. They peppered him with talking points, most of which he seemed to ignore. His assistant, Mary Beth Brown, told him, "And don't be all engineery, all 'It requires twenty-five times the energy to get to orbit that it does to get to space.'"

"Most people think gravity ends when you get two hundred miles above the earth," Musk observed, adding, "Most people don't know much."

It troubles Musk that while few people know that the world's oil supply could plateau by 2020 and run out as early as 2050, nearly everyone knows that electric cars suck. For decades, E.V.s resembled hovercraft or mobile eggs, and their lead-acid battery packs were costly, heavy, and sickly. After investing more than a billion dollars, G.M. in 1996 launched the EV1, an electric subcompact that it leased to several hundred customers in California and Arizona. In 2003, the company began retrieving the cars and crushing them for scrap. The EV1, which could go only about seventy-five miles before needing to be charged, embodied the perennial problem of "range anxiety": if your battery ran down far from home, where would you recharge it?

Last fall, Tesla began making the only highway-capable E.V. now available: the Roadster, a $109,000 sports car that goes from zero to sixty in less than four seconds and has a range of two hundred and forty-four miles. Powered by a lithium-ion battery—the kind used in laptops and cell phones —the Roadster was designed to prove that E.V.s can not just compete but excel. (Lithium is lighter than lead and releases a lot more energy.) Having gained "first-mover advantage"— which is particularly prized in Silicon Valley—Musk plans to cut the price for each of Tesla's succeeding models more or less in half and seize the market from the top down. Bob Lutz, the vice-chairman of G.M. and the champion of its electric Chevy Volt, which will début next year, told me, "All the geniuses here at General Motors kept saying lithium-ion technology is ten years away, and Toyota agrees with us—and, boom, along comes Tesla. So I said, 'How come some teeny little California start-up run by guys who know nothing about the car business can do this, and we can't?' That was the crowbar that helped break up the logjam."

So far, Tesla has built just six hundred cars, or .000002 per cent of the country's two-hundred-and-fifty-million-car fleet, but the Roadster can be found in the multicar garages of George Clooney, Matt Damon, Leonardo DiCaprio, the Google founders Sergey Brin and Larry Page—and David Letterman.

Musk has five hundred employees at Tesla, and they have faith in his abilities as an engineer and an entrepreneur. But some worry about his aptitude for the most difficult part of the job: selling cars. At an unveiling of the Model S for Tesla's employees, in Menlo Park, California, Musk read from a PowerPoint presentation, adding his own taglines a beat late: "What's cooler than making a hot product, a sexy product, that also saves the world!" Pause for applause; not forthcoming. "And also makes money, meeting third-quarter targets!"

In the studio, Brown looked at Musk affectionately, seeming to wonder how to imbue him with the Steve Jobs touch. She warned him, "If you call Dan Neil a douche bag on national television, I'm going to come out and kick your ass."

"But he is a douche bag!" Musk protested, half-seriously. Neil, the Los Angeles *Times'* car columnist, had that morning published a caustic piece calling the Model S "a glorified golf cart," after he'd driven the company's pre-prototype "show car"—a kind of dynamic sketch that lacked windshield wipers and operable windows. And Musk tends to blast journalists who don't see things his way. In early April, he had told an interviewer that Randall Stross, who had written negatively about Tesla in the *Times,* "is a huge douche bag, and an idiot."

Musk was predisposed to be vexed by the Neil article, because, as he'd told me earlier that day, Tesla was about to recall most of its Roadsters to fix some loose bolts in the wheel hubs. "It's bloody Lotus's fault," he said, referring to the British carmaker, which manufactures the Roadster's chassis, "but it'll be seen as 'Tesla, the upstart car company, doesn't know how to make cars.'

"Then there's my own profile," Musk said, referring to Silicon Valley gossip sites such as Valleywag.com, which have portrayed him as paranoid and despotic. A prophet is not without honor, save in his own valley. "The people who know me generally have a good impression. Generally, if I didn't fire them"—he laughed—"then they have a good impression." He fell silent for two minutes, processing. Then he announced, "I'm going to call Dan Neil and say, 'What the fuck?' Starting with a negative conclusion and backfilling the facts is a classic dickhead move—and a classic human fallacy." Humans!

As a boy in Pretoria, Musk was undersized and picked upon, a smart-aleck known as Muskrat. In his loneliness, he read a lot of fantasy and science fiction. "The heroes of the books I read, 'The Lord of the Rings' and the 'Foundation' series, always felt a duty to save the world," he told me.

When Musk was eight, his parents divorced, and he and his two younger siblings lived with their mother and a series of nannies in a succession of South African cities. "I think my mother somewhat overstates her role in raising me," Musk says dryly. Maye Musk, a Canadian-born model and dietician, says, "Elon would accompany me to dinner parties if I didn't have a date. I'd bring him to meet some interesting adults, and he'd hide a book under the table to read if they weren't interesting enough."

When he was eleven—about the time that he sold his first piece of software, a video game called Blastar—Musk told his mother that he was going to move back to Pretoria to live with his father, Errol, an electrical engineer who would later own an auto-parts store and a share in an emerald mine. "You have three kids and Dad has no kids," Musk explained. ("My father is not a fun guy to be around, but it seemed like the right thing to do," he told me.) He hoped that his father would move with him to America, where he'd once taken him on a visit. America was comics, movies, technology—freedom. When that plan failed, Musk immigrated to Canada on his own, at seventeen. There he floated among his mother's cousins' houses, often living on a dollar a day and buying hot dogs and oranges in bulk. He spent two years at Queen's University in Ontario, then finished up at the University of Pennsylvania, where he earned bachelor's degrees in physics and economics, with an unofficial minor in first-person-shooter video games.

In 1995, Musk dropped out of a Ph.D. program at Stanford after two days in order to explore opportunities on the

Internet; four years later, he sold Zip2, a newspaper-hosting platform he'd built with his brother, Kimbal, and netted $22 million. He promptly founded a company that became part of PayPal, and cashed out with $160 million when eBay bought PayPal, in 2002. Then he began thinking about what to do next. George Zachary, a venture capitalist and a friend of Musk's, remembers, "Elon called me up and said, 'Do you think people would think I'm crazy if I sent mice to Mars?' I said, 'Do they come back?,' and he said, 'I don't know.' I said, 'Well, if they don't come back, yes.'"

Musk founded SpaceX in 2002. Last fall, its Falcon 1 rocket became the first privately funded liquid-fuelled rocket to achieve orbit—after three failed launches, including that of a rocket containing the ashes of James Doohan, who played Scotty on *Star Trek*. (Musk says, "Technically, Scotty's ashes did get to space, they just didn't stay there.") The company's larger Falcon 9 will soon begin to resupply the Space Station, and Musk expects that the craft will be ferrying tourists into space by 2014, looping them around the moon for fifty million dollars a head.

Two years before founding SpaceX, Musk married Justine Wilson, a writer of fantasy novels he'd met at Queen's University. The couple went on to have twins, followed by triplets; they separated last year. "Elon's central relationship is with his work," Justine Musk says, and Musk acknowledges that when problems began to multiply at Tesla, in 2007, "I went from working hard to working ridiculously hard. And stress breaks things." Shortly after the couple parted, Musk met the English actress Talulah Riley, and proposed to her. Musk and Riley plan to have children, too, though Musk says his reasons differ somewhat from hers: he believes it's the duty of the intelligent and educated to replicate, "so we don't devolve into a not very literate, theocratic, and unenlightened future." As part of his program for *Homo sapiens,* the beta version, he reminds unfruitful employees, "You should have, on average, 2.1 kids per woman."

In 2004, Musk, who was interested in developing an electric car, met an engineer named Martin Eberhard, proposed to build a sports car with a lithium-ion battery. Musk agreed to underwrite the company, and he and Eberhard planned to release the Roadster within two years, at a development cost of about $25 million. It took four and a half years and $140 million. Eberhard wanted to get the first Roadster out fast, by placing an electric power train in a modified Lotus Elise chassis. Musk believed that the first Roadster had to impress— which meant that it had to have, among several expensive and time-consuming changes, a carbon-fibre body and the ability to reach sixty miles per hour in less than four seconds. (Musk denies that the changes burdened the company.) He also insisted that they focus on future models. "He'd say, 'We're going to be the next G.M.,' and talk about putting a hundred thousand cars on the road by 2009," Eberhard recalls.

Tesla's chief technology officer, J. B. Straubel, says, "We hugely underestimated the challenge—the complexity of supply chains, of manufacturing, of the battery design. It was like working through a maze." The Roadster's battery is a highly engineered arrangement of six thousand eight hundred and thirty-one finger-size laptop cells imported from Japan. Tesla adds two fuses to each cell so they're all triple-fused, packs them in six hundred and twenty-one cell modules, maintains the modules at a constant temperature with radiator coolant, and monitors them with twelve computers, then houses this amphibious latticework in a thick aluminum case shaped like a baby grand piano. The unit weighs half a ton.

Musk and Tesla's board of directors pushed Eberhard out in 2007, as it became evident, just months after the company estimated the cost of producing the first Roadsters at $70,000 apiece, that the figure would actually be a crippling $130,000. (In May, Eberhard filed a lawsuit against Musk and Tesla, claiming that Musk had slandered him by calling him deceitful and had stolen the credit for founding Tesla; in a rebuttal on Tesla's blog, Musk argued that "it would have been forgivable if Eberhard had simply been in over his head," but that Eberhard had sought to keep the cost overruns from the board. Musk says that the parties are now considering mediation.)

Musk tried out two other C.E.O.s. Yet he also kept doubling his bet, putting up a total of $75 million of the company's first $195 million. (He eventually invested ninety per cent of his net worth in Tesla, SpaceX, and SolarCity.) Last fall, he backed his money with a resource even more precious to him: his time. He took the job of C.E.O. himself, and immediately began focussing on price and profit. Relying in part on the fact that the storage density of lithium-ion batteries is increasing about eight per cent a year, and costs are dropping correspondingly, Musk recently vowed that Tesla will offer a third-generation car for less than thirty thousand dollars by 2014. Straubel says, "As the company has matured, it has become more of a worthy adversary for Elon. He constantly wants everything we're doing to be really difficult, but he works really hard to make sure it's not impossible. He almost won't let us fail." Justine Musk observes, "I like to compare him to the Terminator. He sets his program and just . . . will . . . not . . . stop."

As new-car sales in America are expected to fall to ten million this year, down from sixteen million in recent years, and as Chrysler and G.M. struggle after sojourns in bankruptcy, the big automakers are, often reluctantly, developing E.V.s of their own. Ford plans to release the electric Focus in 2011, and Chrysler says it will have five hundred thousand electric cars on the road by 2013, under its new ENVI brand, aimed at "consumers who care about the planet's future." (For everyone else, there's the Jeep Wrangler Unlimited.) Renault, Nissan, and Mitsubishi are soon to release electric models, and the Chinese government, in a bid for its manufacturers to dominate the market, is setting up battery-charging stations in some of its largest cities and offering fleet owners who buy E.V.s and hybrids subsidies of up to eighty-eight hundred dollars.

But the American car buyer's default vehicle is a twenty-thousand-dollar sedan—and that equation doesn't work yet for E.V.s. The Roadster's power train alone costs about fifteen thousand dollars to manufacture, five times what it would cost for a standard car. So a number of automakers have sought cheaper electric options. G.M.'s Volt, for instance, is a "plug-in series hybrid." For longer journeys, a four-cylinder engine will kick in and repower the battery, but most trips will call solely on the battery, which has a range of about forty miles. (Nearly eighty per cent of Americans drive fewer than forty miles a day.)

A number of analysts see plugins as offering customers the best of both worlds: conspicuous greenness backstopped by the good old internal-combustion engine. And most E.V. manufacturers embrace the idea of competition, believing that the more E.V.s that enter the market the more consumers will believe that the concept, finally, isn't going to go away. Nonetheless, Musk can't help pointing out that in his view the Volt is an inelegant compromise; its battery pack is nearly half as large as the Roadster's but has only one-sixth the electric range. After the Volt's battery runs down, Musk says, "You'll have a tiny engine pulling around a big car with a dead battery —you'll be the worst car on the road."

In New York, when Musk got onstage with David Letterman, he perched awkwardly in his chair, half-turned toward the host, who was fighting a cold and was in a particularly sardonic mood. Letterman began a rant about how Detroit's failure to produce electric vehicles had ruined the country's economy, and how the Volt "has a range of forty miles" —a characterization that ignores the repowering provided by the gasoline engine, but one that Musk didn't correct. "That's crap!" Letterman growled. After the Model S was brought out from backstage, to oohs from the audience, Musk elicited applause when he noted that it would cost only $49,900 (after a $7,500 federal tax credit). As Letterman began to step into the car, Musk twice said, "There's one very important point worth making"—intending to explain that recharging with electricity, at the equivalent of roughly forty-five cents a gallon, turns the S into a thirty-five-thousand-dollar car (if you amortize costs over seven years)—after which he'd deliver his kicker: "So would you rather have this car, or a Ford Taurus?"

But Letterman grabbed the car's steering wheel and began flailing around and screaming, pretending that he was being electrocuted. Musk grinned gamely; interview over. Three weeks later, G.M.'s Bob Lutz went on the *Late Show* to correct the record on the Volt. He was allowed several minutes to make his points—and then Letterman grabbed the steering wheel of the Volt prototype and began flailing around and screaming.

In late March, Tesla unveiled the Model S at a cocktail party on friendly turf: SpaceX's headquarters, next to a local airport in Hawthorne, south of Los Angeles. Techno music throbbed as the hangar filled with some five hundred guests—a Bluetooth-sporting, leather-jacket-wearing crew that included the producer Joel Silver, the director Jon Favreau, and the agent Ari Emanuel, who has reserved four of the cars. Twenty Roadsters sat in rows outside, their vanity plates a chorus of eco-jubilation—EV 2, AC POWR, CYA OPEK. The air was tangy with jet fuel and Eau Sauvage.

Anthony Kiedis, the lead singer of the Red Hot Chili Peppers, was telling Musk that the only problem with his Roadster was that "now I never drive my other car"—a Porsche. Rick Rubin, the co-head of Columbia Records, told me, "I want to be a Tesla owner, but when my friend"—he nodded at Kiedis—"tried to pick me up tonight it was painful." Rubin is a distinctly burly man, but many people have found that levering themselves into the Roadster's low cockpit calls to mind a prison break through a ventilation shaft. Rubin said that he was going to put down a deposit for the roomier Model S: "The quiet feels really good, just taking off without a sound."

When Musk slipped the silk cover off the show car, the crowd surged and cell-phone cameras flashed. "This car is going to show what's possible with electric vehicles," Musk promised. "You can fit a surfboard, a fifty-inch TV, and a mountain bike—at the same time." There were gasps. Praising the car's cornering, he boasted, "You'll need a spatula to flip this thing over." And with Tesla's planned QuickCharging—stations that the company intends to place at highway rest stops, where you'll be able to recharge your battery in forty-five minutes—"you could start here at breakfast and be halfway across the country by dinnertime."

For now, if you plug your Roadster into one of Tesla's seventy-ampere wall boxes (which the company will install in your garage for three thousand dollars), it takes nearly four hours to recharge the car completely. When I plugged a Roadster I was test-driving into a standard outlet in my sister's garage, its battery gained only nine miles in two hours. (However, as long as cars are "trickle charged" during off-peak hours, the current grid will be able to handle charging about a hundred and seventy-five million E.V.s.)

When I asked Musk how you could possibly get your Model S halfway across the country before dinnertime, we got into a back-and-forth that included discussion of higher speeds draining the battery faster because the drag increases with the square of the velocity; a possible anode change in the battery cells from graphite to silicon; the daunting logistics of charging an E.V. in the five minutes it takes to gas up a conventional car (it would require an eight-hundred-and-forty-kilowatt connection, which would drain the grid as much as a one-hundred-unit apartment building does in the course of a day)—and, on my end, such considerations as the country's width, and how often people need to eat and visit the bathroom, and the speed limit. "In a twenty-four-hour period," he finally suggested, "you could get halfway across the country, how about that?"

"Using the highway charging stations that haven't been built yet?" I said.

"Right!"

Musk longs to engage people in the mechanics of the constructed world. So when Governor Arnold Schwarzenegger made a late appearance at the launch party, Musk gave him a thorough tour of the car, detailing the location of the battery pack in the floor pan, the eventual rear-facing child seats, the electronic cutoff that caps the speed at a hundred and thirty miles per hour. "Huh," Schwarzenegger said. The Governor slid into the driver's seat and stretched appreciatively (having returned his Roadster because it constrained his mighty deltoids). He swiped a hand across the seventeen-inch dashboard computer. "Haptic screen," Musk said, leaning in. "Digital wireless as well. You can actually browse the Internet and see the Google Maps fly." Schwarzenegger held a pose of keen interest as photographers and videographers jostled for the shot.

"He has no technical understanding whatsoever," Musk said later, with a trace of disappointment. "But he's become very pro-environment—he made a deposit on a Model S." Meanwhile, after his cameo, Schwarzenegger rolled off in a convoy of sixteen-mile-per-gallon Yukon XLs.

Musk spends half the week at SpaceX and half at Tesla, which is headquartered in San Carlos, California. He bounces from meeting to meeting to meeting, never taking notes, nodding briskly as he caches information with a kind of sleep-deprived alertness. In early April, during Tesla's weekly executive staff meeting, Mike Donoughe, a Chrysler veteran, mentioned that a murky set of administrative problems at BorgWarner, the company's transmission supplier, was delaying Roadster production. Tesla needed an uninterrupted flow of cars to boost its thin cash reserves and shaky reputation for dependability, but Donoughe's verdict was gloomy: "If we can get eighty cars to customers this month, it would be a home run, but we're looking more at sixty-five, seventy."

Musk frowned. "This is life or death for us—if Borg-Warner doesn't deliver on time for more than a month, we're dead. Don't shield me from emergencies. I want to know the split second they occur, and have the option of taking a hand." The other executives bent over their notes, eyes averted.

"We believed we had it managed better than we did," Donoughe said.

"Because we're teed up to have a profitable third quarter, before Model S expenses start becoming significant," Musk continued. "So we need to make those cars, deliver them to customers, and have them work. Crazy." Everyone laughed, nervously.

After the meeting, Musk called the head of transmissions at BorgWarner to underscore the seriousness of the problem. Then he sent two employees from Tesla's office in Auburn Hills, Michigan, to BorgWarner's offices, nearby. "Tell them you're here to help," he said. "Be polite but immovable. And, unless the security guard throws you out, they will find the parts you need." The parts appeared, and Tesla delivered eighty-four cars in April.

Musk told me, "It's ironic that we're being held up once

again by the incumbent technology—the transmission—not the new one, the battery." BorgWarner is the company's third transmission maker. Marc Tarpenning, a Tesla co-founder, says, "We learned that the car industry is unbelievably good at delivering what they've done in the past with a little tweak— faster, or in yellow. But if you want something a lot different —a simplified transmission that's electrically actuated—that's too radical. The designers and engineers who can do radical changes all left Detroit forty years ago."

Silicon Valley's E.V. entrepreneurs portray their technology as a fundamental discontinuity, a break from Detroit's hidebound traditions. Yet, at the turn of the twentieth century, electric vehicles outsold all other types of cars. "Electric Road Wagons" and "Electrobats" were popular with women, because, unlike gas-powered vehicles, they required no strenuous cranking to start. (The Columbus Buggy Company proclaimed, "A delicate woman can practically live in her car yet never tire.") Cars with internal-combustion engines gradually took over, because they were easier to refuel and they cost less, as Henry Ford's assembly-line breakthroughs made his cars cheap enough for nearly everyone. Walter Flanders, the efficiency expert behind Ford's Model T, observed, "Henceforth the history of the industry will be the history of the conflict of giants." Over the decades, E.V.s surfaced as an occasional curiosity, but the memorable challenges to the giants were posed by engineers from Detroit, including Preston Tucker, in the nineteen-forties (whose eponymous sedan showcased disk brakes and a rear-mounted engine), and John DeLorean, in the nineteen-eighties (whose eponymous sports car had gull-wing doors and travelled through time in *Back to the Future*). Both companies were unable to scale up production and quickly collapsed. Tucker built only fifty-one cars.

E.V. devotees like to point out that electricity is everywhere, and that the country has more than a billion outlets. But many of those are tucked away behind sofas. What's more, many drivers park on the street: building a recharging infrastructure for them, one that feels as ubiquitous as the country's hundred and sixty thousand gas stations, will pose an expensive challenge. Mark Duvall, the director of electric transportation at the Electric Power Research Institute, says, of the cost of building charging stations, "If you want to use E.V.s to drive between cities, we're probably into the hundreds of billions."

Undeterred, Shai Agassi, a forty-one-year-old software whiz from Israel, plans to build a huge charging network. Agassi's marketing hook is an insistence that E.V.s are just like cell phones: while people like Musk build the phone, Agassi is going to build the network. He'll own your car's battery, and you'll pay only for the miles you drive with it. Two years ago, Agassi founded Better Place, a Silicon Valley–based company that intends to supply customers with E.V.s, built by Renault-Nissan; charging posts; and battery-switching stations for use on long trips. His first network is taking shape in Israel: before Renault's E.V.s arrive there, in 2011, Better Place is working to install a hundred thousand charging posts and build a hundred battery-switching stations, where a giant robotic arm will pull out your depleted battery and replace it with a charged one in less than a minute. He plans similar networks in Denmark, Australia, Hawaii, and Northern California, expanding centers of E.V. support to eventually cover the world.

Musk and Agassi would seem like natural allies, yet each is keenly aware of history's parsimony in recognizing pioneers. Agassi, who is trim, suave, and as relentless as a woodpecker, says of Musk, "Elon made the best car in the world, which is fantastic. But we're going to make the cheapest. Cheap wins." He explained that by 2020 the cost of an "electric mile" will be so negligible that you'll essentially be buying or leasing your E.V. (minus the battery, which he owns) for about the cost of what you used to pay each year for gas. "You can't solve the world's climate problem with two hundred and fifty expensive cars—you need seventy million a year," Agassi says. "It's the difference between building a small device that connects to your TV, called Minitel, or building the Internet. We went out to do the Internet. This is iPod, this is Ford Model T, taking eighty per cent of the market." He drew a graph, one of many he plotted as we talked. "You've got to focus on the twenty-five per cent of cars that drive twenty-K plus a year and emit sixty-six per cent of the emissions." He inked in dots and vectors. "To do that group, you've got to have battery exchange—and you have to give the car to them for free, because they're the average Joes who buy clunkers, drive them a lot every day, and consume them to the end. Forget about these guys"—Agassi gestured to where forty per cent of the cars lay, those which drive fewer than six thousand miles a year—"the George Clooneys and Leo DiCaprios. They give you a lot of publicity, but Leo doesn't drive a lot of miles."

Agassi's projections for the price of electricity and E.V.s in the coming years are aggressive; the main problem he faces, though, is persuading manufacturers other than Renault to build E.V.s with batteries that are easy to detach and exchange. None of the auto executives I spoke with expressed any inclination to build their cars to suit Better Place. They had liability concerns about swapping, and proprietary concerns about their battery's design. Herbert Kohler, the vice-president for E-Drive and Future Mobility at the German automaker Daimler A.G., said tartly, "A standardized battery would have to result from a standardized car, and a standardized car didn't work under socialism in the G.D.R."—East Germany.

Just in case Agassi turns out to be right, Musk has decided to make the Model S's battery swappable. (The swap won't take place at Better Place stations, though; Agassi told me that he would stock batteries only from large automakers.) But Musk says that battery swapping won't really be necessary. Powerful batteries will allay most people's range anxiety, and innovation will make charging fast—or at least fast enough for people to do it while they grab a bite. "Don't build unicorn pastures until there are some unicorns," he said. "I think Shai is going to spend a lot of money and not have a lot to show for it." Still, Musk worries that the course of E.V. adoption may be determined less by the pertinent data than by personal magnetism. He noted, ruefully, "Shai is very charismatic and natural in group settings, so his information is always going to seem overimpressive, whereas mine seems underimpressive."

In early April, Tesla threw a cocktail party at the National Building Museum, in Washington, D.C., to show off the Model S to the only venture-capital firm worth hitting up these days: the federal government. (The Department of Energy alone is giving $27.4 billion in loans to improve fuel economy and encourage the nascent E.V. industry.) Partygoers could ride in the Model S around a sort of giant indoor slot-car track, at speeds of up to thirty-two miles an hour. They could also ride in the Roadster, but only outside, in the rain; when Musk was planning the party with Mary Beth Brown, he told her, "The Roadster hurts us in Washington—we want to deëmphasize it. We don't want to give the sense that this is about toys for rich people."

Diarmuid O'Connell, a former State Department official who acts as the company's government liaison, was buttonholing members of Congress and their aides, hitting Tesla's themes: environmentalism, of course, but also patriotism (innovation defines America); the economy (breakthroughs like the Model S will lift us out of the recession; we transfer trillions of dollars to the Middle East for oil); and national security (our dependence on oil compromises our foreign policy). When Thomas (Mack) McLarty, President Clinton's first chief of staff, emerged from the Model S, O'Connell brought him over to meet Musk, who was wearing a gray suit to fit in. McLarty, whose McLarty Companies owns ten car dealerships, cried, "This is exciting!" Musk gave a vigorous nod, and stood ready to field questions. But that was it.

"Elon's a wealthy, passionate, iconic figure, and it's a fascinating vision," McLarty told me, after he'd moved off. "But he's an independent producer, and my generation saw the DeLorean."

Musk took the microphone and addressed the crowd, ticking off the Model S's qualities. Afterward, he greeted Senator Maria Cantwell, of Washington, who chairs the Senate's energy subcommittee, and asked, "Did you hear my sales pitch?"

"Um, no. But I took your car for a little spin," Cantwell said noncommittally. Musk instantly launched into his latest version of the pitch: "The Roadster is a good car. The Model S is a great car. It's just a giant version of what you have in a laptop. The motor is only nine inches in diameter—you can actually pick it up"—and he was off, talking for four minutes as Cantwell waved at passing acquaintances over his shoulder. "The gear ratio allows more torque, yet the center of gravity is super low, and the battery being in the floor pan allows us to fit seven people—"

Cantwell patted Musk's hand. "Thank you!" she said, gliding off. O'Connell stepped in to debrief her, and she asked, "Why don't you do a minivan?" O'Connell explained that Tesla had struck out with Lou Rhodes, the president of the ENVI program at Chrysler, when it proposed building an electric power train for one of the automaker's minivans. Cantwell shook her head: typical. (When I followed up with Rhodes, he said, "Chrysler owns the minivan market, and we will stand alone on our minivan strategy going forward.")

Cantwell told me that she was concerned that while the Big Three struggle to stay in business China already has two hundred and fifty companies working to build batteries and electric cars and charging infrastructure. "Getting denser, more affordable batteries built here is the whole game," she said. "Otherwise, we're soon going to be as dependent on Chinese batteries as we are now on Middle East oil." But Cantwell acknowledged that there is no political will in Congress to prod consumers to switch to electric by taxing gasoline heavily, as is done in Europe.

Mike Carr, the legal counsel for the Senate Energy and Natural Resources Committee, was also at the party. He said that Senator Jeff Bingaman, of New Mexico, who chairs the committee, had a bill that would introduce a "feebate" on cars according to their energy efficiency: gas guzzlers would be taxed and E.V.s would get a rebate. (The bill was introduced in the Senate in early August.) "But the automakers, while saying they favor gasoline taxes, oppose the idea—which essentially front-loads the cost of a gas tax into the purchase price—because they think it would make their cars more expensive now," Carr said. "These days, the auto industry is rarely in the position to be able to think long term."

At times, between meetings, Musk finds himself daydreaming about building a supersonic electric airplane, or a double-decker highway. Then he catches himself, with a start, and gets back to work. In April, just after resolving the transmission-delivery snafu, Musk met with Deepak Ahuja, Tesla's C.F.O. Ahuja told him that by July the production cost of the Roadster would drop to eighty-two thousand dollars, making the company's margin more than thirty per cent on each car. (The company wound up making its first monthly profit in July.) Ahuja went on, "We'd projected we'd be at three million dollars in Model S reservations by the end of

March, and we're at seven million a week later. So we're exactly double."

Musk spun in his chair like a boy. "Not bad! Not bad for the worst automotive environment since the Great Depression, all the stories about Tesla supposedly going bankrupt, people's net worth having taken a giant kick in the balls, and the fact that the car isn't coming out for two and a half years." And in May, in an important vote of confidence, Daimler A.G. bought nine per cent of Tesla, for fifty million dollars—even as it was relinquishing a twenty-per-cent stake in Chrysler, which it had owned entirely as recently as 2007. "Tesla enables us to skip a generation and get into electric as fast as possible," Daimler's Herbert Kohler told me.

In the ensuing months, however, as Musk shifted his focus to wooing the Department of Energy—which in late June extended $465 million to the company, to build two factories—and to getting the Roadster's 2.0 version out the door, the pace of Model S reservations fell markedly. Winning hearts and minds is a slog. G.M.'s Bob Lutz, who spoke with me on the day that his company announced it was closing thirteen plants and dropping its Pontiac brand, observed that first-mover advantage gets you only so far. "The hubris of Tesla is 'We're not going to fall into the trap of being like Detroit—we're going to be the Silicon Valley guys, nimble and innovative,'" Lutz said. "Everyone who tries to reinvent this business believes that auto companies are populated by dummies who don't understand Moore's Law. But, unlike a silicon chip, the modern automobile has to be a certain size, and carry a certain number of people, at a certain speed. Over thirty-five hundred parts sourced from around the world have to come together at the right place and the right time to produce sixty to seventy of these things an hour. These things are called cars. And to make them you need a large engineering staff, a workforce that demands retirement benefits, a tax staff, a fleet of accountants, and an unbelievable amount of reliability testing that Tesla can't afford to do right now—and we can't afford not to do. Inevitably, Tesla will discover that the only way to succeed on the scale we have is to be exactly like us."

Although more than a quarter of Tesla's employees come from the Big Three, and although the company has begun to cultivate the Stakhanovite mind-set necessary for mass production, Musk argues that Tesla is nothing like G.M., and never will be: "We're still very little, and so while the big automakers won't be afraid of us, they should be afraid of their competitors imitating us. Our success will make Toyota worry about what BMW will do, and G.M. worry about Honda—will create a concern about being late for the party. So our role is as a guiding light, helping bring these cars to market five or ten years faster than they would have otherwise—which could make an important difference for saving the species." He closed one eye to gaze at the ceiling and beyond, calculating. "Still," he added, "we could be selling a million cars a year in ten years. That seems doable." That would require Tesla to increase its current production a thousandfold. It would also be more cars than G.M. will make in the U.S. this year.

James Harkin

Caught in the Net

*Whatever prophets of the net say, information for
its own sake is not power. Power is power. The
relentless gush of electronic information and
invitations to offer feedback which now come our
way can often obscure where real power lies.*

Thursday 26 March 2009, day 66 of Barack Obama's presidency, may be remembered as the moment at which his clean-living administration went to pot. The occasion was the launch of Obama's online town hall, Open for Questions, designed to build on the momentum of his net-fuelled campaign by inviting ordinary Americans to pose questions directly to their new leader. The idea was touted in advance on the White House website, and 92,000 people rolled up online to speak directly to the president.

When the roster of questions bubbled up to the president's monitor at the press conference, however, most were obsessed with the decriminalisation of dope. The imbalance was astonishing. In the middle of a deep recession and with America's armed forces still mired in Iraq and Afghanistan, the top four questions relating to both the economy and the budget were all about marijuana. The issue of dope dominated in the section about "green jobs and energy," too, where the most popular query invited the new president to "decriminalise the recreational/medical use of marijuana so that the government can regulate it, tax it, put age limits on it, and create millions of new jobs and a multibillion-dollar industry right here in the US." After addressing some questions that came in lower down the list, Obama gamely tried to laugh the whole thing off. "I have to say that there was one question that was voted on that ranked fairly high, and that was whether legalising marijuana would improve the economy and job creation," he said. "And I don't know what this says about the online audience."

I wonder what it says about our politicians. The internet is one of the most dazzling inventions of the past 50 years, indispensable to the way we live today. But the truth is that many of those in authority have stopped seeing the internet as a medium by which people send messages and receive feedback via a loop of electronic information. Instead, they have invested the flow of electronic information with a metaphysical significance about human nature and how things work. That is why politicians can talk about the net as a revolution. It's how they can see a game of sending out information into the electronic ether and batting back feedback as having anything to do with democracy. And it's why some thinkers have begun to imagine that online gadgetry might level the economic playing field and might even begin to alleviate inequality—that it might, in the memorable phrase of the *New York Times* columnist Tom Friedman, succeed in making the world flat.

How did this come about? Before the early network of computers that gave rise to the internet was cobbled together by researchers in American universities in the early 1970s, it was inspired by an idea called cybernetics. Cybernetics was the invention of an American mathematician named Norbert Wiener who, while working on an anti-aircraft predictor machine to help shoot down German bombers more efficiently during the Second World War, became fascinated by the philosophical implications of his own research. Looked at from the outside, according to Wiener, it was as if gunner, pilot and their respective instruments had all been fused together via an information loop into a new kind of self-regulating system that constantly righted its errors through feedback from its environment. Wiener concluded that, in the new age of electronic machines, all of us were best thought of as existing on a continuous electronic information loop, constantly sending out messages and rapidly responding to feedback in order to correct our mistakes.

Wiener's cybernetics was always an impoverished idea of how human relationships work. In the immediate aftermath of the Second World War, however, as intellectuals and scientists sought out unsullied new models for understanding human behaviour, it proved enormously influential. The US military would go on to use Wiener cybernetics to build sophisticated systems for air defence in the 1960s. Just as important, however, was the influence of cybernetics on the remnants of the American counterculture in the early 1970s. The momentum of the "revolution in the head" in 1968 quickly overvaulted itself, and many veteran hippies had responded by retreating to a nest of close-knit communes around the San Francisco Bay Area to escape the attention of the authorities. Even more so than the young pretenders of the New Left, the hotchpotch of radicals who made up the counterculture was suspicious of leadership of any kind. For some of them, Wiener's idea of laying an information loop between their various communal hideouts seemed to suggest a way around bureaucratic mechanisms for social control.

Many of those veterans of the counterculture would become enormously influential in the development of the computer industry and of the net in the following decades. As the hi-tech economy of the San Francisco Bay area spread outwards in the 1980s and early 1990s, and computers began to appear in more and more homes and offices, the idea of networks was borrowed by economists and business leaders. While the computer industry seemed to be advancing rapidly, it helped, too, that the old model of production—the traditional, Fordist economy of manufacturing goods on strictly regimented factory lines—was stumbling from recession to recession and that businesses were searching for new ways of operating. It occurred to many futurologists that what they were witnessing was the birth pangs of a whole new economy, one thoroughly networked and constantly adjusting itself to the continuous feedback of its suppliers and customers.

This new kind of economy would be powered by computers and electronic networking devices, to be sure, but it was about much more than just technology. What it demanded was nothing less than the flattening or levelling of the old-fashioned, hierarchical firm into a new, leaner kind of organisation that sat alongside its many and shifting employees and suppliers like a node in a network. By the late 1980s, influential think tanks such as the Global Business Network, staffed by former hippies like Stewart Brand, were offering advice to huge multinationals on how to re-engineer their operations according to cybernetic principles. One study of management literature in western countries, by the French sociologists Luc Boltanski and Eve Chiapello, found that between the 1960s and 1990s the number of mentions of networks increased more than twentyfold. After all, the logic went, if something as flat as a network could be so powerful, why not stretch everything flat so it looked just the same?

The politics of the counterculture had long been eclipsed, but its central idea of bringing about direct communication between peers outside of the reach of authority survived intact. In the course of just a few years at the beginning of this century, as broadband connections became widespread and opened up a permanent window on the web, many of us took to zoning out at work or disappearing into the spare room at home to spend hours watching or communicating with one another online. No longer content with passively absorbing information on the internet, we began to set up our own castles on its turf. As we came together in online social networks such as Facebook and Twitter, and busily ferried messages to and fro between ourselves in a vast online information loop, the idea began to gain ground that this exchange of information between peers in an online network would change everything before it. By laying a vast electronic information loop between all of us, we would put millions of ordinary people back in touch with each other as online peers, thus stretching everything perfectly flat and leaderless—and leaving bureaucracies and hierarchies, without any means of controlling information, to collapse of their own volition.

This picture of ourselves as essentially messaging creatures has now so far inveigled itself into our lives that we barely notice. It began as an idea that we could benefit from being joined together in a continuous loop of instruction and feedback. It is not without its uses. Google's enormous success in the search-engine business owes something to the cybernetic idea. While other online search engines were using human editors to serve us up a range of information, Google's brilliant technicians realised as early as a decade ago that the best way to organise the information out there on the web was to stitch every piece of information together in a series of sophisticated feedback loops.

Every time we choose from the list of hits that Google serves up to us in response to our search, we are helping Google rank the information of our peers, and that information is in turn used to track what the best destinations are on the web. When the company decided to measure the value of a website by looking at how many other people found it worthwhile, it sewed into its operation a feedback loop that helped traffic flow much more easily around its system. As a result, it became one of the richest companies on earth; Google is now capitalised at roughly $100bn. Its machinery makes for an ingenious way of organising our information on the web, but there is no reason to think that it can be of much help in organising the rest of our society.

As computer networks found their way everywhere, however, the idea that we can be treated as information processors on a giant social network was ushered in. One reason that politicians can be reluctant to question all this is that, with the fading of the conventional ideologies of left and right, there seem to be precious few good ideas around for organising the good society. That is why David Cameron was so keen to make the pilgrimage to Google's headquarters, and why Gordon Brown chooses to address Google conferences and be seen under its banner. For the same reason, many mainstream institutions are in thrall to the hokum of a new breed of internet evangelists. At the same time as newspapers in Britain and the US are firing trained journalists and cutting their staff numbers, many of them are also paying huge fees to listen to modish ideas about how net-based collaboration (so-called crowdsourcing) might help to reinvent their operations.

Take a closer look at the fate that befell Obama's online town hall. It turned out that a small Washington-based lobby group, the National Organisation for the Reform of Marijuana Laws, had urged its members to vote for questions supporting the legalisation of cannabis. What happened after that was significant. Lost in the bowels of the White House's website and unsure of how to make their presence felt, most of the nearly four million voters had simply chosen to "buzz up" the questions of the dope-smokers who had arrived just before them. To anyone who has studied how popularity contests work on a closed online information loop, none of this came as any surprise. In an intriguing experiment conducted in the last three months of 2004 and the first three of 2005, three academics at Columbia University in New York used the web to invite as many as 14,000 young people to rate songs by relatively unknown bands and download the ones they liked. The researchers began by dividing their subjects into two groups. They asked the first group to make their decisions independently of each other while they allowed the second to see a rolling chart of how many times, in descending order, each song had been downloaded by others—telling them, in effect, which songs were most popular among their peers.

The results, when they came in, were clear. Those who could see the download charts, the researchers discovered, gave higher ratings to the songs at the top of the chart and were more likely to download those songs. People tended to like songs more if other people liked them. The result was to make the choices of those in the second group unpredictable, with much depending on who rolled up to make their choices first. Identical songs were judged to be hits or flops depending on whether other people had been seen to download them earlier.

There is nothing new about facing pressure from our peers when it comes to making decisions about whether music is good or not. People have always been affected by the taste of those around them, and that susceptibility to influence helps them make up their own minds. The effect discovered by the Columbia University researchers, however, was much bolder and more specific than that. When an electronic feedback loop is called on to make decisions about quality, their work suggests, there arises an effect that throws everything out of kilter and amplifies the decisions of a few early arrivals into a randomly self-reinforcing spiral of continued popularity. Left to fend for ourselves in a sea of online information, with only our online peers for direction, our decisions about quality and taste, it seems, can become snagged in a self-perpetuating feedback loop of follow-the-leader.

American politicians are not the only ones trying to stitch politics back together with the information feedback loops. Two weeks before the inaugural outing of Barack Obama's online town hall, in a paper titled *Working Together,* Gordon Brown announced an initiative whereby people in England would get more powers to rate the performance of GPs, police, childcare and councils on-line. It was a scandal, said the Prime Minister, that online businesses such as eBay had "higher standards of transparency" than those for public services. The British government had thus far been "much too slow to make use of the enormous democratising power of information." To make amends, he said, National Health Service patients would, from this summer, be able to comment on local services and provide feedback on GPs through a new raft of websites.

Are the workings of an online auction site an appropriate model for a mature democracy? Think about how eBay works. Its operation is stitched together by information feedback loops in which buyers and sellers are encouraged to rank each other's honesty and reliability. It works very well, but only by introducing distortions of its own. In an intriguing public statement in February 2008, for example, eBay announced it was overhauling its feedback system to ban sellers from leaving negative comments about buyers. What was happening, it conceded, was that when buyers gave "bad" feedback to sellers from whom they had bought, those sellers responded by leaving negative feedback of their own. Fear of incurring such retaliation had driven both buyers and sellers to award one another excellent but quite unwarranted feedback. The system was in danger of collapsing into one of mutual self-congratulation. Far from being a model of democratic debate, eBay had begun to resemble a kind of robotic dance routine, in which one dancer's decision to step in one direction leads to everyone else automatically following suit.

Just like any other medium, the net has biases which pull our behaviour in peculiar ways. At its worst, making decisions on the net tends towards a self-reinforcing populism, which binds everyone together in an electronic chain gang. It is not hard to decipher these biases, if you analyse our experience online as a medium rather than celebrate it as a revolutionary new political idea. There is nothing wrong with politicians keeping up with new technology and the internet, but everything depends on what they expect that technology to do for them.

In his inspiring campaign for the presidency, Barack Obama used mobile phones and online social networks as a tool to spur his supporters into action. Since he arrived in the White House, however, his enthusiasm for the net has begun to look like an end in itself. Aside from his online popularity contests, Obama has made plans to digitise information about the workings of government and put it online. Our own Cabinet Office, through its Power of Information review, has been doing much the same.

This is all very well, but without directions to guide us through this ocean of electronic information, the danger is that we might drown in the data. Transparency is all very well, but not all of us are investigative journalists. Politicians are supposed to make sense of the mountain of data that comes their way and to shape it into arguments and ideas—not simply throw it back to us in digital form, to see what we think.

It is true that many of our mainstream cultural and political institutions lack legitimacy and are limping from one crisis to the next. They are out of sync with the populace, and they seem to know it. All of this presents exciting possibilities for those of us who are interested in change. Yet we should be wary of letting the information geeks inherit the earth, wary of replacing the crumbling authority of the media and political classes with a glut of electronic information and phantom ideas about democracy and equality.

Whatever the prophets of the net say, information is not power. Power is power, and the relentless gush of electronic information and invitations to offer feedback which now come our way can often obscure where real power lies. Marshall McLuhan's dictum, that the medium is the message, is in danger of becoming a self-fulfilling prophecy. If our rulers seem entranced by the medium of online information, perhaps that is because they have absolutely nothing else to say.

Alexis Madrigal

Telegraphs Ran on Electric Air in Crazy 1859 Magnetic Storm

A tipping point in the history of astronomy.

On Sept. 2, 1859, at the telegraph office at No. 31 State Street in Boston at 9:30 a.m., the operators' lines were overflowing with current, so they unplugged the batteries connected to their machines, and kept working using just the electricity coursing through the air.

In the wee hours of that night, the most brilliant auroras ever recorded had broken out across the skies of the Earth. People in Havana and Florida reported seeing them. *The New York Times* ran a 3,000 word feature recording the colorful event in purple prose.

"With this a beautiful tint of pink finally mingled. The clouds of this color were most abundant to the northeast and northwest of the zenith," the *Times* wrote. "There they shot across one another, intermingling and deepening until the sky was painfully lurid. There was no figure the imagination could not find portrayed by these instantaneous flashes."

As if what was happening in the heavens wasn't enough, the communications infrastructure just beginning to stretch along the eastern seaboard was going haywire from all the electromagetism.

"We observed the influence upon the lines at the time of commencing business—8 o'clock—and it continued so strong up to 9 1/2 as to prevent any business from being done, excepting *by throwing off the batteries at each end of the line and working by the atmospheric current entirely!*" the astonished telegraph operators of Boston wrote in a statement that appeared in *The New York Times* later that week.

The Boston operator told his Portland, Maine counterpart, "Mine is also disconnected, and we are working with the auroral current. How do you receive my writing?" Portland responded, "Better than with our batteries on," before finally concluding with Yankee pluck, "Very well. Shall I go ahead with business?"

In terms of the relationship between the Earth and its star, it is probably the weirdest 24-hours on record. People struggled to explain what had happened.

NASA's David Hathaway, a solar astronomer, said that people in the solar community were beginning to understand that there was a relationship between events on the sun and magnetism on Earth. But that knowledge was not widely disseminated.

Another theory held that auroras were actually atmospheric phenomena, that is to say, weather of a particular type. Proof of various sorts was offered. Auroras apparently had a sound, "the noise of crepitation," or crackling, that marked them as Earth-bound phenomena. Even weirder explanations arose, like meteorologist Ebenezer Miriam's hilariously quacky quote in *The New York Times*.

"The Aurora (*electricity discharged from the craters of volcanoes*) either dissolves in the atmosphere, and is thus diffused through space or concentrated into a *gelatineus* [sic] substance forming *meteors,* called *shooting stars,*" Miriam wrote. "These meteors dissolve rapidly in atmospheric air, but sometimes reach the earth before dissolving, and resemble thin starch."

But some scientists were on the right track. Eighteen hours before the storm hit, Richard Carrington, a young but well-respected British astronomer, had been making his daily sunspot observations when he saw two brilliant spots of light. We know now that what he was seeing was the heating up of the surface of the sun beyond its standard fusion-powered temperature of about 5,500 degrees Celsius. The energy to do so came from a magnetic explosion as a distended part of the sun's magnetic field snapped and reconnected.

"They give off the energy equivalent of about 10 million atomic bombs in the matter of an hour or two," Hathaway said. "[The 1859] one was special, and it was noticed because it was a white light flare. It actually heated up the surface of the sun well enough to light up the sun."

Though back then Carrington didn't know what he was looking at, five years of staring at the sun had taught him that what he was seeing was unprecedented. When in the wee hours of the next night, the skies all over the globe began turning brilliant colors, Carrington knew he was on to something.

"I think that it represents a tipping point in astronomy because for the first time, astronomers had concrete evidence that a force other than gravity could communicate itself across 93 million miles of space," said Stuart Clark, author of the book *The Sun Kings: The Unexpected Tragedy of Richard Carrington and the Tale of How Modern Astronomy Began.*

Still, it would be decades before the scientific theory would catch up with the observations. British heavyweights like Lord Kelvin opined that the sun could never deliver the level of energy that had been observed on Earth. Understanding what was happening without understanding how the sun worked or the nature of particles was not exactly easy.

"It's a great example of where theory and observation don't match up," Clark said. "The scientific establishment tends to believe the theory, but it's usually the other way around, and the observations are correct. You have to build up a critical mass of observations to shift the scientific theory."

Over time, more and more observations did shift the theory, and the sun was held properly responsible for geomagnetic storms. The technological lesson that electrical equipment could be disturbed was largely forgotten, though.

When a geomagnetic storm hits the Earth, it shakes the Earth's magnetosphere. As the magnetized plasma pushes the Earth's magnetic field lines around, currents flow. Those currents have their own magnetic fields and soon, down at the ground, strong electromagnetic forces are in play. In other words, your telegraph can run on "auroral current."

Geomagnetic storms, though, can have less benign impacts. On August 4, 1972, a Bell Telephone line running from Chicago to San Francisco got knocked out. Bell Labs researchers wanted to find out why, and their findings led them right back to 1859 and the auroral current.

Louis Lanzerotti, now an engineering professor at the New Jersey Institute of Technology, went digging in the Bell Labs library for similar events and explanations. Along with field research, the history became the core of a new approach to building more robust electrical systems.

"We did all this analysis and wrote this paper in '74 for the Bell Systems Technical Journal," Lanzerotti said. "And it really made a helluva difference in Bell Systems. They redesigned their power systems."

The fight to secure the Earth's technical systems from geomagnetic anomalies continues. Late last year, the National Academies of Science put out a report on severe space weather events. If a storm even approaching 1859 levels were to happen again, they concluded the damage could range upwards of a $1 trillion, largely because of disruptions to the electrical grid.

The data on how often huge storms occur is scarce. Ice

cores are the main evidence we have outside human historical documents. Charged particles can interact with nitrogen in the atmosphere, creating nitrides. The increased concentration of those molecules can be detected by looking at ice cores, which act like a logbook of the atmosphere at a given time. Over the last 500 years of this data, the 1859 event was twice as big as anything else.

Even so, the sun remains a bit of a mystery, particularly these tremendously energetic events. Scientists like Hathaway are able to describe why one geomagnetic storm might be bigger than another based on the details of how it arose, but they are hard pressed to predict when or why a freakishly large storm might arise.

Scientific understanding of how the sun impacts the Earth and its tech-heavy humans isn't complete, but at least we know when it got its start: the early hours of September 2, 1859.

"It's at that point we realized that these celestial objects affected our technologies and the way we wanted to live our lives," Stuart said.

And it turns out, our burning hot star still does.

Kevin Kelly

Technophilia

Advances in technological therapy.

An acquaintance of mine has a teenage daughter. Like most teens in this century she spends her day texting her friends, abbreviating her life into 140 character hints, flinging these haikus out to an invisible clan of mutual texters. It's an always-on job, this endless encapsulation of the moment. During dinner, while walking, on the toilet, lounging in bed, or in any state of wakefulness, to chat is to live. Like all teens, my friend's daughter tested the limits of her parents' restrictions. For some infraction or another, they grounded her. And to reinforce the seriousness of her misconduct, they took away her mobile phone. Immediately the girl became physically sick. Faint, nauseous, and so ill she couldn't get out of bed. It was as if her parents had amputated a limb. And in a way they had. Our creations are now inseparable from us. Our identity with technology runs deep, to our core.

According to psychologist Erich Fromm (and famed biologist E. O. Wilson) humans are endowed with biophilia, an innate attraction to living things. This hard-wired, genetic affinity for life and life processes ensured our survival in the past by nurturing our familiarity with nature. In joy we learned the secrets of the wild. The eons which our ancestors spent walking to find coveted herbs in the woods or stalking a rare green frog were bliss; ask any hunter/gatherer about their time in the woods. In love we discovered the boons each creature could provide, and the great lessons of hurt and healing organic forms had to teach us. This love still simmers in our cells. It is why we keep pets, and potted plants in the city, why we garden when supermarket food is cheaper, and why we are drawn to sit in silence under towering trees.

But we are likewise embedded with technophilia, the love of technology. Our transformation from smart hominid into Sapiens was midwifed by our tools, and at our human core we harbor an innate affinity for made things. We are embarrassed to admit it, but we love technology. At least sometimes.

Craftsmen have always loved their tools, birthing them in ritual, and guarding them from the uninitiated. As the scale of technology outgrew the hand, machines became a communal experience. By the age of industry, lay folk had many occasions to encounter complexifying technology larger than any natural organism they had ever seen and they began to fall under its sway. In 1900 the historian Henry Adams visited and revisited the Great Exposition in Paris, where he haunted the hall showcasing the amazing new electric dynamos, or motors. Writing about himself in the third person he recounts his initiation:

> To Adams the dynamo became a symbol of infinity. As he grew accustomed to the great gallery of machines, he began to feel the forty-foot dynamos as a moral force, much as the early Christians felt the Cross. The planet itself seemed less impressive, in its old-fashioned, deliberate, annual or daily revolution, than this huge wheel, revolving within an arm's-length at some vertiginous speed, and barely murmuring—scarcely humming an audible warning to stand a hair's-breadth further for re-

spect of power—while it would not wake the baby lying close against its frame. Before the end, one began to pray to it.

Each summer tens of thousands of enthusiasts make a pilgrimage to a nearby town along the Pacifica coast where I live to collectively bestow affection upon beautiful machines. The love-in, called Dream Machines, draws smitten fans of self-powered vehicles: cars, airplanes, steam engines. Rows of restored 1950s Chevys, and vintage Packards, in candy-color deliciousness woo their admirers. Rare species of airplanes, rivets gleaming, recline in a field, their painted propellers and exposed engines beckoning. A parade of oddly mutant motorcycles stream by. Behind one roped-off area a dozen old guys in overalls and greasy baseball caps tend noisy, hissing contraptions. This is the steam-powered zoo. Unlike modern machines, the innards of steam machines are visible, a kind of living transparency which solicits admiration for their mechanical honesty. One capped fellow demonstrates an insanely dangerous steam-powered cross-cut saw. Its naked teeth, as long as fingers, rake across a sacrificial log in a reptilian frenzy. The onlookers nod in approval.

I was there to witness the love. I was born lacking the normal male gene for car-madness. I am oblivious to the subtle differences in automobiles; I can't tell one sedan from another. I don't even know the model of the old van I drive. But I came to see others venerate classic technology. So it was weird to discover in one corner of this teeming rendezvous, three magnificent machines that snagged my soul as I tried to walk by. In an instant I was bewitched. I felt these were the most intoxicating vehicles I had ever seen. I had no idea what they were. A metal circular logo affixed to the front grill on each declared that they were Blastolenes.

Blastolenes are custom-built fantasies. They are oversized

car-like monsters that retained the rough proportions of ordinary vehicles, only at a disturbing larger scale. Imagine your car three times its current size. One Blastolene was strapped down to a flat bed truck as if it were a trophy wild gargantuan captured by hunters, and it might bust its chains at any moment and zoom off. Like many vehicles it was animalish: the Blastolene's exposed circulatory pipes suggested guts, its rounded wheel cases were muscular haunches, and its chrome tie rods were obviously bones. People crowded around, sighing in satisfaction at its remarkable beauty. I was seized with a deep affinity for the creature.

The second Blastolene on display was a convertible sedan built around a hulking M7 Patton Tank motor. The motor emitted percussions rather than sound. Its gigantism was irresistible. I suddenly realized that for 40 years I had been driving baby cars; this was the daddy car. Timidly creeping up to it (can I touch it?), I felt a childlike awe. I could feel its abnormal density; the solid gravity pulling me in toward it, yet its intimidating scale, like an elephant, warning me away.

No doubt much of the attraction of these machines is the way they ape, so to speak, animal life. Maybe our technophilia is merely biophilia in disguise. But some of the magnetism that draws us to them is also due to the dynamo that peeks from their interior. Its rotational energy twirls us. Many decades ago California writer Joan Didion made a pilgrimage to the Hoover Dam, a trip she recounts in her anthology, *The White Album*. She, too, felt the heart of a dynamo.

Since the afternoon in 1967 when I first saw Hoover Dam, its image has never been entirely absent from my inner eye. I will be talking to someone in Los Angeles, say, or New York, and suddenly the dam will materialize, its pristine concave face gleaming white against the harsh rusts and taupes and mauves of that rock canyon hundreds or thousands of miles from where I am.

. . . Once when I revisited the dam I walked through it with a man from the Bureau of Reclamation. We saw almost no one. Cranes moved above us as if under their own volition. Generators roared. Transformers hummed. The gratings on which we stood vibrated. We watched a hundred-ton steel shaft plunging down to that place where the water was. And finally we got down to that place where the water was, where the water sucked out of Lake Mead roared through thirty-foot penstocks and then into thirteen-foot penstocks and finally into the turbines themselves. "Touch it," the Reclamation man said, and I did, and for a long time I just stood there with my hands on the turbine. It was a peculiar moment, but so explicit as to suggest nothing beyond itself.

. . . I walked across the marble star map that traces a sidereal revolution of the equinox and fixes forever, the Reclamation man had told me, for all time and for all people who can read the stars, the date the dam was dedicated. The star map was, he had said, for when we were all gone and the dam was left. I had not thought much of it when he said it, but I thought of it then, with the wind whining and the sun dropping behind a mesa with the finality of a sunset in space. Of course that was the image I had seen always, seen it without quite realizing what I saw, a dynamo finally free of man, splendid at last in its absolute isolation, transmitting power and releasing water to a world where no one is.

Of course dams inspired dread and disgust as well as awe and admiration. Soaring, breathtaking dams frustrate the return of single-minded salmon and other spawning fish, and they indiscriminately flood homelands. In the technium revulsion and reverence often go hand in hand. Our biggest technological creations are like people in that way; they elicit our deepest loves and hates. On the other hand no one has ever been revolted by a cathedral of redwoods. In reality no dam, even Hoover dam, is eternal under the stars since rivers have a mind of their own; they pile up silt behind the dam's wedge so that eventually their waters can crawl over it. But while it stands, the artificial wins our admiration. We can identify with the dynamo revolving forever, as we feel our living hearts must do.

Passions for the made run wide. Almost anything manufactured will have adoring fans. Cars, guns, cookie jars, fishing reels, tableware, you name it. Their fans lavish attention by comprehensively collecting all variants of the technology, or modifying the standard form, or by imitating their own version. Not surprisingly, fans of a feather gather together. I tallied up the number of online forums for manufactured items commonly adored. One might think of these as churches. I found over 40,000 online congregations dedicated to honoring various cars, more than 10,000 different fan groups enamored of motorcycles, 6,000 assemblies really into boats, 5,000 fellowships serving avid gun owners, and 1,000 denominations obsessed with all types of cameras. The list for other artifacts, tools, and machines commanding their own smitten followers would run into the hundreds.

MIT sociologist Sherry Turkle calls a particular specimen of technology that is revered by an individual an "evocative object." These bits of the technium are totems that serve as a springboard for identity, or for reflection, or for thinking. A doctor may love his/her stethoscope, as both badge and tool; a writer might cherish a special pen and feel its smooth weight pushing the words on their own; a dispatcher can love his ham radio, relishing its hard-won nuances, as a magical door to other realms that opens to him alone; and a programmer can easily love the root operating code of a computer for its essential logical beauty. Turkle says, "We think with the objects we love, and we love the objects we think with." She suspects that most of us have some kind of technology that acts as our touchstone.

I am one of them. I am no longer embarrassed to admit that I love the internet. Or maybe it's the web. Whatever you want to call the place we go to while we are online, I think it is beautiful. People love places, and will die to defend a place they love, as our sad history of wars prove. Our first encounters with the internet/web portray it as a very distributed electronic dynamo—a thing one plugs into—and that it is. But the internet is closer to the technological equivalence of a place. An uncharted territory where you can genuinely get lost. At times I've entered the web just to get lost. In that lovely surrender, the web swallows my certitude and delivers the unknown. Despite the purposeful design of its human creators, the web is a wilderness. Its boundaries are unknown, unknowable, its mysteries uncountable. The bramble of intertwined ideas, links, documents, and images create an otherness as thick as a jungle. The web smells like life.

It knows so much. It has insinuated its tendrils of connection into everything, everywhere. The net is now vastly wider than me, wider than I can imagine, so in this way, while I am in it, it makes me bigger too. I feel amputated when I am away from it.

I find myself indebted to the net for its provisions. It is a steadfast benefactor, always there. I caress it with my fidgety fingers; it yields up my desires, like a lover. Secret knowledge? Here. Predictions of what is to come? Here. Maps to hidden places? Here. Rarely does it fail to please, and more marvelous, it seems to be getting better every day. I want to remain submerged in its bottomless abundance. To stay. To be wrapped in its dreamy embrace. Surrendering to the web is like going on aboriginal walkabout. The comforting illogic of dreams reigns. In dreamtime you jump from one page, one thought, to another. First on the screen you are in a cemetery looking at an automobile carved out of solid rock, the next moment, there's a man in front of a black board writing the news in chalk, then you are in jail with a crying baby, then a woman in a veil gives a long speech about the virtues of confession, then tall buildings in a city blow their tops off in a thousand pieces in slow motion. I encountered all those dreamy moments this morning within the first few minutes of my web surfing. The net's daydreams have touched my own, and stirred my heart. If you can honestly love a cat, which can't give you directions to a stranger's house, why can't you love the web?

Our technophilia is driven by the inherent beauty of the technium. Admittedly, this beauty has been previously hidden by a primitive phase of development that was not very pretty. Industrialization was dirty, ugly, and dumb in comparison to the biological matrix it grew from. A lot of that stage of the technium is still with us spewing its ugliness. I don't know whether this ugliness is a necessary stage of the technium's growth, or whether a smarter civilization than us could have tamed it earlier, but the arc of technology's origins from life's evolution, now accelerated, means that the technium contains all of life's inherent beauty—waiting to be uncovered.

Technology does not want to remain utilitarian. It wants to become art, to be beautiful and "useless." Since technology is born out of usefulness, this is a long haul. Robots will proliferate in a million different varieties and levels. Most will never be as smart as a grasshopper, and only few droids will surprise us with their intelligence. But the goal of every robot, and every machine and tool, is to exist for its own sake. To exist not only because it is useful, but because its existence is beautiful. There is evidence of that back on the fields of the Dream Machines, in the rows of mechanical glamour. While the Blastolene and lollipop 1950s Chevys are potentially useful—as transport—few are actually used that way. They are coddled, nursed and nurtured, repaired and improved, adored and honored, and sculpted into longevity by the sheer love of their innate beauty. They are art.

Today, at the start of the 21st century, there are tens of million species of tools and technologies at loose in the world. Assuming a modest increase of only 5% additional new tools and kinds of artifacts every year, by the end of the century our planet will be overrun by manufactured possibilities. Our own human needs are not expanding at this rate. The continual rise in technological variety is propelled by the needs of other technologies. You have a house, then you get a car. Now your car needs a house, too. It doesn't have hands like you do, so it needs a garage-door opener for its house. It needs check up equipment to keep it healthy, and add-ons to keep it comfortable. The same goes for other kinds of hardware. Handheld devices need jackets, houses need paint, computers need peripherals. I estimate that about half of the denizens of the technium are technologies serving other technologies. If you remove a keystone technology from your home—say the computer—how many other devices and equipment would immediately become redundant? Remove your car, and what else can go? Remove your stove, and then count the pieces of gear no longer needed.

But we won't let these subordinate technologies go, based on the evidence so far. We don't "need" a lot of what we maintain. We keep specific technology around not only because it may be useful, but because we like to have it around. The gear, devices, networks form an interdependent ecosystem of interrelated parts, and we have a technophilia for its survival.

We love the jungly mesh of the technium, and the way we can lose ourselves in it. We rebel at the negative costs of this interrelatedness, and its negative externalities such as pollution (global warming is a type of pollution), but we have a deep affinity for its web. We continue to manufacture new ideas and new artifacts, not because we always need them, but because the technium needs them, and because we find the technium attractive.

Most evolved things are beautiful, and the most beautiful are the most highly evolved. Cities display this principle clearly. Newborn, unrefined cities lack depth, and so, throughout history humans find new cities ugly. The first few versions of London were considered heinous eye sores. But over generations, every urban block in that city and all others are tested by daily use. The parks and streets that work are retained; those that fail are demolished. The height of buildings, the size of a plaza, the rake of an overhang are all adjusted by variations until they satisfy. But not all imperfection is removed, nor can it be since many aspects of a city—say the width of streets—cannot be changed easily. So urban workarounds and architectural compensations are added over generations. Additionally, every available opportunity to build within a city is grabbed. The tiniest alley way is utilized for public space, the smallest nook becomes a store, the dampest arch under a bridge filled in with a home. Over centuries, this constant infilling, ceaseless replacement and renewal, and complexification—or in other words, evolution—creates a deeply satisfying esthetic. The most beautiful places are those that reveal layers of time. They accrue forms uniquely fitted to that place. Every corner in a city carries the long history of the city embedded in it like a hologram, glimpses of which unfold as we stroll by it.

The superb special effects magicians working for Hollywood discovered how to exploit the principle of evolutionary beauty when filming made-up worlds. Their fantastic cities and convincing props of the future are in reality new items, having been imagined only days earlier. To give them the convincing heft of reality, and the attractive richness we associate with beautiful things, the effects wizards devise a layered evolutionary backstory for each item or place. Model makers layer on "greeblies," or intricate surface details that reflect a fictitious past history. This artificial evolution produces objects and places that exhibit what George Lucas calls the "used future." For instance a detailed ray gun arrives at its current design via an imaginary backstory in which its predecessors were once longer and powered by a different energy source; the gun thus contains vestigial ridges and tubes. We feel authenticity. A backstory assumes that a 22nd century city had been bombed in a previous age; its earlier primitive steel ruins under gird the foundation of recent crystalline towers. It looks beautiful.

Evolution is not just about complications. One pair of scissors can be highly evolved, and beautiful, while another is not. Both scissors entail two swinging pieces joined at their center. But in the highly evolved scissors, the accumulated knowledge won over thousands of years of cutting is captured by the forged and polished shape of the scissor halves. Tiny twists in the metal hold that knowledge. While our lay minds can't decode why, we interpret that fossilized learning as beauty. It has less to do about smooth lines and more to do about smooth continuity of experience. The attractive scissors, or beautiful hammer, or gorgeous car, carry in their form the wisdom of their ancestors.

Not all stuff will attract our emotions, and the same lifelikeness and sentience will often infuriate us. Professor Sherry Turkle has spent her professional life studying (and worrying about) the human propensity towards technophilia. For the past three decades MIT engineers have designed a series of robots that increasingly take on attributes of human personality. The latest one is called Nexi. When Nexi is not on, the researchers pull a curtain around it. One day a student came in late to work on the robot, but found no one else around, so she pulled back the curtain. She was startled and confused to find Nexi blindfolded. What did it mean? As Turkle relates the story: "It raised the question in the mind of the perplexed student, are we protecting the people around the robot, or are we protecting the robot? The blindfold immediately brought up the fantasy of torturing the robot. You know, if it's alive enough to need a blindfold, then maybe it's alive enough to be tortured."

We are so eager to love technology that Turkle is worried this love blinds us. In her laboratory Turkle observes how ordinary people feel about anthropic technology. She has been surprised at how little encouragement humans need to surrender love for machines. The merest suggestion of humanlike eye movement, the tiniest hint of active eyebrows, and the roughest ready smile on an otherwise obviously metal machine can make a person melt before it. Even feel bad about turning it off. Humans will treat any minimally anthropomorphized droid like it not only deserves our affections, but in some strange way is returning our love. That worries Turkle because she is concerned whether we will diminish our own humanity in order to match this minimal humanity we spy in our creations. If we let robots take care of the elderly as they want do in Japan, will the elderly become robot like to meet them? As computer scientist Jaron Lanier, another worrier of technophilia, puts it: "We make ourselves stupid in order to make computers seem smart. I don't worry about computers getting intelligent, I worry about humans getting dumber."

In the future, we'll find it easier to love technology. Machines win our hearts with every step they take in evolution. Like it or not, anthropic robots (at the level of pets at first) will gain our affections, since even minimal life-like ones do already. The internet provides a hint of the maximal passion possibilities of the technium. The global internet's nearly organic interdependence, and emerging sentience make it wild, and its wildness draws our affections. No human can turn away from the trick of anthropomorphism, and not be seduced by the humanity we project onto look-alikes, but the attraction of highly evolved technology is not only in its reflection of our faces. We are deeply attracted to its beauty, and its beauty resides in its evolution. Humans are the most highly evolved organs we have experienced, so we fixate on imitations of this form (quite naturally), but our technophilia is fundamentally not for anthropy, but for evolution. Humanity's most advanced technology will soon leave imitation behind and create obviously non-human intelligences, and obviously non-human robots, and obviously non-earth-like life, and all these will radiate an attractiveness that will dazzle us.

As it does, we'll find it easier to admit that we have an affinity for it. In addition the accelerated arrival of tens of millions more artifacts will deposit more layers onto the technium, polishing existing technology with more history, and deepening its embedded knowledge. Year by year, as it advances, technology, on average, will increase in beauty. I am willing to bet that in the not-too-distant future the magnificence of certain patches of the technium will rival the splendor of the natural world. We will rhapsodize about this technology's charms, marvel at its subtlety, travel to it with children in tow, to sit in silence beneath its towers.

And this is as it should be because technology wants to be loved.

Joshuah Bearman

Can D.I.Y. Supplant the First-Person Shooter?

The burgeoning fringe of indie designers who may be transforming the future of games.

The face of the enemy flashed across a 20-foot screen. "That's right," Jason Rohrer announced. "It's Roger Ebert." There were a few boos, as several hundred people stirred in their seats. The film critic's cherubic face stared at the audience. "Ebert said video games can't be art," Rohrer said. "He issued all of us a direct challenge. And we need to find an answer."

Rohrer was addressing the Game Developers Conference, one of his industry's premier trade events. Each spring, the conference convenes in San Francisco, and among the tens of thousands of people who attend is a burgeoning fringe of independent designers like Rohrer who hope to radically transform their medium. "A realization is dawning that games can be much more than what they are now," Rohrer told me later. "They even have the potential to be meaningful in deep, fundamental ways."

These game designers, a self-described indie scene, form a tightly knit group with a do-it-yourself culture and a rebellious spirit—something like a 'zine movement for video games. New and cheap technologies have enabled the movement's rise. New tools for production and distribution—through smartphones, over the Web and via downloadable services on PlayStation, Wii and Xbox consoles—now make it possible for individuals to conceive, develop and publish their own games.

Rohrer himself is a kind of Thoreauvian game designer, a 31-year-old back-to-the-land programmer-philosopher who lives in Las Cruces, N.M., where he codes his eccentrically engrossing games, which can feel like digitally mediated poetic moods, on an ancient computer and makes them available free online. "Now anyone can do it," he says, "which is not how the mainstream video-game industry works."

Video-game companies were once nimble trailblazers born in the countercultural spirit of the 1970s. But it didn't take long for the industry to grow into a kingdom of conglomerates, spending tens of millions of dollars on big titles. Soaring development costs squeezed out small publishers and stifled creativity. "There are some great mainstream games, but they are getting to be fewer and further between," says Rob Auten, who used to run video-game production for 20th Century Fox. "Our industry is probably more risk-averse than Hollywood. It is extremely difficult to break the patterns of the establishment."

Hence the growing opposition. At the conference, the indie community gathered daily, halfway down one wing of the basement, in Room 131, where Rohrer and dozens of other speakers discussed what you might call games for games' sake. It was a diverse group, including teenagers who make Web games for fun; fine-arts refugees who create digital esoterica; and indie success stories, like Jenova Chen, the co-creator of the PlayStation 3 hit Flower, and Jonathan Blow, who almost single-handedly created Braid, perhaps the most successful independent game of all time. Although theirs is a loyal opposition—they say it is because they love video games so much that they are called to action—there is a playfully polemical attitude among indie gamers, some of whom wore matching eyepatches around the conference as a sign of solidarity. They are activists, people who want to take on juggernauts with two-megabyte downloads. For them, games are software manifestos.

The industry is starting to take notice. Two years ago, almost no one had heard of Jason Rohrer. Then he made Passage, a brief but powerful meditation on mortality that created a stir even before it caused Clint Hocking, the creative director at Ubisoft, the world's fourth-largest game company, to shed tears. Hocking used Passage to publicly indict his colleagues at last year's conference. "Why can't we make a game that . . . means something?" Hocking asked. "A game that matters?"

Many of the mainstream designers who heard Hocking's lecture a year ago now piled into Room 131 to hear Rohrer ask those questions again. "Other media are capable of masterpiece-level works of art," Rohrer said. Behind him, a slide showed Picasso's *Guernica,* a poster for the movie *Blue Velvet* and the cover of *Lolita.* "The question we have to ask is: How can we follow in their footsteps?"

Video games are too big for their own good, Rohrer told me as we walked through one of the several convention-hall floors —some 300,000 square feet of screaming bells and digital whistles: supernaturally enhanced combat, turbocharged vehicles, many-eyed monsters with seemingly phlegm-covered fangs and the expensive software that makes it all possible. The conference was a preview of the next incremental step in the industry's quest to make video games bigger, louder, more realistically violent.

Showcasing these flashy graphics requires bigger teams and more money, which has guided the industry toward safe prospects like licensed properties and sequels. Even when working on more original fare, the enormous teams that create today's video games dilute artistic intention. There are exceptions like Will Wright, whose legacy includes The Sims, but they stand out because they are exceptions. "For the most part," Rohrer said, "there's no single person trying to bring a specific vision to life."

Making matters worse, according to Rohrer and others, video games fall into the trap of using the wizardry and craft of those big teams to emulate movies—bad movies at that. The narrative elements in today's big games tend to be retreads of film-genre clichés. Or they're extensions of actual film brands, like *The Godfather*. Rohrer calls this cinematic approach to video games "asymptotic": in his view there's no point in making video games as good as movies, because we already have movies. "Just as early film production copied the stage," he said, video games have yet to escape the influence of film. "Eventually film figured out editing, camera movement —the tools that made movies movies. Video games need to discover what's special and different about their own medium to break out of their cultural ghetto."

This is something that Eric Zimmerman, an independent game designer, has been thinking and writing about for years. Zimmerman, who studied painting as an undergraduate, co-wrote *Rules of Play,* a well-regarded textbook on game design. "Maybe games are not about communication the way movies are," Zimmerman says. "They're about interaction—with a system or other players, with rules."

At the Game Developers Conference, the avant-garde assembled itself around the Independent Games Festival, a patch of convention floor where more than two dozen idiosyncratic titles were on display. Not far away, cheers rose as gamers played blockbuster releases like Street Fighter IV, but there was still healthy traffic around whimsical, mostly two-dimensional games with titles like I Wish I Were the Moon. Because of their lo-fi graphics, these titles might look like kids' games to the casual viewer. Or they may not look much like games at all, abandoning conceits like competition and levels, winning and losing. Osmos appeared to be an amoebic adventure in space. Coil begins by piloting a sperm in search of an ova. Blueberry Garden, a floor favorite that was named the best game in the festival, looked like a surreal moving storybook with a flying, beaked protagonist.

Billed by its programmer, Erik Svedang, as a game of "curiosity and exploration," Blueberry Garden features little instruction and no puzzles—other than the question of what exactly to do next—but roaming among the garden's flora and fauna to the sounds of a Debussy-like soundtrack is captivating. "Dude, you just kind of float around and get those blueberry power-ups," one player explained to his friend. But the directionless dream world of the garden turns out to be a seductive trap. The garden is slowly filling with water; only once it's inundated do you realize how to escape. Blueberry Garden's quick denouement makes it more of a clever ruse than a great game, but the emotional arc—being lulled into a dream and then forced awake for survival—was original. Most important to the indie admirers, the game demonstrated what one person can do to make something new and sell it for just $5.

Simplicity prevails among indie games and not just because developers lack the resources for complexity. Stripping to the fundamentals, indie game designers say, allows them to innovate. "Designing a game can be like a Japanese garden," Jenova Chen says. "It's not what you put in but how much you take away." In 2005, while at the University of Southern California's graduate program for interactive media, Chen and Kellee Santiago created Cloud, a daydream of a game where a boy stuck in a hospital imagines himself floating in the sky, corralling clouds into shapes of his choosing. When Cloud went online, it was downloaded 500,000 times. "It crashed the school's server several times," Chen says.

Chen and Santiago formed their own boutique developer, Thatgamecompany, and signed a three-game contract with Sony. Their company now has 10 employees. Flower, the second title from Thatgamecompany, was released this year over the PlayStation Network. There is some debate in the indie scene over whether a deal with Sony means that you've moved on to the mainstream, but Chen says indie gamers should be happy that companies like Sony are starting to respond to the movement's successes. "Flower is like an ambassador for the rest of the indie world," Jason Rohrer says. "It shows you that what we're doing can appeal more broadly."

Flower is striking to behold. In it, you gather and pilot a stream of flower petals through a series of landscapes by turning the controller in your hands, somewhat like a steering wheel. Flying along the rows of bulbs growing in the grass releases more petals to join your caravan. As you green the grass and bring color to the wind, the game gives the sensation of unlocking spring. And vividly so: unlike most indie games, Flower's visuals are as sophisticated as any big title. As many as 200,000 individual blades of grass can ripple in your wake. "I like technology," Chen says, "but the blockbuster games use it for the same thing over and over again. What we tried to innovate was the emotional content."

Flower has an environmental message, about the fragility of life, but more important is the primal experience of playing. You can experience it like a film, passing through a whole range of emotions from beginning to end. "Flower," Chen says, "is about the sublime." It is a game to be played in one sitting, he said, and preferably "alongside your lover."

If Chen is a sensualist, evoking feeling with focused graphics, Rohrer is the genre's minimalist. Rohrer's most influential game, Passage, is two megabytes and can be downloaded in seconds. All the action is displayed in a horizontal window 12 pixels tall. Your character and environs are two-dimensional, about as vivid as Pac-Man. The game lasts just five minutes.

Navigating the game is not the challenge: you control the protagonist with simple keyboard strokes. You sense the world is big, but it can be glimpsed only through a small window that scrolls along as your little blurry figure encounters little blurry obstacles (walls, trees, stones, etc.) and occasional little blurry treasures (actual treasure, in boxes). There is only one other person, and you meet her almost immediately. You can choose to go on by yourself or to become forever bonded by freeing her little pixilated heart. Together, the game is harder but more rewarding: navigating the dense obstacles is more difficult as a pair, but the treasure and the distance traveled yield more points. You have a companion in a lonely world.

And that world is changing. At the start you are on the far left of the window. On the other side is a rippling, dotted haze. As you head toward this uncertain future, your perspective shifts, inexorably sliding forward. Eventually you and your companion are balding, stooping, growing old. There is only so much time, for togetherness, treasure or both. As you reach the right side of the window, the dotted haze is now behind you, a past, receding into the distance. Then your wife dies. Then you die.

"And then you can start over," Rohrer says. "Which you have to do to get everything out of Passage." Only through multiple attempts can you fully appreciate the consequences of your choices. By the third run, the finitude starts to settle in. No matter how well you do, you'll cross that screen until it goes blank. The revelation is not in the game's story; rather, it resides in the player's agency. With 300 seconds of rudimentary graphics, Passage created the first interactive memento mori.

"People are starting to realize that games can't survive on narrative and character," Rohrer says. "It's not what video games are meant to do. It doesn't explore what makes them unique. If they are going to transcend and have real meaning, it has to emerge from game mechanics. Play is what games offer."

The response to Passage was mixed. Some called it a pretentious failure, neither art nor a game. Others thought it was a strange but sweet exercise. And then there were those who declared it a giant step forward, an unlikely demonstration of the power of video games. Rohrer's champion Hocking, in his speech the previous year, sharply chided his entire industry for failing to innovate as much as indie designers like Rohrer who are "tinkering away in their spare time."

Hocking told me: "These games have used what is innate to games—their interactivity—to make a statement about the human condition. And we in the industry seem to not be able to do that."

Jonathan Blow, a near celebrity at the conference, spent more than two years and $180,000 of his own money to create a captivating game called Braid. Blow is intense and intellectual, a vocal critic who has repeatedly compared the gaming mainstream to cigarettes and junk food. He burnishes his critique with language you might expect from a critical-theory seminar, attacking the "Skinnerian reward scheduling" of games like World of Warcraft, the hugely successful online game, as "unethical" and "predicated on a kind of player exploitation."

Blow's prickly antagonism toward mainstream games has been amplified by the commercial and critical success of Braid, which he released first on Xbox Live. Now available on personal computers and the PlayStation, Braid has been downloaded—and paid for—more than 400,000 times. "It is a revelation," Rohrer says. "In terms of a game that deals with complex, subtle and multifaceted themes, the kind of themes you would encounter in a novel, there's nothing like it."

Braid involves a two-dimensional world of levels, not unlike the worldwide classic Super Mario Brothers. But unlike most platformers, neither the chronology nor the game play is linear. As the game opens, we learn that Braid's male protagonist has lost a girl and wants her back. As the character moves through the worlds of Braid, he can manipulate time in several ways: for example, to undo mistakes; to repeat actions through a ghostly doppelgänger; to slow the present. Blow has said that Braid takes its inspiration from, among other sources, Italo Calvino's *Invisible Cities* and David Lynch's *Mulholland Drive.*

Resolving Braid's mysteries often requires creating doubles of yourself and then cooperating with them in intricate plans. Beyond the metaphysical suggestions, Braid is unusually satisfying as game play. It is also an aesthetic experience: Braid was designed by Blow and then rendered by David Hellman, an illustrator. The delicate watercolors and haunting soundtrack combine with the game play to create a penetrating melancholy.

"Braid is something you could show to Roger Ebert and say, 'Here is a work of authorial intention,'" Rohrer says. "It captures something about the modern zeitgeist." It is also a postmodern work, reiterating traditional features—puzzles, princesses, levels—to comment on the medium itself. And it achieves all of this with very little conventional story. Rohrer likens the game to Thomas Pynchon's *V.* But in a novel or a movie, Rohrer says, the meaning emerges from the characters and the situations they find themselves in. Whereas in Braid, the meaning emerges from the game mechanic.

Braid is about the tragedy of time and the impermanence of memory; the time-reversal feature functions as a metaphor for loss and learning from mistakes. Blow denies the widely circulated theory that the game is about a breakup, suggesting that it is instead about a much more primary aspect of human experience. A practitioner of kung fu and tai chi, Blow has said that his character's four-dimensional journey is about the existential problems that arise from quantum mechanics. That may sound like quite a lot of intellectual pretension to wrap around a little cartoon man in a maze. But it does reflect the fact that Braid is both a game and the artistic vision of a single person.

Some observers say the success of Braid is an *Easy Rider* moment for video games. The industry is stagnating; the megastudio Electronic Arts lost a billion dollars in the last fiscal year. Along comes a game that takes artistic chances and shows there's a market for it. It's not the same market as the one for, say, the Halo franchise, whose latest offering sold 1.5 million copies in its first month. But for a lone developer, it turns out that a game like Braid—more than 400,000 downloads, about $15 apiece—can make you rich.

For the industry's major studios, the Independent Games Festival is now a place to scout talent, to buy new games and to hire new designers. Jason Rohrer agreed to be represented by a production company to make games for potential advertising campaigns, and he also signed up to create his first commercial release: a strategy game for Nintendo's hand-held console that will explore the trade in conflict diamonds in Africa.

But among indie designers, there is a wide spectrum of commercial engagement, from Jenova Chen's small shop under the banner of Sony to Jonatan Soderstrom, a 24-year-old designer who is content to transmit his bizarre output free to the world. "Yeah, the big publishers come around and want to talk to you," said Soderstrom, who until a few weeks ago lived in his childhood bedroom in his parents' house in Gothenburg, Sweden, and goes by the handle Cactus. Soderstrom, who has made more than 40 video games in the past five years, gave a talk in a filled-to-capacity Room 131: How To Make a Game in Four Hours. ("Games don't need to be fun," he said. "They can get intensely weird and freak you out.")

Now he and some friends were wandering down Haight Street holding a case of Pabst Blue Ribbon and drinking from paper bags. "I don't care about money," Soderstrom said. "I just want games to be something like art." The indie scene was leading his medium in the right direction, he said, but "games are still not like great films or books that really affect a lot of people in a special way."

Last year, Soderstrom had a game in the Independent Games Festival that generated interest from the big publishers. "They all wanted to talk to me about my games," he said, but he was too busy hanging out with his friends, drinking, staying up all night, playing and talking about video games. Several companies at the conference, he said, left their cards at his booth. He never called them.

The Placebo Problem

Placebos are getting more effective. Drugmakers
are desperate to know why.

Merck was in trouble. In 2002, the pharmaceutical giant was
falling behind its rivals in sales. Even worse, patents on five
blockbuster drugs were about to expire, which would allow
cheaper generics to flood the market. The company hadn't introduced a truly new product in three years, and its stock price
was plummeting.

In interviews with the press, Edward Scolnick, Merck's
research director, laid out his battle plan to restore the firm to
preeminence. Key to his strategy was expanding the company's reach into the antidepressant market, where Merck had
lagged while competitors like Pfizer and GlaxoSmithKline
created some of the best-selling drugs in the world. "To remain dominant in the future," he told *Forbes,* "we need to
dominate the central nervous system."

His plan hinged on the success of an experimental antidepressant codenamed MK-869. Still in clinical trials, it
looked like every pharma executive's dream: a new kind of
medication that exploited brain chemistry in innovative ways
to promote feelings of well-being. The drug tested brilliantly
early on, with minimal side effects, and Merck touted its

game-changing potential at a meeting of 300 securities analysts.

Behind the scenes, however, MK-869 was starting to unravel. True, many test subjects treated with the medication felt their hopelessness and anxiety lift. But so did nearly the same number who took a placebo, a look-alike pill made of milk sugar or another inert substance given to groups of volunteers in clinical trials to gauge how much more effective the real drug is by comparison. The fact that taking a faux drug can powerfully improve some people's health—the so-called placebo effect—has long been considered an embarrassment to the serious practice of pharmacology.

Ultimately, Merck's foray into the antidepressant market failed. In subsequent tests, MK-869 turned out to be no more effective than a placebo. In the jargon of the industry, the trials crossed the futility boundary.

MK-869 wasn't the only highly anticipated medical breakthrough to be undone in recent years by the placebo effect. From 2001 to 2006, the percentage of new products cut from development after Phase II clinical trials, when drugs are first tested against placebo, rose by 20 percent. The failure rate in more extensive Phase III trials increased by 11 percent, mainly due to surprisingly poor showings against placebo. Despite historic levels of industry investment in R&D, the US Food and Drug Administration approved only 19 first-of-their-kind remedies in 2007—the fewest since 1983—and just 24 in 2008. Half of all drugs that fail in late-stage trials drop out of the pipeline due to their inability to beat sugar pills.

The upshot is fewer new medicines available to ailing patients and more financial woes for the beleaguered pharmaceutical industry. Last November, a new type of gene therapy for Parkinson's disease, championed by the Michael J. Fox Foundation, was abruptly withdrawn from Phase II trials after unexpectedly tanking against placebo. A stem-cell startup called Osiris Therapeutics got a drubbing on Wall Street in March, when it suspended trials of its pill for Crohn's disease, an intestinal ailment, citing an "unusually high" response to placebo. Two days later, Eli Lilly broke off testing of a much-touted new drug for schizophrenia when volunteers showed double the expected level of placebo response.

It's not only trials of new drugs that are crossing the futility boundary. Some products that have been on the market for decades, like Prozac, are faltering in more recent follow-up tests. In many cases, these are the compounds that, in the late '90s, made Big Pharma more profitable than Big Oil. But if these same drugs were vetted now, the FDA might not approve some of them. Two comprehensive analyses of antidepressant trials have uncovered a dramatic increase in placebo response since the 1980s. One estimated that the so-called effect size (a measure of statistical significance) in placebo groups had nearly doubled over that time.

It's not that the old meds are getting weaker, drug developers say. It's as if the placebo effect is somehow getting stronger.

The fact that an increasing number of medications are unable to beat sugar pills has thrown the industry into crisis. The stakes could hardly be higher. In today's economy, the fate of a long-established company can hang on the outcome of a handful of tests.

Why are inert pills suddenly overwhelming promising new drugs and established medicines alike? The reasons are only just beginning to be understood. A network of independent researchers is doggedly uncovering the inner workings—and potential therapeutic applications—of the placebo effect. At the same time, drugmakers are realizing they need to fully understand the mechanisms behind it so they can design trials that differentiate more clearly between the beneficial effects of their products and the body's innate ability to heal itself. A special task force of the Foundation for the National Institutes of Health is seeking to stem the crisis by quietly undertaking one of the most ambitious data-sharing efforts in the history of the drug industry. After decades in the jungles of fringe science, the placebo effect has become the elephant in the boardroom.

The roots of the placebo problem can be traced to a lie told by an Army nurse during World War II as Allied forces stormed the beaches of southern Italy. The nurse was assisting an anesthetist named Henry Beecher, who was tending to US troops under heavy German bombardment. When the morphine supply ran low, the nurse assured a wounded soldier that he was getting a shot of potent painkiller, though her syringe contained only salt water. Amazingly, the bogus injection relieved the soldier's agony and prevented the onset of shock.

Returning to his post at Harvard after the war, Beecher became one of the nation's leading medical reformers. Inspired by the nurse's healing act of deception, he launched a crusade to promote a method of testing new medicines to find out whether they were truly effective. At the time, the process for vetting drugs was sloppy at best: Pharmaceutical companies would simply dose volunteers with an experimental agent until the side effects swamped the presumed benefits. Beecher proposed that if test subjects could be compared to a group that received a placebo, health officials would finally have an impartial way to determine whether a medicine was actually responsible for making a patient better.

In a 1955 paper titled "The Powerful Placebo," published in *The Journal of the American Medical Association,* Beecher described how the placebo effect had undermined the results of more than a dozen trials by causing improvement that was mistakenly attributed to the drugs being tested. He demonstrated that trial volunteers who got real medication were also subject to placebo effects; the act of taking a pill was itself somehow therapeutic, boosting the curative power of the medicine. Only by subtracting the improvement in a placebo control group could the actual value of the drug be calculated.

The article caused a sensation. By 1962, reeling from news of birth defects caused by a drug called thalidomide, Congress amended the Food, Drug, and Cosmetic Act, requiring trials to include enhanced safety testing and placebo control groups. Volunteers would be assigned randomly to receive either medicine or a sugar pill, and neither doctor nor patient would know the difference until the trial was over. Beecher's double-blind, placebo-controlled, randomized clinical trial—or RCT—was enshrined as the gold standard of the emerging pharmaceutical industry. Today, to win FDA approval, a new medication must beat placebo in at least two authenticated trials.

Beecher's prescription helped cure the medical establishment of outright quackery, but it had an insidious side effect. By casting placebo as the villain in RCTs, he ended up stigmatizing one of his most important discoveries. The fact that even dummy capsules can kick-start the body's recovery engine became a problem for drug developers to overcome, rather than a phenomenon that could guide doctors toward a better understanding of the healing process and how to drive it most effectively.

In his eagerness to promote his template for clinical trials, Beecher also overreached by seeing the placebo effect at work in curing ailments like the common cold, which wane with no intervention at all. But the triumph of Beecher's gold standard was a generation of safer medications that worked for nearly everyone. Anthracyclines don't require an oncologist with a genial bedside manner to slow the growth of tumors.

What Beecher didn't foresee, however, was the explosive growth of the pharmaceutical industry. The blockbuster success of mood drugs in the '80s and '90s emboldened Big

Pharma to promote remedies for a growing panoply of disorders that are intimately related to higher brain function. By attempting to dominate the central nervous system, Big Pharma gambled its future on treating ailments that have turned out to be particularly susceptible to the placebo effect.

The tall, rusty-haired son of a country doctor, William Potter, 64, has spent most of his life treating mental illness—first as a psychiatrist at the National Institute of Mental Health and then as a drug developer. A decade ago, he took a job at Lilly's neuroscience labs. There, working on new antidepressants and antianxiety meds, he became one of the first researchers to glimpse the approaching storm.

To test products internally, pharmaceutical companies routinely run trials in which a long-established medication and an experimental one compete against each other as well as against a placebo. As head of Lilly's early-stage psychiatric drug development in the late '90s, Potter saw that even durable warhorses like Prozac, which had been on the market for years, were being overtaken by dummy pills in more recent tests. The company's next-generation antidepressants were faring badly, too, doing no better than placebo in seven out of 10 trials.

As a psychiatrist, Potter knew that some patients really do seem to get healthier for reasons that have more to do with a doctor's empathy than with the contents of a pill. But it baffled him that drugs he'd been prescribing for years seemed to be struggling to prove their effectiveness. Thinking that something crucial may have been overlooked, Potter tapped an IT geek named David DeBrota to help him comb through the Lilly database of published and unpublished trials—including those that the company had kept secret because of high placebo response. They aggregated the findings from decades of antidepressant trials, looking for patterns and trying to see what was changing over time. What they found challenged some of the industry's basic assumptions about its drug-vetting process.

Assumption number one was that if a trial were managed correctly, a medication would perform as well or badly in a Phoenix hospital as in a Bangalore clinic. Potter discovered, however, that geographic location alone could determine whether a drug bested placebo or crossed the futility boundary. By the late '90s, for example, the classic antianxiety drug diazepam (also known as Valium) was still beating placebo in France and Belgium. But when the drug was tested in the US, it was likely to fail. Conversely, Prozac performed better in America than it did in western Europe and South Africa. It was an unsettling prospect: FDA approval could hinge on where the company chose to conduct a trial.

Mistaken assumption number two was that the standard tests used to gauge volunteers' improvement in trials yielded consistent results. Potter and his colleagues discovered that ratings by trial observers varied significantly from one testing site to another. It was like finding out that the judges in a tight race each had a different idea about the placement of the finish line.

Potter and DeBrota's data-mining also revealed that even superbly managed trials were subject to runaway placebo effects. But exactly why any of this was happening remained elusive. "We were able to identify many of the core issues in play," Potter says. "But there was no clear answer to the problem." Convinced that what Lilly was facing was too complex for any one pharmaceutical house to unravel on its own, he came up with a plan to break down the firewalls between researchers across the industry, enabling them to share data in "pre-competitive space."

After prodding by Potter and others, the NIH focused on the issue in 2000, hosting a three-day conference in Washington. For the first time in medical history, more than 500 drug developers, doctors, academics, and trial designers put their heads together to examine the role of the placebo effect in clinical trials and healing in general.

Potter's ambitious plan for a collaborative approach to the problem eventually ran into its own futility boundary: No one would pay for it. And drug companies don't share data, they hoard it. But the NIH conference launched a new wave of placebo research in academic labs in the US and Italy that would make significant progress toward solving the mystery of what was happening in clinical trials.

Visitors to Fabrizio Benedetti's clinic at the University of Turin are asked never to say the P-word around the med students who sign up for his experiments. For all the volunteers know, the trim, soft-spoken neuroscientist is hard at work concocting analgesic skin creams and methods for enhancing athletic performance.

One recent afternoon in his lab, a young soccer player grimaced with exertion while doing leg curls on a weight machine. Benedetti and his colleagues were exploring the potential of using Pavlovian conditioning to give athletes a competitive edge undetectable by anti-doping authorities. A player would receive doses of a performance-enhancing drug for weeks and then a jolt of placebo just before competition.

Benedetti, 53, first became interested in placebos in the mid-'90s, while researching pain. He was surprised that some of the test subjects in his placebo groups seemed to suffer less than those on active drugs. But scientific interest in this phenomenon, and the money to research it, were hard to come by. "The placebo effect was considered little more than a nuisance," he recalls. "Drug companies, physicians, and clinicians were not interested in understanding its mechanisms. They were concerned only with figuring out whether their drugs worked better."

Part of the problem was that response to placebo was considered a psychological trait related to neurosis and gullibility rather than a physiological phenomenon that could be scrutinized in the lab and manipulated for therapeutic benefit. But then Benedetti came across a study, done years earlier, that suggested the placebo effect had a neurological foundation. US scientists had found that a drug called naloxone blocks the pain-relieving power of placebo treatments. The brain produces its own analgesic compounds called opioids, released under conditions of stress, and naloxone blocks the action of these natural painkillers and their synthetic analogs. The study gave Benedetti the lead he needed to pursue his own research while running small clinical trials for drug companies.

Now, after 15 years of experimentation, he has succeeded in mapping many of the biochemical reactions responsible for the placebo effect, uncovering a broad repertoire of self-healing responses. Placebo-activated opioids, for example, not only relieve pain; they also modulate heart rate and respiration. The neurotransmitter dopamine, when released by placebo treatment, helps improve motor function in Parkinson's patients. Mechanisms like these can elevate mood, sharpen cognitive ability, alleviate digestive disorders, relieve insomnia, and limit the secretion of stress-related hormones like insulin and cortisol.

In one study, Benedetti found that Alzheimer's patients with impaired cognitive function get less pain relief from analgesic drugs than normal volunteers do. Using advanced methods of EEG analysis, he discovered that the connections between the patients' prefrontal lobes and their opioid systems had been damaged. Healthy volunteers feel the benefit of medication plus a placebo boost. Patients who are unable to formulate ideas about the future because of cortical deficits, however, feel only the effect of the drug itself. The experiment suggests that because Alzheimer's patients don't get the benefits of anticipating the treatment, they require higher doses of painkillers to experience normal levels of relief.

Benedetti often uses the phrase "placebo response" instead of placebo effect. By definition, inert pills have no effect, but under the right conditions they can act as a catalyst for what he calls the body's "endogenous health care system." Like any other internal network, the placebo response has limits. It can ease the discomfort of chemotherapy, but it won't stop the growth of tumors. It also works in reverse to produce the placebo's evil twin, the nocebo effect. For example, men taking a commonly prescribed prostate drug who were informed that the medication may cause sexual dysfunction were twice as likely to become impotent.

Further research by Benedetti and others showed that the promise of treatment activates areas of the brain involved in weighing the significance of events and the seriousness of threats. "If a fire alarm goes off and you see smoke, you know something bad is going to happen and you get ready to escape," explains Tor Wager, a neuroscientist at Columbia University. "Expectations about pain and pain relief work in a similar way. Placebo treatments tap into this system and orchestrate the responses in your brain and body accordingly."

In other words, one way that placebo aids recovery is by hacking the mind's ability to predict the future. We are constantly parsing the reactions of those around us—such as the tone a doctor uses to deliver a diagnosis—to generate more-accurate estimations of our fate. One of the most powerful placebogenic triggers is watching someone else experience the benefits of an alleged drug. Researchers call these social aspects of medicine the therapeutic ritual.

In a study last year, Harvard Medical School researcher Ted Kaptchuk devised a clever strategy for testing his volunteers' response to varying levels of therapeutic ritual. The study focused on irritable bowel syndrome, a painful disorder that costs more than $40 billion a year worldwide to treat. First the volunteers were placed randomly in one of three groups. One group was simply put on a waiting list; researchers know that some patients get better just because they sign up for a trial. Another group received placebo treatment from a clinician who declined to engage in small talk. Volunteers in the third group got the same sham treatment from a clinician who asked them questions about symptoms, outlined the causes of IBS, and displayed optimism about their condition.

Not surprisingly, the health of those in the third group improved most. In fact, just by participating in the trial, volunteers in this high-interaction group got as much relief as did people taking the two leading prescription drugs for IBS. And the benefits of their bogus treatment persisted for weeks afterward, contrary to the belief—widespread in the pharmaceutical industry—that the placebo response is short-lived.

Studies like this open the door to hybrid treatment strategies that exploit the placebo effect to make real drugs safer and more effective. Cancer patients undergoing rounds of chemotherapy often suffer from debilitating nocebo effects—such as anticipatory nausea—conditioned by their past experiences with the drugs. A team of German researchers has shown that these associations can be unlearned through the administration of placebo, making chemo easier to bear.

Meanwhile, the classic use of placebos in medicine—to boost the confidence of anxious patients—has been employed tacitly for ages. Nearly half of the doctors polled in a 2007 survey in Chicago admitted to prescribing medications they knew were ineffective for a patient's condition—or prescribing effective drugs in doses too low to produce actual benefit—in order to provoke a placebo response.

The main objections to more widespread placebo use in clinical practice are ethical, but the solutions to these conundrums can be surprisingly simple. Investigators told volunteers in one placebo study that the pills they were taking were "known to significantly reduce pain in some patients." The researchers weren't lying.

These new findings tell us that the body's response to certain types of medication is in constant flux, affected by expectations of treatment, conditioning, beliefs, and social cues.

For instance, the geographic variations in trial outcome that Potter uncovered begin to make sense in light of discoveries that the placebo response is highly sensitive to cultural differences. Anthropologist Daniel Moerman found that Germans are high placebo reactors in trials of ulcer drugs but low in trials of drugs for hypertension—an undertreated condition in Germany, where many people pop pills for *herzinsuffizienz,* or low blood pressure. Moreover, a pill's shape, size, branding, and price all influence its effects on the body. Soothing blue capsules make more effective tranquilizers than angry red ones, except among Italian men, for whom the color blue is associated with their national soccer team—*Forza Azzurri!*

But why would the placebo effect seem to be getting stronger worldwide? Part of the answer may be found in the drug industry's own success in marketing its products.

Potential trial volunteers in the US have been deluged with ads for prescription medications since 1997, when the FDA amended its policy on direct-to-consumer advertising. The secret of running an effective campaign, Saatchi & Saatchi's Jim Joseph told a trade journal last year, is associating a particular brand-name medication with other aspects of life that promote peace of mind: "Is it time with your children? Is it a good book curled up on the couch? Is it your favorite television show? Is it a little purple pill that helps you get rid of acid reflux?" By evoking such uplifting associations, researchers say, the ads set up the kind of expectations that induce a formidable placebo response.

The success of those ads in selling blockbuster drugs like antidepressants and statins also pushed trials offshore as therapeutic virgins—potential volunteers who were not already medicated with one or another drug—became harder to find. The contractors that manage trials for Big Pharma have moved aggressively into Africa, India, China, and the former Soviet Union. In these places, however, cultural dynamics can boost the placebo response in other ways. Doctors in these countries are paid to fill up trial rosters quickly, which may motivate them to recruit patients with milder forms of illness that yield more readily to placebo treatment. Furthermore, a patient's hope of getting better and expectation of expert care—the primary placebo triggers in the brain—are particularly acute in societies where volunteers are clamoring to gain access to the most basic forms of medicine. "The quality of care that placebo patients get in trials is far superior to the best insurance you get in America," says psychiatrist Arif Khan, principal investigator in hundreds of trials for companies like Pfizer and Bristol-Myers Squibb. "It's basically luxury care."

Big Pharma faces additional problems in beating placebo when it comes to psychiatric drugs. One is to accurately define the nature of mental illness. The litmus test of drug efficacy in antidepressant trials is a questionnaire called the Hamilton Depression Rating Scale. The HAM-D was created nearly 50 years ago based on a study of major depressive disorder in patients confined to asylums. Few trial volunteers now suffer from that level of illness. In fact, many experts are starting to wonder if what drug companies now call depression is even the same disease that the HAM-D was designed to diagnose.

Existing tests also may not be appropriate for diagnosing disorders like social anxiety and premenstrual dysphoria—the very types of chronic, fuzzily defined conditions that the drug industry started targeting in the '90s, when the placebo problem began escalating. The neurological foundation of these illnesses is still being debated, making it even harder for drug companies to come up with effective treatments.

What all of these disorders have in common, however, is that they engage the higher cortical centers that generate beliefs and expectations, interpret social cues, and anticipate rewards. So do chronic pain, sexual dysfunction, Parkinson's, and many other ailments that respond robustly to placebo treatment. To avoid investing in failure, researchers say, pharmaceutical companies will need to adopt new ways of vetting drugs that route around the brain's own centralized network for healing.

Ten years and billions of R&D dollars after William Potter first sounded the alarm about the placebo effect, his message has finally gotten through. In the spring, Potter, who is now a VP at Merck, helped rev up a massive data-gathering effort called the Placebo Response Drug Trials Survey.

Under the auspices of the FNIH, Potter and his colleagues are acquiring decades of trial data—including blood and DNA samples—to determine which variables are responsible for the apparent rise in the placebo effect. Merck, Lilly, Pfizer, AstraZeneca, GlaxoSmithKline, Sanofi-Aventis, Johnson & Johnson, and other major firms are funding the study, and the process of scrubbing volunteers' names and other personal information from the database is about to begin.

In typically secretive industry fashion, the existence of the project itself is being kept under wraps. FNIH staffers are willing to talk about it only anonymously, concerned about offending the companies paying for it.

For Potter, who used to ride along with his father on house calls in Indiana, the significance of the survey goes beyond Big Pharma's finally admitting it has a placebo problem. It also marks the twilight of an era when the drug industry was confident that its products were strong enough to cure illness by themselves.

"Before I routinely prescribed antidepressants, I would do more psychotherapy for mildly depressed patients," says the veteran of hundreds of drug trials. "Today we would say I was trying to engage components of the placebo response—and those patients got better. To really do the best for your patients, you want the best placebo response plus the best drug response."

The pharma crisis has also finally brought together the two parallel streams of placebo research—academic and industrial. Pfizer has asked Fabrizio Benedetti to help the company figure out why two of its pain drugs keep failing. Ted Kaptchuk is developing ways to distinguish drug response more clearly from placebo response for another pharma house that he declines to name. Both are exploring innovative trial models that treat the placebo effect as more than just statistical noise competing with the active drug.

Benedetti has helped design a protocol for minimizing volunteers' expectations that he calls "open/hidden." In standard trials, the act of taking a pill or receiving an injection activates the placebo response. In open/hidden trials, drugs and placebos are given to some test subjects in the usual way and to others at random intervals through an IV line controlled by a concealed computer. Drugs that work only when the patient knows they're being administered are placebos themselves.

Ironically, Big Pharma's attempt to dominate the central nervous system has ended up revealing how powerful the brain really is. The placebo response doesn't care if the catalyst for healing is a triumph of pharmacology, a compassionate therapist, or a syringe of salt water. All it requires is a reasonable expectation of getting better. That's potent medicine.

David Carr

The Fall and Rise of Media

For media, a sunset is followed quickly by a sunrise.

Historically, young women and men who sought to thrive in publishing made their way to Manhattan. Once there, they were told, they would work in marginal jobs for indifferent bosses doing mundane tasks and then one day, if they did all of that without whimper or complaint, they would magically be granted access to a gilded community, the large heaving engine of books, magazines and newspapers.

Beyond that, all it took to find a place to stand on a very crowded island, as E. B. White suggested, was a willingness to be lucky. Once inside that velvet rope, they would find the escalator that would take them through the various tiers of the business and eventually, they would be the ones deciding who would be allowed to come in.

As even casual readers of media news know, those assumptions now sound precious, preposterous even. Calvinistic ideals are no match for macromedia economics that have vaporized significant components of the business model that drives traditional publishing.

The most popular books of the holiday season have become cat toys in a price war between online and offline retailers. Newspapers still hang onto a portion of seasonal ads, but the retail chains that place them have consolidated into a much smaller cohort, and much of their spending is bifurcated between old and new media marketing. Magazines intended to help the reader primp for Christmas parties are, in many cases, half as big as they were just a few short years ago.

Pages are down, spending is down, revenues are down, and the biggest feature of this holiday season in the media kingdom has been layoffs and buyouts at Condé Nast, Time Inc., The Associated Press, and yes, The New York Times.

(And it's not just Manhattan-centric endeavors. Published ambition has been diminished by new realities elsewhere, most recently in the announced closing of The Washington Post's remaining domestic bureaus. Last week, in an interview with Howard Kurtz, the executive editor, Marcus Brauchli, said it plainly: "We are not a national news organization of record serving a general audience." Yeow.)

That feeling of age, of a coming sunset, is tough to avoid in all corners of traditional publishing. Earlier in November, the New York comptroller said that employment in communications in New York had lost 60,000 jobs since 2000, a year when the media industry here seemed at the height of its powers.

I arrived in New York that same year as part of Inside .com, a digital news site conceived to cover a media space that was converging and morphing into something wholly new. The site covered the mainstream media's efforts to come to grips with new realities and efforts by new players to cash in on emerging technology.

Few of us could have conceived that in the next decade some of the reigning titans of media would be routed. Profligate dot-com ad money that had fattened print went away in a digital wipeout, and when digital media came back, it was to dine on the mainstream media rather than engorge it. After 2000, jobs in traditional media industries declined at a rate of about 2.5 percent annually and then went into a dive in 2008 or so. (Inside.com, an idea before its time—hey, let's charge for high-quality, business-oriented content—disappeared after about 18 months.)

That carnage has left behind an island of misfit toys, trains whose cabooses have square wheels and bird fish who are trying to swim in thin air. The skills that once commanded $4 for every shiny word are far less valuable at a time when the supply of both editorial and advertising content more or less doubles every year.

Where do all the burgeoning pixels come from? Everywhere, and cheap at that. An outfit called Demand Media now tests headlines for reader salience and cranks out thousands of articles and videos daily that it pays about $20 apiece for.

Web crawlers grab expensive content and replicate it far away from the organizations that produce it. Various media labs are now testing algorithms that assemble facts into narratives that deliver information, no writers required. The results would not be mistaken for literary journalism, but on the Web, pretty good—or even not terrible—is often good enough.

For those of us who work in Manhattan media, it means that a life of occasional excess and prerogative has been replaced by a drum beat of goodbye speeches with sheet cakes and cheap sparkling wine. It's a wan reminder that all reigns are temporary, that the court of self-appointed media royalty was serving at the pleasure of an advertising economy that itself was built on inefficiency and excess. Google fixed that.

Certain stalwart brands will survive and even thrive because of a new scarcity of quality content for niche audiences that demand more than generic information. The chip that was implanted in me when I arrived at this newspaper—you might call it New York Times Exceptionalism—leads me to conclude that this organization will be one of those, but the insurgency continues apace.

Those of us who covered media were told for years that

the sky was falling, and nothing happened. And then it did. Great big chunks of the sky gave way and magazines tumbled —Gourmet!?—that seemed as if they were as solid as the skyline itself. But to those of us who were here back in September of 2001, we learned that even the edifice of Manhattan itself is subject to perforation and endless loss.

So what do we get instead? The future, which is not a bad deal if you ignore all the collateral gore. Young men and women are still coming here to remake the world, they just won't be stopping by the human resources department of Condé Nast to begin their ascent.

For every kid that I bump into who is wandering the media industry looking for an entrance that closed some time ago, I come across another who is a bundle of ideas, energy and technological mastery. The next wave is not just knocking on doors, but seeking to knock them down.

Somewhere down in the Flatiron, out in Brooklyn, over in Queens or up in Harlem, cabals of bright young things are watching all the disruption with more than an academic interest. Their tiny netbooks and iPhones, which serve as portals to the cloud, contain more informational firepower than entire newsrooms possessed just two decades ago. And they are ginning content from their audiences in the form of social media or finding ways of making ambient information more useful. They are jaded in the way youth requires, but have the confidence that is a gift of their age as well.

For them, New York is not an island sinking, but one that is rising on a fresh, ferocious wave.

Michael James Massimino

Tweet from Space

From orbit: Listening to Sting on my ipod watching the world go by—literally

About the Contributors

Sam Anderson is the book critic for *New York Magazine*. He lives in the Hudson Valley with his wife and two children.

Joshuah Bearman has written about CIA missions, aspiring Fabios, cat burglars, the Great Chinese Rodent Disaster of 2003, and the world's greatest Pac-Man player. He has published articles in *Harper's, Wired, Rolling Stone, New York Times Magazine, McSweeney's,* and *Believer,* and contributes to *This American Life.* He is currently working on a book to be published by Riverhead.

Burkhard Bilger has been a staff writer at *The New Yorker* since 2000. His articles have appeared in the *Atlantic, Harper's, New York Times,* and other publications, and his book, *Noodling for Flatheads,* was a finalist for a PEN-Faulkner Award. Bilger lives in Brooklyn with his wife, Jennifer Nelson, and his children, Hans, Ruby, and Evangeline.

Mark Bowden is a journalist and author whose books include *Black Hawk Down* and *Guests of the Ayatollah.* He is a contributing editor to *Vanity Fair.*

David Carr is a culture reporter and the media columnist for the *New York Times.* He is the author of *The Night of the Gun.*

Douglas Fox is a freelance writer based in California. He frequently writes about neuroscience and climate. He has reported extensively from Antarctica in the last couple of years, most recently for *National Geographic.* His stories have appeared in *Discover, New Scientist, Popular Mechanics, Science, Conservation, Science News for Kids, Natural History, Los Angeles Times, Christian Science Monitor,* and *The Best American Science and Nature Writing.* His story "Where Rivers Run Uphill" garnered the AAAS Kavli International Award for Children's Science Writing in 2010.

Tad Friend is a staff writer for *The New Yorker* and writes the magazine's "Letter from California." He is the author of *Cheerful Money: Me, My Family, and the Last Days of Wasp Splendor* (Little, Brown). His articles have also appeared in *The Best American Travel Writing, The Best American Sports Writing,* and *The Best American Crime Reporting.*

Ben Greenman is an editor at *The New Yorker* and the author of several acclaimed books of fiction, including *Superbad, Please Step Back,* and *What He's Poised to Do.* His journalism and essays have appeared in *The New Yorker, New York Times, Washington Post,* and elsewhere. He lives in Brooklyn with his wife and sons.

Vanessa Grigoriadis is a contributing editor at *New York Magazine, Rolling Stone,* and *Vanity Fair.* She won the National Magazine Award in Profile Writing in 2007 for a profile of Karl Lagerfeld. She was also nominated for the 2008 Award in Feature Writing for a *New York Magazine* cover story, "Gawker and the Rise of the Creative Underclass."

James Harkin is a writer and social forecaster, and the author of *Cyburbia* (Little, Brown).

Adam Higginbotham has written extensively about crime for publications in the United States and United Kingdom; his work has appeared in the *Daily Telegraph, Observer, GQ,* and *Details,* where he is a contributing editor. He lives in New York City.

Alex Hutchinson is a National Magazine Award–winning writer and contributing editor at *Popular Mechanics* whose writing also appears in such publications as the *Globe and Mail* and the *New York Times.* He runs the SweatScience.com blog on the intersection of sports and fitness with science and technology. This is the second time his writing in *The Walrus* has been selected for the Best Technology Writing series.

Steven Johnson is the author of six books, including the recent best-sellers *The Invention of Air, The Ghost Map,* and *Everything Bad Is Good for You.* He writes for the *New York Times Magazine, Wired,* the *Guardian, Discover,* and other publications and has made numerous appearances on *Charlie Rose, The Daily Show,* and *The Colbert Report.* He lives in Brooklyn.

Kevin Kelly is senior maverick at *Wired*. He is the author of *Out of Control* and the upcoming book *What Technology Wants*.

Jill Lepore is the David Woods Kemper '41 Professor of American History at Harvard University and a staff writer at *The New Yorker*. Her books include *The Name of War*, winner of the Bancroft Prize, and *New York Burning*, a finalist for the Pulitzer Prize.

Alexis Madrigal is the author of a forthcoming book on the history of green technology in America. He writes about energy and science for Wired.com.

Javier Marías is a Spanish novelist, translator, and columnist. He has published twelve novels, two collections of stories, and a number of essay collections and has received a large number of international literary awards. His work has been translated in forty-seven countries, and more than six million copies of his books have been sold worldwide. He lives in Madrid.

Michael James Massimino is an American engineer and a NASA astronaut. He is a veteran of two Space Shuttle missions, including the historic final Hubble Space Telescope repair mission.

Evan Ratliff is a Brooklyn-based writer whose work has appeared in *Wired, The New Yorker, New York Times Magazine, Outside,* and other magazines. He is a contributing editor at *Wired* and the story editor for *Pop-Up* magazine, a live event.

Daniel Roth is the managing editor of Fortune.com. Roth has spent his career writing long-form features about the biggest names in business—and the innovators who aim to unseat them —most recently as a senior writer at *Wired* and Condé Nast *Portfolio.*

Clay Shirky writes, teaches, and consults on the social effects of the Internet, and especially those places where our social and technological networks overlap. He is on the faculty of New York University's Interactive Telecommunications Program and has consulted for Nokia, Procter and Gamble, NewsCorp, the BBC, the U.S. Navy, and Lego. Over the years, his writings have appeared in the *New York Times, Wall Street Journal, Wired, Har-*

vard Business Review, and *IEEE Computer Review.* His first book, *Here Comes Everybody: The Power of Organizing without Organizations,* was published by Penguin in 2008.

Steve Silberman is a freelance writer in San Francisco. His articles on science, literature, and music have appeared in *Wired, The New Yorker, Nature, Shambhala Sun,* and many other national publications. He is currently writing a book on neurodiversity.

Anne Trubek is associate professor at Oberlin College. Her book *A Skeptic's Guide to Writers' Houses* is forthcoming from the University of Pennsylvania Press in 2010, and she is coeditor of *Writing Material: Readings from Plato to the Digital Age* (Longman, 2003). She writes a literary column for *GOOD* magazine, and her writing has appeared in the *Believer, Oxford American, Washington Post,* and numerous other publications.

Lawrence Weschler, formerly of *The New Yorker,* is currently director of the New York Institute for the Humanities at New York University. His dozen-plus books include *Everything That Rises: A Book of Convergences* (winner of the National Book Critics Circle Award for Criticism, 2007) and, most recently, a pair of biographies of two diametrically opposite artists, a massively expanded edition of his first book, *Seeing Is Forgetting the Name of the Thing One Sees* (Robert Irwin), and *True to Life* (David Hockney).

Acknowledgments

Grateful acknowledgment is made to the following authors, publishers, and journals for permission to reprint previously published materials.

"In Defense of Distraction" by Sam Anderson. First published in *New York Magazine,* May 17, 2009. Copyright © 2009 by *New York Magazine.* Reprinted with permission.

"Can D.I.Y. Supplant the First-Person Shooter?" by Joshuah Bearman. First published in the *New York Times Magazine,* November 13, 2009. Reprinted by permission of the author.

"Hearth Surgery" by Burkhard Bilger. First published in *The New Yorker,* December 21, 2009. Reprinted by permission of the author.

"A Crime of Shadows" by Mark Bowden. First published in *Vanity Fair,* December 2009. Reprinted by permission of the author.

"The Fall and Rise of Media" by David Carr. From The New York Times © November 29, 2009 The New York Times All rights reserved. Used by permission and protected by the Copyright Laws of the United States. The printing, copying, redistribution, or retransmission of the Material without express written permission is prohibited.

"Thinking Machine" by Douglas Fox. Originally published in *Discover,* October 2009. Reprinted by permission of the author.

"Plugged In" by Tad Friend. First published in *The New Yorker,* August 24, 2009. Reprinted by permission of the author.

"Naked Truth" by Ben Greenman. Copyright © 2009 Condé Nast Publications. All rights reserved. Originally published in *The New Yorker,* November 30, 2009. Reprinted by permission.

"Do You Own Facebook? Or Does Facebook Own You?" by Vanessa Grigoriadis. First published in *New York Magazine,* April 5, 2009. Reprinted by permission of the author.

"Caught in the Net" by James Harkin. First published in *New Statesman,* April 30, 2009. Reprinted by permission of the author.

337

"The Inkjet Counterfeiter" by Adam Higginbotham. First published in *Details,* September 2009. Reprinted by permission of the author.

"Global Impositioning Systems" by Alex Hutchinson. First published in *The Walrus,* November 2009. Reprinted by permission of the author.

"Why We Tweet" by Steven Johnson. First published as "How Twitter Will Change the Way We Live" in *Time,* June 5, 2009. Reprinted by permission of the author.

"Technophilia" by Kevin Kelly. First published in The Technium on kk.org, June 8, 2009. Reprinted by permission of the author.

"Baby Food" by Jill Lepore. First published in *The New Yorker,* January 19, 2009. Reprinted by permission of the author.

"Telegraphs Ran on Electric Air in Crazy 1859 Magnetic Storm" by Alexis Madrigal. Copyright © 2009 Condé Nast Publications. All rights reserved. Originally published in Wired.com, September 2, 2009. Reprinted by permission.

"Airships" by Javier Marías. First published in *Granta,* Summer 2009. Copyright © 2009 by Javier Marías. Reprinted by permission of the author.

"Tweet from Space" by Michael James Massimino. Originally published on Twitter, May 19, 2009.

"Vanish" by Evan Ratliff. First published as "Writer Evan Ratliff Tried to Vanish: Here's What Happened" in *Wired,* November 20, 2009. Reprinted by permission of the author.

"The Answer Factory" by Daniel Roth. Originally published in *Wired,* November 2009. Copyright © 2009 Condé Nast Publications. All rights reserved. Reprinted by permission.

"Newspapers and Thinking the Unthinkable" by Clay Shirky. First published in shirky.com, March 13, 2009. Reprinted by permission of the author.

"The Placebo Problem" by Steve Silberman. First published in *Wired,* September 2009. Reprinted by permission of the author.

"Handwriting Is History" by Anne Trubek. First published in *Miller-McCune,* December 17, 2009. Reprinted by permission of the author.

"David Hockney's iPhone Passion" by Lawrence Weschler. First published in the *New York Review of Books,* October 22, 2009. Reprinted by permission of the author.